Robert Lowell

Robert Lowell

Nihilist as Hero

Vereen M. Bell

Harvard University Press

Cambridge, Massachusetts and London, England   1983

Publication of this book has been aided by a grant from
    the Andrew W. Mellon Foundation

LIBRARY OF CONGRESS CATALOGING IN PUBLICATION DATA

Bell, Vereen M., 1934-
    Robert Lowell, nihilist as hero.

    Includes bibliographical references and index.
    1. Lowell, Robert, 1917–1977—Criticism and
interpretation.   2. Nihilism in literature.
3. Pessimism in literature.   I. Title.
PS3523.O89Z58   1983   811'.52   82–9336
ISBN 0–674–77585–6   AACR2

FOR JANE

ACKNOWLEDGMENTS

Helen Vendler's contribution to this work and to my spirits has been immeasurable. George Core gave badly needed tactical support and editorial guidance. Frank Bidart, in his characteristically selfless way, gave invaluable help with the manuscript materials under his care. Rodney Dennis and the staff in the Houghton Library were patient, attentive, and hearteningly civilized. I thank them all.

V.M.B.

CONTENTS

ROBERT LOWELL

INTRODUCTION

Robert Lowell's poetry is identifiable by nothing so much as its chronic and eventually systematic pessimism. One is hard pressed to come forward with even remotely sanguine or assuaging poems from Lowell's canon, and the few that we might call forth seem in the end to be momentary aberrations in an otherwise desolate philosophical context. Whatever spirit of affirmation that we think we perceive in Lowell's work we must always suspect ourselves of projecting upon it, being less willing than Lowell himself to yield to the implications of a nihilism of such an absolutized form—being, as it were, more Nietzschean than Lowell was able to be. What encourages us to find such pictures in the clouds is the element in his work that I consider to be fully as significant as its chronic pessimism (by which I contradict myself slightly); this feature is Lowell's conditioned and wholly understandable reluctance to accept the consequences of his own vision—a kind of scruple that causes him to consider again and again what life might be if it were not in fact what it is. But the reservation is only in the background, oblique, issuing from ontological nostalgia. In his very darkest moments, IS or Being, becomes for Lowell "the whited monster"—not white, but whit*ed*, by us; monstrous and whited.

In his preface to *Land of Unlikeness*, Allen Tate represented Lowell as one of the few poets of his generation who retained "at least a memory of the spiritual dignity of man." For Tate a concept such as "spiritual dignity" necessarily implied a teleology, Christian or otherwise, without which auxiliary and dependent concepts such as dignity and heroism become increasingly subjective, debatable, and ambiguous. Once the teleology unravels, the personal idealism that it sustained begins to seem merely conditioned and vestigial, and this process results in the kind of demoralized ambivalence that is the salient characteristic of Lowell's work. Nietzsche regarded all teleologies and metaphysical systems as expressions of nihilism in disguise, since they were indications that "man [had] lost faith in his own value," and he exhorted his audience to transform the nihilism of despair—which occurs when religious and philosophical systems fail to support belief and identity—into a nihilism of affirmation.[1] In his early poems Lowell was working his way through the crises of nihilism that Nietzsche describes, but he was never able to break through fully to the other Nietzschean side, to give credence to the exaltation of subjectivity or to the desirability of the human reappropriation of the world. The secular Augustinian scruple prevails in his thought as well.

As he moves painfully along the metaphysical spectrum implied in my title—which, of course, is really his—Lowell in the poems becomes increasingly problematic to himself, as an artist and as a human being, and this effect is evident in his work as markedly in its technique as in its content. Form and value in Lowell's work do not so much collaborate and cohere as test and challenge each other, continually. Frank Kermode might say of Lowell's career, as he has said of Sartre's *La Nausée*, that it represents a "crisis in the relation between fiction and reality, the tension of dissonance between paradigmatic form and contingent reality."[2] Lowell's nihilism is complicated by the unregulated intervention of internally surviving paradigms. Hayden Carruth addresses precisely this issue in his tribute to Lowell just after Lowell's death. Carruth calls attention to the number of poets of Lowell's generation who died early, as if broken finally by an indefinable anxiety and guilt.

> They had inherited from their elders—Eliot, Pound, Stevens, Williams, Auden, even Frost—an enormous metaphysical awareness, an enormous apparatus for moral, psychological, and aesthetic inquiry, without anything to use it on. They were in a vacancy ("the unredeemable world"). They had neither faith nor doubt, neither art for its own sake nor the natural environment. Everything had been used up... [Finally] they came to understand, one way or another, that their sin was their own existence.

How could it be in this great universe—great no matter how you conceive of it, an order or a disorder, an act or an accident—how could it be that such a monstrous thing as human intelligence had arisen? It was too absurd. It was nothing really, a trifle of unmeaning; yet it was everything too. For it was the sin of presumption, the worst sin of all.[3]

If the first negational stage of nihilism is a necessary transition, as Nietzsche argued, to the affirmational—"the sign of a crucial and most essential growth, of the transition to new conditions of existence"—it stands to reason that this first dangerous phase might also never be wholly transcended. Lowell was somehow perpetually in transition, between the negation of old values and the affirmation of new ones, and he makes Nietzsche by comparison seem ingenuously romantic.

This brings us to the point of the title of this study and to the poem from Lowell's *Notebook* from which it is appropriated.

The Nihilist as Hero

"All our French poets can turn an inspired line,
but which has written six passable in sequence?"
said Valéry. That was a happy day for Satan....
One wants words meat-hooked from the living steer,
but the cold flame of tinfoil licks the metal log,
the beautifully unchanging fire of childhood
betraying a monotony of vision.
Life by definition breeds on change,
each season we scrap new cars and wars and women.
Sometimes when I am ill or delicate,
the pinched flame of my match turns living green,
the cornstalk in green tails and seeded tassel....
A nihilist has to live in the world as is, gazing the impossible
    summit to rubble.

Several things are relevant here. The poem, like so many in *Notebook*, and like all of the poems in the section in which it appears, is about writing and life. Valéry in paraphrase is speaking for the primacy of craft and "intelligent labor" against mere inspiration, which is accidental. To the extent that discipline in craft serves the ends of "la poésie pure," the Satan here must be Valéry's Satan of "Ébauche d'un serpent," whom Alan

Williamson quotes Lowell as calling "the spirit that insists on perfection."[4] When we come to the last lines of Lowell's poem, that spirit has been rejected, not in absolute terms, but on behalf of the nihilist, who has different needs, who cannot contemplate perfection and needs instead to live authentically in his language, in words not polished but "meat-hooked from the living steer"; "life by definition breeds on change." A demeaning irony underlies this: only in illness, or most often in illness, do those inspired visions of change occur. The normative or healthy is the child's stylized seeing, a "monotony of vision." The other is closer to life by its very strangeness. So to say that the nihilist has to live in "the world as is" means that he has no choice and must justify his existence only by intensifying his experience of it. "Gazing the summit to rubble" implies an unwillingness to cave in but also an unwillingness to be naive about the value of the world—a minimal existential gesture, assertion with no object. The hero of this context is a very small hero indeed, and seems meant to appear so. One could not guess whether Lowell had the last lines of Auden's "Autumn Song" in his mind when he wrote his own couplet, but they certainly come to mind for the reader, by way of the contrast:

> Cold, impossible, ahead
> Lifts the mountain's lovely head
> Whose white waterfall could bless
> Travellers in their last distress.

The difference between the two images is that where Auden's idealism is dualistic and pessimistic (the waterfall is *there* at the summit but at the same time unattainable) Lowell's is overtly monistic and therefore not only pessimistic but hopeless. In *Day by Day*, his last volume, Lowell's position seems at times closer to Auden's: he seems to have become able at last to imagine a mode of being other than the thwarted human one, but even that remains elusive, opaque, and suspect. Meanwhile, in *Notebook*, another memorable epigram has been appropriated to be cynically devaluated. Nietzsche's injunction "Become what you are!" has become, for the title of the section in which "The Nihilist as Hero" appears, "We Do What We Are."

It is worth making a point of the "echoes" because in Lowell's work it is mostly echoes of idealism that we hear, which phenomenon gives us a different reading of Tate's observation that Lowell was among the few poets who retained "at least the memory of the spiritual dignity of man." I take this sonnet of Lowell's to be a bedrock statement about how a nihilist with heroic presumptions remains an inescapable irony to himself, a helpless oxymoron, an ambivalent Laforgue two generations farther on, with different problems; and the evolution of Lowell's style shows, I think, that whatever else was murky in his understanding, his perception of this irony was grimly clear. It seems possible, even, that toward the end of his career the awkwardness and unfinished quality of his writing, and its willful banality, were quite deliberate and contrived expressions of the defeatedness of spirit felt by the character he had made of himself in his poems.

One thing above all a poet must take care not to do is lose morale, since poetry is, if nothing else, morale apotheosized. Yet very few of the traditional consolations of the poet seem to have had any therapeutic relevance for Lowell at any point in his life. The facsimile of Christian theism that motivates his early work is, in its way, more terrifying an implication than the glum agnosticism of the later, and is not at all orthodox. Eastern religions seem not to have interested him at any stage. Romantic supernaturalism, like Roethke's or Dickey's, is virtually absent from his work. He could neither sentimentalize his own childhood nor, therefore, childhood in general or the myth of innocence. His view of history was antimelioristic. Sexual love was, in the poems at any rate, at least as problematic as redemptive. Most of the friends he writes about, by the time they get written about, are either dying or dead. Any infatuation with the Nietzschean will to power he might have cherished in his younger days seems to have dissipated altogether by the time of *Notebook* and *History*, where historical and mythological *übermenschen* are systematically debunked and vulgarized. Over the long haul his compulsive sincerity produces in him an ambiguous attitude even toward art. Lowell was a studious and learned man. Mythology, literature, music, painting constituted for him an alternative universe, one that was not irrational and that therefore absorbed him powerfully. On the other hand, his own style grew increasingly less "literary," and thus indirectly he expressed a distrust of literature's ability to affirm anything usefully meaningful or truthful about human life. In *Notebook* the allure of posterity is mocked repeatedly. So all that is left finally, when this is summed up, is an art which, as Sartre said, reclaims "the world by revealing it as it is but as if it had its source in human liberty,"[5] and not only does this minimal, stubbornly human thing but calls attention at every stage to the fact that that is what it is doing.

In the memorable last sentence of the "Afterthought" appended to *Notebook* Lowell said: "In truth I seem to have felt mostly the joys of living, in remembering, in recording, thanks to the gift of the Muse [an ironic shading here], it is the pain." This statement calls attention to the fact that, naive views of confessional poetry notwithstanding, the Robert Lowell in life and the Robert Lowell in the poems were substantively different people, the Lowell in life—in and often out of health—having been a considerably more vivid and robust figure than his readers, extrapolating, might be expected to conjure. The divergence is not easy to account for, but it suggests that Lowell the poet was a watchful, Kierkegaardian critic of Lowell the man, analytical and unappeasable. One might suppose that a good many people live perfectly satisfactory and productive lives without being able to call up much more justification for doing so than Lowell has, and without thinking much about it. But poetry when it is not morale apotheosized is a form of condensed thinking, an intensifying of the real. In any event this is what it seems to have become for Lowell, or what he was unable, for whatever reason, to keep it from becoming. Without the writing he might have achieved more peace, and hence his ambivalence about it, about his Muse. The human liberty that Sartre speaks of, after all, has its bright and dark, or manic and depressive, sides, and so one might expect that a world that had even such a source as that would be as problematic as one with no source at all.

A related point that needs to be raised here is that Lowell's identity, at least his poetic one, was uniquely and inextricably entwined with the history of his own time, and with human history generally. To say "uniquely" is not to overstate it. He is most like Pound in this respect, though Pound managed, until Pisa at any rate, to convey the impression of having transcended historical process and of knowing pretty clearly how it ought to be directed. For Lowell, history denied the autonomy of the self and confirmed that public and private events were simply expressions on a different scale of the same human motivations; and with Lowell this self was not someone else's, or an abstraction, but his own. It was an expression of his nihilist's integrity that he could not pretend to inhabit a different planet in order to make a separate poetic peace. What was happening in the world affected him to the point that the borders between his own identity and the human world outside became progressively more indistinct—hence, for example, a volume called *Notebook* becomes another volume called *History*.

Auden in the thirties was involved in history in a way similar to Lowell's, but grew more rather than less insular. Stevens by comparison was like a Villiers de l'Isle–Adam paragon. Eliot and Tate wrote about history in a formal mode that distances us—and them, as personae—from its unmediated circumstantiality. When Lowell writes about World War II he and his father both are strangely, obliquely implicated ("I ask for bread, my father gives me mould; / His stocking is full of stones").[6] His mother's casket, containing her body, on the way home from Italy, is observed to resemble Napoleon's at the Hôtel des Invalides.[7] When he thinks of the death of Che Guevara he is conscious at the same moment that he is illicitly involved with the woman whose hand he is holding, and he thinks, in a characteristically baroque connection, of Charles I in hiding.[8] When he writes about Colonel Shaw's unwavering integrity and sense of purpose and of the disintegration of Boston into "civic sandpiles," it is he himself who is Colonel Shaw's foil, pining for "the dark downward and vegetating kingdom" of the old South Boston Aquarium and taking some comfort from the next-best thing, his television set, crouching before it to watch the "drained faces of Negro schoolchildren rise like balloons" on the screen. "For the Union Dead" is in fact a model of the way in which history and the poet's life interact in Lowell's poems. The poet in that poem is more like Boston than he is like Colonel Shaw, an aspect of the process that he deplores; and the tone of the poem, consistent with the behavior of the poet *in* the poem, is not that of moral outrage but that of an observer who seems to be content to be different to the extent that he observes. This effect is very carefully managed, and it produces something near to the reverse of the covert sanctimoniousness that compromises most such cultural criticism. It also deepens the sense of hopelessness by which we and the poet participate in the dehumanizing process.

David Kalstone has written of John Ashbery that he emphasizes "the unique power of language to reveal how much of the external life the inner life displaces."[9] In Lowell's poetry, as a rule, the inner life cannot displace the external, and the external in fact introjects so deeply that it infects the very language that might be used to displace it. The effect of the pressure of history is to narrow the gap for Lowell between art and life and therefore to foreclose any chance of redemption through mere sensibility. Jarrell wrote about this long ago: Lowell, he said, "seems to be condemned both to read history and to repeat it."[10] One cannot achieve human authenticity finally without being historical; but to achieve authenticity at the expense of repeating the history of this particular century, and of having it internalized, virtually ensures an unwinnable contest with moral despair and self-contempt.

Describing what he calls Lowell's "poetry of experience," Steven Gould Axelrod says that "Lowell did not write poems in hopes of achieving immortal fame, 'grass on the minor slopes of Parnassus'...His 'open book,' he suggests in *History*, amounts to no more than an 'open coffin,' doomed like his corporeal self to perish in time, though more slowly. Poetry had an entirely different value for Lowell, an existential value: it proved its maker was 'alive.'"[11] Axelrod quotes Lowell as saying that in America "the artist's existence becomes his art. He is reborn in it, and he hardly exists without it." Lowell's comment comes in an interview with A. Alvarez in which the main subject becomes America's famous cultural schizophrenia. On the one hand it is a country whose "democracy was based, theoretically, on certain abstract principles that were lacking in Europe" (Alvarez), founded "on a constitution" rather than "on a history and a culture." "We were founded," Lowell says, "on a Declaration, on the Constitution, on Principles, and we've always had the ideal of 'saving the world.'" On the other hand it is a country whose "moral sense" seems thwarted by its own "general rootlessness and mobility," because of which "nothing seems to last, neither objects, nor relationships, nor even the landscape" (Alvarez). For Lowell this abstracted quality of American life is epitomized by the city of New York.

> You can't touch a stone in London that doesn't point backwards into history; while even for an American city, New York seems to have no past. And yet it's the only city that sort of provides an intellectual, human continuum to live in... [If] you removed it, you'd be cutting out the heart of American culture. Yet it is a heart with no past. The New York of fifty years ago is utterly gone and there are no landmarks; the record of the city doesn't point back into the past. It has that sheer presence which, I think, is not the image of mobility you talk about.
>
> *Alvarez:* This kind of driving force, moving into the future all the time, without a past at all, as though the wake were closing up behind it...
>
> *Lowell:* And it has a great sheer feeling of utter freedom. And then when one thinks back a little bit, it seems all confused and naked.[12]

It is in this context that Lowell offers his observation about the American artist's existence becoming his art. The language in places is curiously Nietzschean. The remarks describe a country that is simultaneously idealistic and nihilistic and a poet, living in history, who is all too aware of how deeply identified he and his native country are.

Axelrod does not comment upon the odd circumstance that what "proves its maker is alive" (a honeycomb, in the first instance) is also described as an "open coffin." Lowell's commentators tend to want to make the poems seem more conventionally affirmative than they truly are. The irony in this case is very dark and represents Lowell at a low point in existential morale, where being alive is next to being dead, and where the poem alone is the sign that the poet has kept going nevertheless. It is thus also a sign—as silence would not be—that the poet, with every possible reason to do so clearly before him, has not been willing to give up on experience or on his wavering commitment to extort from experience some unmediated value that remains for him imaginable but stubbornly undisclosed.

1. Subduing Disorder

In his "Afterthought" for *Notebook 1967–68* Lowell describes himself as leaning "heavily to the rational" while being "devoted to surrealism."[1] He cites examples of the surrealistic style and then concludes with this general observation: "Surrealism can degenerate into meaningless clinical hallucinations, or worse, into rhetorical machinery, yet it is a natural way to write our fictions." The offhand manner of this statement does not do justice to its importance. The thought is after *Notebook* but its implications and relevance reach back through Lowell's work to *Land of Unlikeness*, where the rational faculty strains toward the "union with God" which "is somewhere in sight in all poetry" through and against the opposing confusion of *regio dissimilitudinis*. The rational faculty is the custodian of the "memory of the spiritual dignity of man," which Allen Tate speaks of in his preface for that first volume; but even there it is more a memory than a living conviction, and even the memory is painfully sustained in the face of the evidence, the land of unlikeness, the theological surreal. The rational faculty begins by seeking to discover order and succeeds only in imposing it—an order that is strenuous, explosive, and deranged because the poet who achieves it is equally a witness to God and an honest witness of history and experience.

The order of the early poems is violently formal, not God's but the poet's—the order of a poet who leans "heavily to the rational" but finds surrealism "a natural way to write our fictions." As a persona, that poet is manifest in a formalized hallucination as an avatar of both God and man at once, in command and helpless, shaper and misshapen, the hero as nihilist edging already toward the nihilist as hero. Lowell's form of surrealism is the evidence in his style of the continuing crisis of his unstable epistemology—a perceptual affliction at its source in the mind, causing everything to be seen at once, all of time coexisting in any one instant, all planes of perception and cognition collapsed into a single surface, no dimension or space, only the illusion of dimension and space in the massively baroque motion, derived from Milton, and described by Jarrell as "things wrenched into formal shape, organized under terrific pressure."[2] This is surrealism in one respect; in another it is cubism's epistemology gone berserk. In *Pity the Monsters* Alan Williamson points out that what Lowell means by "surrealistic" is significantly different from what is ordinarily meant by the term, that his surrealism, in fact, is

> the opposite of much dream- or fantasy-based art (the paintings of Dali or De Chirico, for instance), which tends to de-realize experience by artful exclusions, reducing us to the simple relation of a very few sensations . . . Such art often regains in atmospheric unity what it loses in logic, and leaves us with an odd sense of lucidity, even of rest. Lowell's poems turn, rather, to the unruliness of the moment, showing us how many separate strands of sensation it contains, how weirdly the mind shuttles between them and its own equally abrupt and mysterious patterns of fantasy-thought. Lowell struggles, in short, to overcome a monistic fastidiousness that is all but essential to the descriptive process, whether its conventions are realistic or surrealist; and to deliver the feeling, if not the literal contents, of a basic mind-flux.[3]

In the half-dozen enduring poems in *Lord Weary's Castle*, the rule imposed upon disorder is masterful; but it is the rule of will rather than faith, of reason muscling chaos, unlikeness, into shape. In complex ways the difference between Lowell's poems of the forties and his poems of the early seventies is one of syntax. Syntax in *Lord Weary's Castle* is the order-making force, the instrument of will and reason, the organizing system that contains and creates the pressure. When the syntax breaks, the rational will has yielded, the union with God has failed, and the poet has entered time to contend with chaos—if such is possible—on its own terms.

In that early baroque and surrealistic manner, the condensation, the arresting conceits, and the jolting prosody produce an intensity that is, in effect, feeling sublimated or displaced, a facsimile of feeling where there is no human source. The Lowell persona in the early work is first a poet or prophet and only then a man, mostly on the outer periphery of time; in the later poetry he is first a man, then a poet and diffident prophet who is awkwardly wedged into time. Neither is a desirable position. In the one station his response to experience is synoptic, and in the other paratactic, it being marginally easier—we understand from the work itself—to comprehend and command existence from without than it is from within. Lowell's poetry wavers and veers between a psychic control over experience and defeated capitulations to or appeals from it. The poems then imitate in their forms of feeling the heroic motive in conflict with the encroaching nihilist perspective which threatens to undermine it. In Lowell's career as a whole, ambivalence is visible as a process, an unsteady but continuous process of erosion—from the heroic and formal posture of *Lord Weary's Castle* to the existential disorientation of *Notebook, History, For Lizzie and Harriet, Dolphin,* and *Day by Day.* In the poems and in isolated phases of his career this ambivalence is visible in the form as abrasive tension and conflict, expressed both in the fluctuating levels of idiom and in the poems' irresolute structures.

In the concluding section of "In Memory of Arthur Winslow" (in both the *Land of Unlikeness* and *Lord Weary's Castle* versions) there erupts this famous invocation to "Our Lady":

O Mother, I implore
Your scorched, blue thunderbreasts of love to pour
Buckets of blessings on my burning head. . . .

In part four of *Life Studies,* the elegiac "Grandparents" turns abruptly upon another form of invocation, equally arresting in its own way: "Grandpa! Have me, hold me, cherish me!" The difference between the two passages shows the result of a reluctant journey into demythologized experience. Both apostrophes express a distressed spirit on the edge of terror, an elegiac hysteria barely subdued in the face of different voids. The second is directed to a once-living person who was loved and now is dead and beyond reaching to for help, and the first to a fiction, a grotesque icon, whose identity in the poem is both remote and bizarre. In the first passage the personage appealed to is excessively stylized and in the second excessively unstylized; and for the reasons implied in the presentation, each potential intercessor is powerless, for the first is merely a fanciful icon made of words and the second is irretrievably dead. The poet of *Life Studies*, in fact, goes on to make a point of the futility of his childish feeling by reverting as suddenly to a mature and jaded detachment:

> I hold an *Illustrated London News*—;
> disloyal still,
> I doodle handlebar
> mustaches on the last Russian Czar.

The implied analogy between Grandfather Winslow and Nicholas II suggests an ambivalent attitude toward his grandfather to begin with. In any case, there is no help, and never was, to be derived from an appeal to the human or superhuman.

In the earliest of these two poems about Arthur Winslow, the death of Lowell's grandfather becomes, callously one feels, an occasion for meditation upon themes of material pride and the death of both humanistic and spiritual idealism. Historically the poem ranges as far back as the early colonial settlement; its idiom—erratically distributed—is an unstable compound of classical mythology, Catholic liturgy, English neoclassical poeticisms, and modern American colloquial speech. Arthur Winslow is barely visible through the opulent verbal screens, except in his generic role as an American patriarch whose dying concludes a family tradition and for whom death by cancer is implied to be a kind of divine retribution. Insofar as he is sympathetically portrayed at all, he is shown to be closed in upon by forces outside his control—his relations, ethnically impure Boston, cancer, Charon, Jesus—despite his own rapacious, capitalistic bravado. Otherwise the meanings considered in the poem are not directly related to the actual death of the actual man.

The earliest (later discarded) version of the poem was begun less than a year after Arthur Winslow's death. On the evidence of the devotion expressed in *Life Studies*, the event of this death must surely have been a painful personal loss; but intent on being a Poet who is entitled to inhabit a symbolic rather than a natural world—a world of essence, Allen Tate would call it—Lowell is impelled by the death to express only the bookish passion of a prophetic vision. His despair is displaced into a rejection of the world, which, curiously and inhumanly, Arthur Winslow is made to symbolize. Microtime yields mysteriously to macrotime, and in the process the poet himself is absorbed into a vividly stylized idiom that is idiosyncratic, private, and austerely impersonal. This labored discontinuity between time and the self is indigenous to Lowell's early style, and one of its main impulses seems to be the extinction rather than the validation of the empirical self, a projection of the self outward beyond history rather than the reverse. At the level of imaginative activity the surrealistic mode already expresses the anxiety of an unsettled perspective and the tension of a groping toward any available pattern of order.

The first section of the Arthur Winslow elegy veers abruptly from one spatial perspective to another, and from circumstantial to mythic modes, in an effect that approximates the experience of hallucination:

> This Easter, Arthur Winslow, less than dead,
> Your people set you up in Phillips' House
> To settle off your wrestling with the crab—
> The claws drop flesh upon your yachting blouse
> Until longshoreman Charon come and stab
> Through your adjusted bed
> And crush the crab.

The phrase "longshoreman Charon" exemplifies in miniature the peculiar idiom of the poem's splayed, perceptual disorientation. Apart from the problem of the very cryptic symbolism in this image, the contexts from which "longshoreman" and "Charon" are imported are so divergent that the two terms of the vehicle virtually cancel each other out. Wrenching them together (Jarrell's phrase again comes to mind) is the aesthetic equivalent of uniting the positive poles of two magnets. The poem's other images may contain less semantic pressure, but their dynamics are essentially the same. In isolation the ironically associated details of the "yachting blouse" and the "adjusted bed" are laconic signs of life's own mocking surrealism; in context they, along with other details—"*This* Easter," "Phillips House," and the morbidly clinical "less than dead"—fix a naturalistic point of reference for the otherwise densely mythological rhetoric, the "longshoreman" level for the "Charon" level of the rest.

This form of rhetorical action is epitomized in the concluding stanza of this section, a single walloping, operatic sentence of ten lines. The first main clause depicts the vulgar Irish in the Public Garden engaged in their idle Sunday diversion of pursuing "the dusky chub" (an oddly Augustan phrase and brief time-warp in itself). Then suddenly in the second clause, pivoting violently on a single conjunction, the poem hurtles into an arena of an altogether different activity (where, incidentally, Arthur Winslow's yachting blouse has one last ironic role):

> and the ghost
> Of risen Jesus walks the waves to run
> Arthur upon a trumpeting black swan
> Beyond Charles River to the Acheron
> Where the wide waters and their voyager are one.

The apparent symbolic function of the coordination in this entire stanza (showing the world unable to hear the Word) is partially subverted by the more striking effect of the explosion of the syntax in the second clause out of the relative quiescence of the first. The focus then seems further dissipated as Jesus becomes Charon to escort Winslow in triumph to a pagan underworld, perhaps Purgatory (but if so, why not say so?). The pageantry seems to have overrun its own allegorical import. Arthur Winslow has been transported from a stylized reality to begin with into the verbal otherworld of a polymythic apparition.

There are, in a sense, two levels of the empirical element in this poem. One is the phenomenal world where Arthur Winslow dies. The other is orthodox Christian doctrine. The language of the poem diverts us from both into itself. Thus, Stephen Yenser cites Allen Tate, who rebukes his protégé, in a general class of poets, for succumbing to the excesses of the "angelic imagination": "Catholic poets have lost, along with their heretical friends, the power to start with the 'common thing': they have lost the gift for concrete experience. The abstraction of the modern mind has obscured their way into the natural order." Yenser adds: "The poet who in pursuit of essence cannot turn part of his attention to nature turns it all upon his words and the figures they make in the hope that the latter, more abstract than nature [and more private, I would add, than doctrine] will bring him nearer Reality."[4] We might consider further whether the evasion, by the words, of the two realms of reference does not, in fact, entail a rejection of both and the substitution in their place, filling a vacuum, of a symbolist mirage. The extraordinary verbal intensity of this poem, and of the others like it, suggests a vividness of feeling so intense that it must create its own solipsistic environment into which it can be displaced, its own retroactive objective correlative. Words have been used deliberately to distort reference to nature and meaning.

In the next two sections of the elegy—"Dunbarton" and "Five Years Later"—the idiom is less surrealistically vivid. The poem returns to an identifiable natural world (the site of the family burial ground) and a fairly ordered (because evaluated) past. Although five years pass between the first section and the next two, the themes are continuous: the failure of the Puritans' hope to create, in God's service, an Eden on earth and the ascendancy in its place, symbolized by Arthur Winslow's misguided capitalistic enterprise, of a modern Babylon. Then as the cities of Columbus and Boston shade subtly into Babylon (by implication), and as Babylon finally recovers local form as Trinity Church and then mythic form as Atlantis, the apocalyptic tempo mounts once more. The speaker of section four (Winslow or the poet or both) broods upon the grotesque demise of the Puritan dream. He invokes the Virgin for intercession. Then, in a vision as if out of the *Book of Revelation*, he beholds Trinity Church with its merely "painted Paradise" "Sink like Atlantis in the Devil's jaw." The speaker is spared this judgment upon materialized spiritual pride ("I strike for shore"); but without the assurance of a movement in history toward God and no longer responsive to the debased coinage of iconography, he finds himself without bearings for the will. He therefore can only pray for absolution.

> "I find no painted idols to adore:
> Hell is burned out, heaven's harp-strings are slack.
> Mother, run to the chalice, and bring back
> Blood on your finger-tips for Lazarus who was poor."

The idiom of this section is less bizarre than that of the first only because its frame of reference is primarily Christian. But even within that frame of reference, the idiom is mixed in a kind of ecumenical Esperanto. Hence the famous *ad hoc*, surrealistic Mariolatry, born of the confused occasion and of mixed feelings toward religious understanding:

> O Mother, I implore
> Your scorched, blue thunderbreasts of love to pour
> Buckets of blessings on my burning head. . . .

Here, the refuge of sinners has become one with the angry God of Jonathan Edwards, and therefore difficult to respond to with single-minded devotion. It may be that this image expresses a powerful ambivalence in Lowell's religious feeling, or it may be simply a flourish of erudition; in any case, no very decisive epiphany is available within a framework of so many variant mythic systems. The poem is resolved, musically speaking (as in section one) within the borders of its own verbal realm; but for a poem that represents itself as an ethical and spiritual meditation, that form of resolution seems self-defeating. The chief conflict of Lowell's early poems, and the source of their intensisty, is an abrasion between existentialist and formalist modes of understanding. In this elegy the meaning of Arthur Winslow's death is pressed toward an uncertain teleology of history and myth—in the abstract, a conventional mission of elegy—but in that process, meaning of any form becomes obscured, and the personal meaning of the personal event is evaded or disregarded altogether.

Although poetic vision that is clouded in this way by erudition borders on being alien to its own underlying theistic doctrine, it is emphatically *life*-alien and emotionally unresponsive to the simpler events of the phenomenal world. (Even in this context, the poet's posing as the poor leper Lazarus from the parable in *Luke* 16:19–25 is an extraordinary affectation.) We learn the full human implication of this from the Robert Lowell of *Life Studies*, where memory and the selective attention of the imagination carry the poet more directly into the pattern of his own experience:

> The farm's my own!
> Back there alone,
> I keep indoors, and spoil another season.
> I hear the rattley little country gramophone
> racking its five foot horn:
> "O Summer Time!"
> Even at noon here the formidable
> *Ancien Régime* still keeps nature at a distance. Five
> green shaded light bulbs spider the billiards-table;
> no field is greener than its cloth,
> where Grandpa, dipping sugar for us both,
> once spilled his demitasse.
> His favorite ball, the number three,
> still hides the coffee stain.
>
> Never again
> to walk there, chalk our cues,
> insist on shooting for us both.
> Grandpa! Have me, hold me, cherish me!

If the rhetorical structure of "In Memory of Arthur Winslow" could be called, in Stevens' terms, a violent order (and therefore a disorder), the arrangement in "Grandparents" is a tamed disorder, its details organized casually, abstracted only by observation, so that the modest truth of it is made to seem revealed from within rather than imposed. This effect is symbolized, in a way, and reinforced, by the casual and seemingly coincidental rhymes, which fall gracefully and responsibly into place. The grandfather's presence is expressed through associated objects that simultaneously declare his absence. Time has stopped and time has gone on. Nature has been "kept at a distance"—apparently a dynastic enterprise—but not at bay. Nothing beyond the realm of life and death, and the love exchanged within it, is called upon or envisioned, and the unembarrassed invocation is an expression of the awkward pain of knowing that one is restrained absolutely by that finitude. Both this invocation and the one to "Our Lady" in the earlier elegy are futile, but in "Grandparents" the lost grandfather is the focus of an ambiguous feeling for existence in time. In "In Memory of Arthur Winslow" the same man and the quality of existence he is called upon in "Grandparents" to symbolize are displaced in favor of surrealistic eschatology. Between these two stages of Lowell's career, the extreme claims of art and of human understanding remain competitive.

In *Lord Weary's Castle*, "Colloquy in Black Rock" is the one poem that seems theologically and emotionally unambivalent, a conventional devotional utterance, and I present it here in its entirety because its comparative simplicity of language and theme and its harmony of parts serve as an instructive contrast to the ambiguities, theological and otherwise, of the rest of the volume's work.

> Here the jack-hammer jabs into the ocean;
> My heart, you race and stagger and demand
> More blood-gangs for your nigger-brass percussions,
> Till I, the stunned machine of your devotion,
> Clanging upon this cymbal of a hand,
> Am rattled screw and footloose. All discussions
>
> End in the mud-flat detritus of death.
> My heart, beat faster, faster. In Black Mud
> Hungarian workmen give their blood
> For the martyre Stephen, who was stoned to death.

Black Mud, a name to conjure with: O mud
For watermelons gutted to the crust,
Mud for the mole-tide harbor, mud for mouse,
Mud for the armored Diesel fishing tubs that thud
A year and a day to wind and tide; the dust
Is on this skipping heart that shakes my house,

House of our Savior who was hanged till death.
My heart, beat faster, faster, In Black Mud
Stephen the martyre was broken down to blood:
Our ransom is the rubble of his death.

Christ walks on the black water. In Black Mud
Darts the kingfisher. On Corpus Christi, heart,
Over the drum-beat of St. Stephen's choir
I hear him, *Stupor Mundi,* and the mud
Flies from his hunching wings and beak—my heart,
The blue kingfisher dives on you in fire.

It is a difficult notion to become adjusted to, but Nietzsche would regard this poem's statement as classically nihilistic, which indeed, given Nietzsche's flamboyantly perverse criteria, it is. The colloquy of the poem is between the heart and the self or "I," and this can only mean, it seems to me, that the heart, without speech except in rhythms, is the body, and the heart's rhythm joins the rhythm of the jack-hammer breaking up the land to break up the flesh toward the certain end, personal death, which renders one speechless and all things pointless along its way. The larger subject of the poem is entropy and the pervasiveness of its forms: what is true of the land being broken up is true of the body, is true of speech, is true for the indentured Hungarian workers; it is true even of time and place, for Black Rock, Connecticut, abruptly becomes and remains Black Mud, a kind of metropolis of inertia, mutability's dark side. The symmetrically central stanza is a musical rendering of this theme, in which the three letters of the word "mud" are relentlessly reiterated in different patterns so that all detail is absorbed symbolically into the sound. But on the other side of that secular apparition awaits epiphany, and with it the poet's and poem's conversion. For the body ("house") of the self and of the savior are suddenly perceived to be one, and St. Stephen's death, as a consequence, to be magical, not merely rubble like the rest. Christ—as in Milton's image in *Lycidas* of "the dear might of Him that walked the waves"—is understood to have transcended mere nature, Black Mud, and the kingfisher comes suddenly as a revelation of the beauty of the sheer power of salvation—the antithesis of the "mud-flat detritus"; coming in flames, the kingfisher is also the gift of the Holy Spirit which gave the Apostles the power of utterance. So the end of all discussion is in turn ended.

It scarcely needs saying that if this were the definitive Lowell, the body of his work, even his early work, would be markedly different. What *is* carried forward into the other poems is the fear and rejection of unmediated existence. What becomes clouded almost immediately is the unified theistic vision, the "monism," as Nietzsche put it, the faith in "some supreme form of domination and administration" which enables man to see "himself as a mode of the deity" and thus "*to be able to believe in his own value.*" "Colloquy in Black Rock" is an extraordinarily effective poem structurally, and its shapedness is dependent entirely upon its clear-cut devotional form; that is, resolution and catharsis are available to the poem because resolution and catharsis are made available to the spirit. In this way, aesthetic and religious values have been mutually reinforcing (and confused with one another) in the past. But this is not to be Lowell's dispensation; and once the traditional recourse to faith from the nihilistic pressure becomes uncertain, it becomes dangerously and then fatally absorbed into the nihilistic vision itself. That is to say, the one kind of nihilism (the kind Nietzsche speaks of) that is a release from the other is instead overcome by it, and the traditional pattern of despair and redemption is, in effect, reversed. This is not a process that takes place in clearly delineated stages. It is more like a metastasis, and the ideational confusion that results prevails in the style of *Lord Weary's Castle*.

The major themes of Lowell's early work derive from a revulsion toward the world—a revulsion that is imperfectly relieved only by fleeting and ambiguous visions of Christian redemption. Whether their subjects are mammon, war, New England's life-denying Puritan history (which the poet himself is a product of), or his own family, the poems are saturated in the fallen state. The interest in Jonathan Edwards that caused Lowell to begin a biography of Edwards was clearly an interest born of identification. Edwards' precisely rationalized fatalism served as the galvanizing in-fluence. In Lowell's poems of this period, as in Edwards' sermons and meditations, the temporal state is both corrupt and joyless. The difference between the two men's views is that for Edwards grace is assured to the penitent in a way that reflects the majesty of God, whereas for Lowell grace is already hypothetical and nostalgic, a residual image in the mind, to be recovered, if at all, from the future and otherwise not remarkably different from the state of childhood for Dylan Thomas, for example, or even erotic love for Keats. What Lowell appears to have derived from Christian doctrine in this period was not so much a view of the world as, first, a pattern of feeling that converts readily into an idiom of poetic expression, and, second, a closed cosmic system that enhanced the acoustics of the poems and the resonance of themes that came naturally to him in the first place. The first adaptation is apparent in the pressure-and-release pattern identified by Randall Jarrell;[5] the second, together with the classical influences, is the authority for Lowell's aggressively anachronistic formal tone.

The explicitly religious poems strain with the pressure from the evil of the world, human and inhuman, then typically seek their release in epiphany. The range of reference available in Lowell's surrealistically allusive idiom intensifies the pressure as well as extends the implication of his themes, and the dense texture that results is in itself a presemantic image of a terrible spiritual claustrophobia.

> Tonight a blackout. Twenty years ago
> I hung my stocking on the tree, and hell's
> Serpent entwined the apple in the toe
> To sting the child with knowledge. Hooker's heels
> Kicking at nothing in the shifting snow,
> A cannon and a cairn of cannonballs
> Rusting before the blackened Statehouse, know
> How the long horn of plenty broke like glass
> In Hooker's gauntlets.

These first lines of "Christmas Eve under Hooker's Statue" range both through history and through different forms of time primarily in order to unite different perspectives upon the same human experience. The blackout stipulates the poem's historical present—America, World War II—and also its prevailing irony, the coincidence of the historical event and the ritual season. The next sentence carries us, in the first clause, into the poet's personal past and, in the second, back outward into a mythic and generic past. Despite the reach back into mythic time there is no illusion of historical space here but instead the flat, atemporal surface of conflicting planes. Hooker's statue evokes yet another war at another point of time.

The "blackened Statehouse" (referring, apparently, to the blackening of the gold dome during World War II as an air raid precaution)[6] fuses modern and eighteenth-century Boston and implies a clash between real and ideal politics. The image of the horn of plenty (prototype of the Christmas stocking) disperses particulars again and universalizes the image of Hooker as the man of war in all times as despoiler of man's good.

In the second stanza Hooker recedes into *his* prototype, the "war-god" Mars, a "blundering butcher" who "rides on Time." Then the poet's helpless station is reinvoked, then his father's, only to imply that there is nothing in time to be passed forward (an even bleaker view than in Jesus' parable):[7]

> I am cold:
> I ask for bread, my father gives me mould;
>
> His stocking is full of stones.

The Santa of childhood seemingly has become the Mars of maturity, crowned with "wizened berries" and addressed as "man of war." The ancient image of Eden is then evoked rhetorically and characterized as it is now negatively transvalued, a bed where "the speckled serpent" and "the black-eyed susan" both forever coexist. The final lines of the last stanza recall Chancellorsville (and Hooker) as an epitome of war's futility, and then Melville's ironic commentary, "All wars are boyish." "But we are old," adds the poet, "our fields are running wild." Men are morally boyish, this means, and therefore naively warlike; but man in time is old, and therefore responsible, but doomed by his nature to continue to despoil his original Eden. The poem concludes with the tentative, visionary hope for the future, "Till Christ again turn wanderer and child."

Invoking Christ as a child brings the poem's theme full circle, back to the Christmas season and its significance (the birth of the child who is a savior, the new beginning) and the idea of threatened innocence which is expressed in the title itself. The characterization of the world's corruption and the desolation of the lost son, who is the poet seeking comfort from the lost father within it, sets all beyond any hope of humanistic or personal redemption; the only stay against despair is the promise of divine intercession. In the abstract this Christian assessment of man's state seems appropriately orthodox, as in "Colloquy in Black Rock," but, in fact, in this resolution the poem is less dependent upon the logic of doctrine than the doctrine is upon the logic of the poem. In *Lycidas* the vision of Edward King's bodily resurrection is not as important, to the poem, as the dignity that Christ's love bestows upon the dead. In "Christmas Eve under Hooker's Statue" the return of Jesus is not as important as the form of childhood Lowell calls upon His advent to symbolize. Christ's returning as a child is quite a different matter, as an image, from his returning "to judge the quick and the dead." Examined closely and taken literally, this Blakean epiphany would seem as heterodox theologically as the resolutions of the first and final sections of "In Memory of Arthur Winslow."

Characteristically, "Christmas Eve under Hooker's Statue" is closed in one way and left unresolved in another. The figure of Christ is introduced abruptly into the context, almost as if to provide a happy ending. Structurally the poem resolves more persuasively with the penultimate line. The effect is like that of many of Shakespeare's mutability sonnets, those which for twelve lines marshal powerful images of time's action, of the decay of beauty and the death of joy, then in the last two assert unpersuasively a faith in art's power to transcend time (Sonnet 65 is a pure example). For the Shakespeare of the sonnets, the consolations of art are not always compelling, and if this analogy is fair, the same might be said for Lowell and the consolations of Christian redemption. To the extent, as I suggested before, that doctrine is a form of empirical reference, this poem is a radical, symbolist transformation.

This strange tension between closure and irresolution, between formal completion on the one hand and affective and intellectual suspension on the other, in itself expresses another dimension of the poem's theme. Faith, which might be expected to resolve the issues, appears to have failed but is rescued tentatively by the more stubborn idealism of the imagination—an idealism that clings to the possibility of peace, simplicity, and innocence which Christ as child signifies. It is not simply the state of childhood toward which Lowell's imagination reaches here; that naive possibility is precluded by the irreversibility of time. It is, rather, an envisioned recovery of innocence of perspective and love within the mature intelligence for which the figure of Christ in the poem as man-child-god provides both a symbol and a mythic and historic authorization. Since the crisis is both personal and cultural, it would seem that the resolution must be personal and cultural as well. And since the dominant vision is complex and harrowing, this countervision, fragile and vulnerable as it is, represents an escape not so much from the reality alone but from the derangement of apprehending it, a tentative liberation into a kind of mental still point.

In Lowell's early religious poems, one consistently visible sign of his imperfect adjustment to orthodoxy is his idiosyncratic, virtually Manichaean distortion of Christian doctrine.* On the one side are God (the God of Calvin and of Jonathan Edwards), man, and nature, and on the other the child Christ and his mother—a scheme that obviously has as much psychoanalytical as theological significance. In this dualistic system, Christ the child is most often the redeemer, whereas Christ crucified is the victim whose death epitomizes the recurring predation upon innocence throughout history. It is even implied in this version of man's history that God transmogrified beyond recovery collaborates in and authorizes the form and meaning of this action:

> Joseph plucks his hand-lines like a harp,
> And hears the fearful *Puer natus est*
> Of Circumcision, and relives the wrack
> And howls of Jesus whom he holds. How sharp
> The burden of the Law before the beast:
> Time and the grindstone and the knife of God.
> The child is born in blood, O child of blood.

This seems pretty clear-cut, and it is not reverent. And the action of Joseph in the scene as a type of the poet is revealing—making, or going through the helpless motions of making, a kind of music to ward off the pain. Structurally, "New Year's Day" is another historical and metaphysical centrifuge, and those who are living in present time from which the spiral begins suffer in recurrence under the same, though more abstractly cruel, dispensation as Joseph: the new year is "born / To ice and death"; a kitten dies in the snow "as if fouled," is bent into and buried in a "Christmas box," and thus becomes a grotesque type of Christ. The "snake-tailed sea-winds" cough and howl "for alms" outside a church whose door is double-locked.

---

*Commentators who read as a type of Christ the "Lambkin" in the ballad from which the title *Lord Weary's Castle* is taken tend to overlook in the original texts the gratuitously malevolent and vengeful character of that figure—more like Lowell's God than his Christ—by comparison with whom Lord Weary, supposed to stand for sinful man, is merely stingy.

The prevailing environment of *Lord Weary's Castle* is a single generic, punishing New England winter—rock, wind, snow, and sea; and if that setting expresses its creator, that creator is disposed toward a malevolence that pervades all dimensions of nature and time. When Lowell has his fierce Quaker whalemen chant,

> "If God himself had not been on our side,
> When the Atlantic rose against us, why,
> Then it had swallowed us up quick"

the ironic thrust may be deeper and more caustic than it first appears, since God, the Atlantic, and the whalemen are continuous in their common murderous attributes. When he conceives a Christ turned "wanderer and child," the "wanderer" may be intended to imply that Christ was and is homeless and alien in the cosmos as well as in the world. The somehow appealing isolation of that last image, in "Christmas Eve under Hooker's Statue," a faint and ambiguous affirmation in the twenty-seventh and final line, causes that poem to take the shape of a moral microcosm.

"The world out-Herods Herod." At the thematic center of *Lord Weary's Castle* is the prototypical image of slaughtered innocents and the child Christ, their representative and potential redeemer. In the poem "The Holy Innocents," where this cold assertion appears, the innocents are oxen, identified with Jesus "in harness" throughout—the child, "Lamb of the sheperds," lies still. In "Christmas at Black Rock," against the strident chaos and clamor of defense plants and drunken Polish workers the Christ Child's "lips are lean and evergreen." But "the spiralling years / Slither with child and manger to a ball / Of ice," and "the green needles nail us to the wall." The forces of redemption have been transformed into forces of pain. The sonnet, "Concord," is more explicit:

> Crucifix,
> How can your whited spindling arms transfix
> Mammon's unbridled industry, the lurch
> For forms to harness Heraclitus' stream!

For Lowell's exhaustive pessimism, the tragedy of the crucifixion seems to lie not only in the death of the good (the child), which it symbolized, but also in the hopelessly perverse way in which the morbid power of its image appears to have infected and preoccupied man's spiritual imagination—particularly, of course, the spiritual imagination of the founders of Lowell's nation and, through their influence, Lowell's own. This point is grimly reiterated at the end of "Concord" by the abrupt intrusion into the present of a typological event from the American past:

> This church is Concord—Concord where Thoreau
> Named all the birds without a gun to probe
> Through darkness to the painted man and bow:
> The death-dance of King Philip and his scream
> Whose echo girdled this imperfect globe.

As a noble innocent, King Philip serves in Lowell's reading of history as one of a number of figures (as widely varied as buttercups, oxen, Abel, the whale in "Quaker Graveyard," and the poet himself as a generic child) whose destruction recapitulates and confirms the meaning of the fate of Jesus—the transvalued if not the doctrinal meaning. King Philip and the pious atrocity of his murder are the main subject of "At the Indian Killer's Grave," and as the poet broods upon the corrupt heritage of that event, his mind and heart move inevitably toward the imagination's lost spiritual home:

> I ponder on the railing at this park:
> Who was the man who sowed the dragon's teeth,
> That fabulous or fancied patriarch
> Who sowed so ill for his descent, beneath
> King's Chapel in this underworld and dark?
> John, Matthew, Luke and Mark,
> Gospel me to the Garden, let me come
> Where Mary twists the warlock with her flowers—
> Her soul a bridal chamber fresh with flowers
> And her whole body an ecstatic womb,
> As through the trellis peers the sudden Bridegroom.

The image here of the magical mother twining flowers into the warlock of Philip's severed head—consoling and restoring—is both gothic and poignant, and it wrenches a psychoanalytical and moral disturbance into a painfully simple form. The other details of this strangely primitivist composition—the simplicity of "gospel me back," the Garden itself, the ecstatic womb, the bridal chamber, the Bridegroom—represent the yearning of regression, a relief from the barely tolerable moral sophistication, from the coming into mature consciousness of the world, which is the burden of the poem's preceding sections. The naively pictorial spectacle evokes the chaste, childlike spirit of the devotional iconography of the Middle Ages—as though the poet were straining toward the cultural form of personal childhood to recover the idiom that best expresses his spirit's immediate need.

The range of Lowell's religious imagination at this stage of his career tends to be limited to the poles of the nativity on the one hand, representing simplicity and peace, and the Crucifixion on the other, foreshadowing the endless recurrence of death and suffering. Resurrection and atonement are not prominent concepts in the pattern of his thought, though "Colloquy in Black Rock" is a striking exception. "Colloquy in Black Rock" in fact represents one of the rare occasions in Lowell's early work when death and guilt are temporarily disassociated in the poet's meditation. The resulting cleanness of line in both concept and execution is atypical, for although the risen Christ may conquer death, death alone is not the issue of *Lord Weary's Castle*. Indeed, death might be considered a deferred anxiety for those living in a world which Lowell's Jonathan Edwards feared abandoned to Satan:

> Content was gone.
> All the good work was quashed. We were undone.
> The breath of God had carried out a planned
> And sensible withdrawal from this land. . . .
> ("After the Surprising Conversions")

The response of his parishioners, Edwards wrote, was a suicidal hysteria. They would hear voices groaning: "'My friend, / Cut your own throat. Cut your own throat. Now! Now!'" And like those early ancestors, it is not redemption beyond the world that Lowell envisions in *Lord Weary's Castle*, but redemption *in* the world, a New Canaan either within the self or without. This nostalgia for Eden the poet has, in a sense, inherited, and it has not yet wholly dissolved in his imagination, despite his own chronic despair. *Lord Weary's Castle* is, after all, a young poet's volume and its pessimism is that of a young man, looking toward the future for openings rather than point-blank at its closure.

The baffled issue of that dream of the New Canaan, and of the perverse enterprise it inspired, is one of the hidden themes of "A Quaker Graveyard in Nantucket," an ambitious, groping poem that is organized finally, however, to express a spiritual and epistemological stalemate to which there appears to be no solution. The character of both men and nature in its setting brutally testifies to God's "planned. . . withdrawal from this land." There is even the lurking and fearsome implication that to name it "withdrawal" may be a euphemistic evasion, that God is indeed present in the sea voices: in the "winds' wings" that "beat upon the stones, / . . . and scream. . . and the claws that rush / At the sea's throat"; in "the high tide" muttering "to its hurt self" as the waves wallow and recede, to leave "only the death rattle of the crabs"; in the thunder that "shakes the white surf and dismembers / The red flag hammered in the masthead." As in "The Dry Salvages," the sea in this poem is the destructive element, more relentlessly concrete than symbolic; but Lowell's Atlantic is barely superior in power to the murderous innocence of the men who pit themselves against it. The seamen in time are overwhelmed, the destroyers destroyed by the elements and their own spiritual pride. The destructive element is within them as well as without and they have no more mastery over the one than the other.

Ensnarled in Lowell's rhetoric, both man and sea, though adversaries, seem finally to function as the agents of a single inexorably ruthless force. In the fifth section, which culminates in the evisceration and dismemberment of the captured whale, the source of the action is ghostly; the seamen have become one with their implements of destruction, and the implements themselves do the work as if motivated by a malign force beyond human origin.

> The fat flukes arch and whack about its ears,
> The death-lance churns into the sanctuary, tears
> The gun-blue swingle, heaving like a flail,
> And hacks the coiling life out: it works and drags
> And rips the sperm whale's midriff into rags,
> Gobbets of blubber spill to wind and weather. . . . .

The calculated violence of language and syntax in this section impels the spectacle beyond empirical or moral understanding and therefore, by implication, beyond any remote possibility of control. The effect is similar to the one in "Skunk Hour," where the "love-cars" on the "hill's skull" are themselves doing the lovemaking, lie together "hull to hull" or, later, bleat their own love songs: "Love, O careless Love." This effect is reinforced throughout the poem, especially in the earlier sections, by the disorienting association of naturalistic with obscure antinaturalistic detail, so that the poem happens in one place and in all places—as the Quaker's "bones abide / There, in the nowhere," in one time and in all of time. Too many dreadful things happen in this poem's world—such as the drowned sailor's grappling the net "With the coiled hurdling muscles of his thighs"—for it to be an empirical, that is, potentially manipulable, world. And it is fearsome for the voyager in it: "The winds wings beat upon the stones, / Cousin, and scream for you." Moreover, a baroque vaulting in the next clause from a simple but significant conjunctive adverb ("where") extends the process to implicate the entire cosmos:

> and gulls go round the stoven timbers
> Where the morning stars sing out together
> And thunder shakes the white surf and dismembers
> The red flag hammered in the mast-head.

Lowell's Christ makes his archetypal appearance at the end of this section almost as an afterthought, an innocent victim of murderous innocence: "Hide, / Our steel, Jonas Messias, in Thy side." There is probably no way to make certain sense out of this passage, but if the punctuation is to be taken seriously it means not that our steel should be hidden, but that "Jonas Messias" should hide. Thus, transposed: Hide, Jonas Messias, (with) our steel in Thy side. (In Matthew's and Luke's gospel accounts Christ identified himself with Jonah, though less explicitly in the latter.) This would suggest that Christ and what he represents will or should recede in the face of an opposing force so absolute. (Jonah did, naively, strive to hide from Yahweh, and Christ asked not to be crucified.) And the whale implied here is not, of course, "IS, the whited monster" but an innocent—that is, unallegorized—beast, or, again, innocence itself.

The movement that follows logically from this thought, "Our Lady of Walsingham," is dramatically stylized by comparison and verbally restful after the intensity of the preceding four sections. But although the pictorial quaintness is mysterious and suggestive, we learn nothing substantive from it except that the ways of God are ultimately mysterious, and that life in any case is not a cheering, pastoral dream. Our Lady of Walsingham, "Expressionless, expresses God." If the world is to come to Walsingham, that is also as far toward God as it is likely to be able to go. Moreover, *there*, Walsingham, is another still point, and as such in personal experience it is merely an eye in the storm.

In the poem's concluding section the wind and tide have ebbed momentarily but they are gathering again, and, now transported in the mind from the vale of the shrine at Walsingham back to the austere New England coast, the poet draws the terms of his paradox into four vividly isolated and juxtaposed assertions.

> You could cut the brackish winds with a knife
> Here in Nantucket, and cast up the time
> When the Lord God formed man from the sea's slime
> And breathed into his face the breath of life,
> And blue-lung'd combers lumbered to the kill.
> The Lord survives the rainbow of His will.

The rhetorical compression of this passage is extraordinary. "Knife" and "life" associate by rhyme, as do "slime" and "time" and finally "kill" and "will." The irony of the progressions is even more explicit: man is formed from the sea's slime (man and sea once again identified); he is inspired with God's own breath; then, as if by perverse prearrangement, the combers lumber in to kill. In context, the famous concluding line seems antiphonal in response to the other three; but if it expresses faith, it is a faith so uncertain as to be virtually agnostic. The line is ambiguous enough to be read in two not quite mutually exclusive ways. The first would be as the simple Kierkegaardian assertion of faith that it is generally taken to be: God may not be manifest in the world, and the covenant with man is broken and obsolete; but He exists. The other reading is more foreboding and issues logically from, rather than reverses, the momentum of the poem: God has rescinded the benign promise of the "rainbow" of the covenant and survives, instead, as the omnipresent, destructive element of Lowell's sea. In this poem, as perhaps in no other in his early work, Lowell's feeling and thought are firmly adjusted to each other. The ambiguities elsewhere, made plainer by their bleak restatement here, are finely and precisely calibrated.

The occasion of "Quaker Graveyard" is ostensibly elegiac, but its scale and tone express a recusant tragic vision. Even the catharsis (elegiac or tragic) toward which the poem moves is coldly arrested and withheld. Like Arthur Winslow in the other elegy, Warren Winslow himself disappears early into the more impersonal engagement of the poet and his materials. When he appears for the last time, veiled in a grim allusion to the sea-burial, he has become all men: "This is the end of running on the waves; / We are poured out like water." There may, indeed, be an intentional echo in this passage of the end of the first section of the Arthur Winslow elegy, where Arthur is ferried to "where the wide waters and their voyager are one"—where oblivion, in effect, is to be the best we may hope for, in keeping with the defeated promise in life.

The traditional rationalization in classical theology for God's causing man to suffer is that Love (as in Eliot's version in *Four Quartets*) "devised the torment" so that we might be turned by it away from the world toward God, "be redeemed from fire by fire." That Lowell does not avail himself of this apologia seems enormously significant, in that it leaves us in a world without joy and without real hope. It is, in effect, Christian nihilism, and it will cause the impending falling away from faith to come as a relief, for

> Here the Lord
> Is Lucifer in harness; hand on sword,
> He watches me for Mother, and will turn
> The bier and baby-carriage where I burn.
> ("Between the Porch and the Altar")

The "bier and baby-carriage" recall the harshly ironic praise of the Feast of Circumcision, from "New Year's Day": *"Puer natus est"*—the child is born.

2. EFFIGIES OF KINGS AND QUEENS

In his review of *Four Quartets* in 1943, Lowell had asserted that *"union with God* is somewhere in sight in all poetry, though it is usually rudimentary and misunderstood."[1] By the time of *The Mills of the Kavanaughs* (1946–1951), this envisioned union for Lowell appears to be dead, and one aspect of the fate of the characters in that volume's monologues is that they live, avatars of the poet who creates them, suspended in a transitional dispensation. The rhetoric of their imaginations is a mythic and prelapsarian, misshapen clouds of glory, and they struggle within it, to live up to it, as ordinary blighted creatures, case histories in ceremonial vestments. In "David and Bathsheba in the Public Garden," Bathsheba's lament epitomizes the crisis of the volume:

> We blew our bubbles at the moon, . . .
>   and the lion caught
> The moonbeams in its jaws.

David and Bathsheba have played at being children, thinking themselves immune to guilt and responsibility until that fantasy is acted upon in life. They live on into the present in arrested misery, like Tiresias or the Sibyl at Cumae, as if in Hell or Purgatory, haunted by Uriah, unable not to see and unable to die, playing with boats in the fountain pool of the Public

Garden. They are figures wrought on the heroic scale, reduced as revenants to the size of their present habitat in time and place, ordinary thwarted adulterers in modern Boston—reduced to their real moral stature within their mythic mold.

The book's other characters enact and are undone by their own versions of the same imperfectly adjusted understanding of imagined selves and psychic realities. For the speaker of "Her Dead Brother," what her brother *was* has been hypostasized in his portrait, barely visible through the varnish. She says, with perhaps conscious irony,

> All's well that ends:
> Achilles dead is greater than the living;
>
> My mind holds you as I would have you live. . . .

The irony is doubled. The brother has achieved perfected stasis only in death; and the glib analogy with Achilles evades by heroic association the central point of their experience together—the inevitable frustration of incestuous love, the perishable naiveté of sexual narcissism, the lion's catching the moonbeams in its jaws. "My Brother, / I've saved you in the ice-house of my mind." The sister's monologue is laced with stylizing, life-evading imagery, and the varied levels of her representation signify conflicting modes of experience within which the pair have struggled to exist. In the beginning, an escutcheon with religious heraldry filters the waning sunlight into the chamber where the portrait hangs ("The Lion of St. Mark's upon the glass / Shield in my window reddens"); the brother's portrait poses him in classic naval regalia ("The fingers on your sword knot are alive"); the myths of Troy and Achilles recur in an allusion to Cressida. But the brother's sloop has been left to rot; and its sails, which bore "the colors of the rainbow," now, in her mind, flap in the failing wind. She dreams of a "Stygian Landing," as she dies by her own hand by the simplest of household means—the gas from an oven burner. "The Lord is dark," she says, making the best of a mostly sordid circumstance, "and holy is His name." Her revelation is that they could not live as they *would* live—simultaneously as stylized figures of their imagination and as complex creatures of reality—and so the ambiguous grandeur of death becomes for her the resolving alternative.

The demented wife in Michael's dream in "Thanksgiving's Over" conceives that she is possessed by the Holy Spirit in the form of birds, that she has achieved a perfected Franciscan union with nature as creation, and that she is guarded in her sodality by an effigy of the Christ Child; but later she is guarded by Venus and becomes Venus in her mind. All of this she reports to Michael from beyond death from the asylum in which she died. She has plunged, before, from her window into authentic time, "Into the neon of the restaurant— / clawing and screaming." Where she in her frenzy plunges is where Michael dwells without hope of remission. Third Avenue is deserted, but the cars of the Third Avenue El rattle the scaffolding, rattle his window, reminders of where he lives and who in fact he is. In the last phase of his dream he has achieved an apathetic equilibrium; he clutches the demystified objects, "the cowhorn beads from Dublin" and grinds them: "*Miserere?* Not a sound." Outside, the "red cement St. Francis"—a petrified St. Francis in a hostile sister snow—feeds cement birds and children before a cement Christ Child, measuring an impossibly remote distance.

The same atrophied dissociation in Anne Kavanaugh's monologue takes the form of a pitifully grand mythic paradigm. Her vision of herself as Persephone (in blue jeans and a sealskin toque) and Harry Kavanaugh as Hades is the only consoling order left to her as she sits stalled in the ruins of her and Harry's wretchedly deflected romantic dreams. The mythic is a form of understanding that comes to her logically enough, since her own fate has been as inexplicable as ancient narrative mythology itself, events befalling simply, unpredictably, without the rational order of causation. Since the conventional recourse of analysis and understanding is useless, there is nothing else for her to do, and the ironic accessibility of metaphor becomes her only consolation. The vague mythic parallel is a dead end: it aggrandizes the pathetic but illumines nothing. Even more forbidding is the implication that Anne has absorbed this mode of thinking from the example of Harry himself; and if anything could be said to explain Harry's grotesque collapse into schizophrenia, self-delusive mythmaking would be it. Harry is literary, Roman Catholic, self-consciously the scion of an ancient family, wholly absorbed in the fabulous shapes and sources of the near and distant past. The setting itself is Harry's mind objectified: the Kavanaugh estate in decay, the millpond with its discolored statues of gods and goddesses surrounding it and seemingly rising from it. He is unequipped for inhabiting the present, let alone transforming it, as he and Anne have dreamed they would. Even as a naval officer, we infer, he has simply entered a traditional role; and when the cruel fact of Pearl Harbor breaks into his consciousness, his fanciful world and his unstable sanity break with it. After this, the heroic transfigurations he suffers in his madness are caricatures of the discontinuity and the ironic contrast of his identities, which prevailed portentously even when he was sane.

> "You lived. Your rocker creaked, as you declined.
> To the ungarnished ruin of your mind
> Came the persona of the murderous Saul
> In dirty armor, followed by a boy,
> Who twanged a jew's-harp
>
> . . . . .
>
> 'Where is my harper? Music! Must I beg
> For music?' Then you sucked your thumb for joy,
> And baby-smiled through strings of orange juice."

Anne thinks for a moment, obliquely perceiving a truth, that the cards she plays with "are Kavanaughs, / Or sinister, bewildered effigies / Of kings and queens." Anne only dimly understands that her and Harry's terrible innocence, out of which grew their naively grand ambitions for the house of Kavanaugh, was the threshold of a terrible pain: "Harry, . . . we are far from home— / A boy and girl a-maying in the blue / Of March or April." The two are prototypical in this volume. They have played role-games in their minds. Anne is Persephone, Anne is Daphne, Anne is Cinderella. They are Adam and Eve in "the time of marriage!—worming on all fours / up slag and deadfall" against Jehovah's torrent. Harry is Hades, Harry is Apollo, Harry is Atlas, Harry is dragon slayer, Harry is demon-lover, Harry is Saul, Harry is finally Harry Tudor ("He died outside the church"). In the final stage of Harry's decline, Anne sees herself pathetically once more as a bride, "a daisy choired by daisies," and she sings: "My life / Is like a horn of plenty gone to grass."

The dreadful games of identity in *The Mills of the Kavanaughs* are played out in a theater of the mind that is like a city of God evacuated and left to the occupation of garbled mythologies and heroic chimeras. This setting in the minds of the characters—a gestalt of allusion, symbol, and rhetoric—implies a spacious and majestic reach of human potential, which their own experience proves does not exist. The stricken, afflicted inhabitants are mocked and diminished by the contrast. The poems themselves seem inhibited and forced at least partly because the poetry has been taken into the custody of the characters. The stiff iambic phrasing of their monologues tends to reinforce our sense of their near-pathological formality. The impression sustained throughout is one of a nightmarish rigidification; and appropriately enough for its theme of desymbolization and decay, the rhetoric of *The Mills of the Kavanaughs* echoes *Lord Weary's Castle* like receding stage thunder.

"Falling Asleep over the Aeneid" and "Mother Marie Therese" are the two poems in the volume that confront its themes most directly, and both are desolate with loss; but they deal with losses of a different order, from different ends of the spectrum of values implied when the concepts *reality* and *myth* are thought of as antithetical. Like the volume's other characters, the old man of the first poem dreams a heroic dream: that he is Aeneas presiding over the grandly ceremonial funeral of Pallas. Passional love, *comitatus*, manly warfare of historic consequence, and religious pageantry parade majestically across his vision. Then he is awakened (by church bells) to a wizened sphere of time. This is the inevitable systolic contraction of the Lowell persona's imagination. He is in his own childhood, recalls the narrow aggressive piety of his great aunt, and then, by association with the funeral of Pallas, the funeral of his own Uncle Charles, a Civil War hero. This occasion's surfacing in memory is again an event worthy of commemoration, but the coherence of the ceremony has unraveled into tension and ambiguous feeling. The exotic bird-priest of the rites for Pallas and the plumage laid upon his bier have been transmogrified into the "Blue-capped and bird-like" corpse of Uncle Charles in his coffin and the stuffed birds in the parlor overlooking him. Outside, the thousand warriors who bear Pallas to the priest become the march of Uncle Charles's "colored volunteers." Grotesquely reviving images of Pallas's "careless yellow hair that seemed to burn / Beforehand," the aunt "laughs, and tells her English maid / To clip [Charles's] yellow nostril hairs." The funeral of Pallas is opulent with action and feeds into a swelling stream of time and history. By contrast, the funeral of Uncle Charles seems oppressive, nugatory, and terminal. The old man recalls that as a child he had held his uncle's sword, as he does now in his mind, "to keep from falling"—out of mythic into authentic time:

> for the dust
> On the stuffed birds is breathless, for the bust
> Of young Augustus weighs on Vergil's shelf:
> It scowls into my glasses at itself.

But as the old man seems to have perceived through the oblique arrangement of his reverie, the gesture of holding the sword is forlornly symbolic. The fall is already accomplished. What has died is not heroism itself, for Uncle Charles has clearly died a hero (both Phillips Brooks of Episcopal Boston and General Grant are there as mourners), but an ancient, spacious vision and a resonant context which had kept heroism, as well as honor and love, viable and sacred in the imagination. The privation of the imagination has broken the union with its forms. "Vergil must keep the Sabbath," the aunt has said sternly, implying a narrow Puritanical distrust of "fictions" and thus a representative collaboration in their dispersal. The old man and new Aeneas searches for a home that no longer exists.

Stephen Yenser finds another dimension to this theme. He points out that the bust of Augustus is not scowling at the old man but at its own reflection—

> and one reason for the scowl is not far to seek, for it is implicit in the sonics, which link "dust" (with its overtones of mortality) and "bust" (with its pun) to "Augustus" (a title that is therefore ironic). The disillusionment here derives not from contemplation of the least of mankind as modern man tends to see himself, but rather from consideration of the greatest, as Octavius, Augustus Caesar, in fact saw himself. Augustus is Lowell's enlightened Ozymandias, and the theme of the poem is, not the demise of heroism, but its futility.[2]

Yenser's point is well taken, and if we accept its implication, then the old man's "dream" must be understood to be not only his but history's as well.

In "Mother Marie Therese," the available elegiac feeling that tends to remain abstract in "Falling Asleep over the Aeneid" is given, as it were, flesh and blood. The poem's coherent progression, its precise reconstruction of historical milieu and character, and its supple modulation of speech rhythms and the formal heroic couplet measure give it a domesticated, being-in-the world quality that has been missing from Lowell's poetry up to this point. Thematically it prefigures *Life Studies*, and at the same time it is the center of value for the volume in which it appears. In relation to the volume's other figures, Mother Marie Therese serves as an imposing norm. For the poem's narrator, the aging nun, her friend, who has survived her and now warms herself before memories, Marie Therese had embodied an unapologetic Renaissance vitality that had made her an anachronism even when alive and a robust abrasion within the convent over which she presided—"Like Proserpina, who fell / Six months a year from earth to flower in hell." Grieving in the vacuum left by Marie Therese's death, the nun has held herself firm with a resentful stoicism:

> For we were friends of Cato, not of God.
> This sixtieth Christmas, I'm content to pray
> For what life's shrinkage leaves from day to day....

The shrunken life she refers to is not simply her own, but the world's as well, as though the entire spirit of the life force has failed abruptly with the drowning of Marie Therese, its incarnation.

> Our world is passing; even she, whose trust
> Was in its princes, fed the gluttonous gulls,
> That whiten our Atlantic, when like skulls
> They drift for sewage with the emerald tide.
> Perpetual novenas cannot tide
> Us past that drowning.

The promise of the afterlife is an austere consolation for the devotee of Marie Therese's disciplined vitalism: "we are ruinous; / God's Providence through time has mastered us." For Marie Therese, Christ has been the giver of life in this world as well as the next, and it is toward this world she is imagined to be yearning from beyond death:

> Without bed-fellows, washed and bored and old,
> Bilged by her thoughts, and worked on by the worms,
> Until her fossil convent come to terms
> With the Atlantic....
> The bell-buoy, whom she called the Cardinal,
> Dances upon her. If she hears at all,
> She only hears it tolling to this shore,
> Where our frost-bitten sisters know the roar
> Of water, inching, always on the move
> For virgins, when they wish the times were love....

So the grief of the two nuns comes together in a final, ironically secular, epiphany, a vivid projection of the surviving sister's humanistic imagination: "My mother's hollow sockets fill with tears."

Marie Therese's tears, the dancing bell buoy, and her bawling billy goat (himself an expressive sign), left keeping watch on the headland are her response to the dreadful silence of Michael's "*Miserere?* Not a sound." They show that she would despise despair. Her being described in the memorial mass as "An emigrée in this world and the next" links her in a way with the other characters in *The Mills of the Kavanaughs*, but her ambivalence is a disciplined ambivalence and also an ambivalence of positive forces, an embrace as opposed to a rejection or evasion; the traction of her identity is firmly secured in the life of colors, textures, action, friends. With her Rabelais, wedding ring, hunting trophies, and Damascus shotguns—signs of her aristocratic lineage in literature as well as in life—Lowell's Mother Superior exerts a powerful life-affirming authority upon the bleakness of his thought. Getting under the nets of fable and self-delusion, her presence implies, is what the other characters have failed to achieve. That failure is personal and cultural, spreads like an epidemic through all of these slightly deranged poems about helplessly deranged people, and Marie Therese is the only resistant force in the volume. She is therefore a stage in a journey of conviction that will continue in *Life Studies* in "Beyond the Alps" from Rome to Paris and then from that "black classic" already "breaking up" to the "rich air" of "Skunk Hour" and the mother skunk with her "moonstruck eyes' red fire" who "will not scare."

3. DISSOCIATION AND AUTHENTICITY

Life Studies is an easy book to sentimentalize, and it continues to encourage the projection upon it of positive, life-affirming values, if only the cold comfort of romantic, Sartrean existentialism. Thus, Charles Altieri sees it as representative of "the bed-rock zero" of postmodernism, "where experience of value can replace interpretations of it," and sees "confessional poetry" in general as "an attempt to solve value problems . . . without reference to philosophical, cultural, or mythic universals."[1] Steven Gould Axelrod writes that "Lowell's goal is a sense of continuity, an identity that has withstood time's incomprehensible flow, . . . a unified, enduring, and valuable 'I am,'" and adds that in reliving the pain of his childhood, "[Lowell] thereby recovers what Roethke calls 'the lost self,' not the past self only but present self as well . . . Rooted in Lowell's painful personal life, *Life Studies* affirms the value of human experience. . . And as a result the dove of experience has brought him new wisdom, a new olive branch to eat."[2] M. L. Rosenthal, less credulous, nevertheless says that "*Life Studies*. . . is the volume in which the poet at last 'finds himself.'"[3] These appraisals, fairly characteristic of the mainstream of Lowell criticism, tend to ignore the forbidding implications of Lowell's having said of his own work that after he had finished it he felt "suspended upon a question mark," and that he did not know whether the question mark were "a lifeline or a deathrope." That remark alone should direct our attention to the fact that *Life Studies* is racked by irresolution and, also, to the more apparent fact that the self "found" there is in most ways the very reverse of the Sartrean "hero" that Axelrod makes him out to be—"'at once. . . totally free and. . . not able to derive the meaning of the world except as coming from myself.'"[4] The self of *Life Studies* is, on the contrary, fearfully determined, only free to the extent that he can perceive his unfreedom. Lowell is direct about this. As a child he is sullen and truculent, gratuitously disloyal and cruel toward his friends, smugly Oedipal toward his father, violent, moody, and self-despising. As an adult he is either indentured to "the kingdom of the mad," a "hell" to himself, "free-lancing out along the razor's edge," or, remorsefully, "cured" and therefore "frizzled, stale and small." As the adult reconstructing his own life in the poems, he is able to show compassion for the closest members of his family—in retrospect—but he shows no compassion or respect for himself.

Admittedly, both courage and humility are required for achieving such dispiriting self-revelation, and these are real virtues. It is true, also, as Rosenthal says, that Lowell's object in *Life Studies* "is to catch himself in process of becoming himself." But the point that appears to need emphasizing is that the self he becomes is no worthy center of value, redeemed by a psychoanalytical epiphany, but is, on the contrary, continuous with the world that he is repeatedly compelled to reject; and this, in effect, leaves nothing at the center. Considered as a narrative of a quest for values, *Life Studies* leads nowhere. Once one is bereft of confidence in God or nature or history or civilization or people as a source of meaning for existence—from all possible sources of essence that existence is supposed to precede—then, it is true, Sartre's isolated self-sufficiency or Nietzsche's "self-overcoming" or an extension of the "will to power" would seem to be the only available recourses for spiritual motivation. Even in a round existential world, though, mere authenticity is not a goal one would choose if there were a halfway attractive alternative, not much of a consolation if one is talking about actual living rather than about writing books or theories about living. But Lowell's existential world is not round to begin with, and both his bondage to it and rebellion against it have the effect, by his account, of misshaping him as well, thus undermining the morale required to achieve radical freedom. This, if it is a just reading, leaves us curiously with a *Life Studies* that, simply by existing, is testimony to the symbolist conviction that when life is without meaning, art alone, in and of itself, has value; and coming from Lowell, of all poets, this is an oddly ambiguous affirmation.

"Beyond the Alps" is an appropriate prologue for *Life Studies* for several reasons, one of the main ones being the way in which Lowell presents in the poem the spectacle of pervasive cultural disintegration while maintaining a measure of composure and detachment from it. In respect to the relation between values, the self, and the world, this will be one pole or parameter for *Life Studies* and "Skunk Hour" the other. "Skunk Hour" fulfills the volume's downward curve into chaos and takes the poet along with it. In "Beyond the Alps" he is still resisting assimilation—"the blear-eyed ego kicking in my berth / lay still." He leaves "the City of God where it belongs," but does so "much against" his "will"; and he envies the intellectual innocence of "our grandparents on their grand tours— / long-haired Victorian sages" who "accepted the universe, / while breezing on their trust funds through the world." The dissolving connection with the "grandparents" is his being on the train and therefore insulated in a way that encourages detached meditation. But the cold intensity of his meditation leaves virtually nothing standing, not even—it is hinted at the end—his own justification in the role of poet.

The City of God "belongs" in Rome because Rome is also the city of Mussolini, a center of cultural confusion. Where, only a decade before, Mussolini had evoked childlike adulation from the masses, now the Pope, all too human behind the scenes with his pet canary and electric razor, taps the same hysteria by means of pronouncing the wholly gratuitous dogma of the assumption of Mary. "The Duce's lynched, bare, booted skull still spoke," Lowell says sardonically, as though Mussolini's ghost had been resurrected. The allusion is to the circumstance of Mussolini's death and revilement: when his body was displayed, in a pile of bodies, in Milan, angry apostates kicked repeatedly at his face and famous jaw until his features were disfigured, so that when he was hung by his feet to afford a better view he seemed grotesquely, with his arms outstretched, to be once again exhorting a crowd. "God herded his people to the *coup de grace.*" Lowell interweaves points in time and the Duce, the Pope, the Church and the "monstrous human crush" (from the Vatican's point of view?) of the idolatrous masses in such a way as to ritualize the principle that the more things change the more they remain the same.

When the train reaches the Alps, a series of random associations brings to mind classical Greece, another high point of civilization, and thus Minerva, who prevailed, by eventual identification with the Olympian Athena, as a goddess of both the arts and war—"pure mind and murder," Lowell calls her, "miscarriage of the brain." The poem by this point has become fixated by the thought that humanity's highest and basest impulses are mutually reinforcing. Deities and art serve merely to sanctify murder. Murder turns us nervously and piously ("O Pius!") back to deities and art. And this point is brought up to date by the train's arriving at its destination: "Now Paris, our black classic, breaking up / like killer kings on an Etruscan cup." The simile is clearly intended as a statement about the dubious relationship between life and art. Jonathan Raban has glossed these and the earlier lines about Minerva persuasively: "Lowell clearly means us to take the implication that literature thrives on destruction. What is bad for man in history—the greed and courage of empire—may be meat for the poet. Later in Lowell's work, especially in *Notebook*, this life-in-death paradox becomes a central concern, and the poet is often observed feeding from the carrion of his own dead flesh."[5] We may be reminded by this now of the lines in *Day by Day* for Robert Penn Warren:

> Can poetry get away with murder,
> its terror a seizure of the imagination
> foreign to our stubborn common health?
> It's the authentic will to spoil,
> the voice,
> haunted not lost,
> that lives by breaking in
> berserk with inspiration. . . .
>
> ("Louisiana State University in 1940")

The poet-speaker of "Beyond the Alps" does not say so outright, for it is essential for his ironic role in that poem that he seem to remain unimplicated, but it seems clear that the series of identifications linking Paris, the funerary art of the Etruscans, killer kings, and, with his arrival, the poet himself, all of which are implicitly "breaking up," puts him into considerable existential jeopardy. The die of *Life Studies* has been cast, but its protagonist has not yet acknowledged it.

"Beyond the Alps" is an indicative poem for *Life Studies*, but it is not a wholly satisfactory one. It is obscure on what must have been in Lowell's mind a fairly straightforward theme, mainly because of an undisciplined proliferation of metaphor, a tendency carried forward from the symbol-burdened style of *Lord Weary's Castle*. The Alps at sunrise are described in sequence as "morning's thigh," "a Parthenon" and "firebranded socket of the Cyclops' eye," associations that are barely intelligible in context. The poem's cynicism threatens to become smug and literary. Its pessimism is unearned in exactly the same way that Eliot argued that Hamlet's was— without clear objective correlation in the text. Pius XII, Mussolini, the vagaries of Roman Catholic dogma, and the unpredictable Italian capacity for exaltation seem too eccentric and too vaguely absurd finally to serve as the basis for a comprehensive philosophical judgment. They are presented in such a way as to seem more an effect of the poet's attitude than the cause of it. But this, too, will prove to be prefigurative, for the strongest poems of *Life Studies* will turn this confusion of Lowell's to advantage by suggesting structurally an immanent absurdity, horror, and sadness at the core of life, which finally eludes our understanding or description.

Causation is never reduced in *Life Studies* to psychoanalytical or sociological formulas, although as readers we tend to be nudged in that direction only to be persuaded that such order-making impulses are primarily aesthetic and based upon a human need to organize our experience at any cost. It was Kierkegaard who said that, in this respect, poetry itself is "a victory over the world. It is through a negation of the imperfect actuality that poetry opens up a higher actuality, expands and transfigures the imperfect into the perfect, and thereby softens and mitigates that deep pain which would darken and obscure all things."[6] In "Beyond the Alps" we anticipate a satisfactory point of arrival only to discover that in the poem there is none, but instead the formal pseudoresolution of a couplet that imitates the order it mocks. The boy Lowell in "91 Revere Street," in his arbitrary inexplicable cruelty and violence, and the husband of "To Speak of Woe That Is in Marriage" are more continuous with the life represented in these poems than we are when we try to impose a logical, coherent pattern upon them. Stephen Yenser is addressing a slightly different aspect of this point when he discusses the techniques of the "intentionally mixed metaphor," which he says characterizes a persona in the poems "who is or has recently been unbalanced" by conveying "the distortion in perspective that accompanies this state": the night attendant of "Waking in the Blue" rousing from "the mare's-nest of his drowsy head" to "catwalk...down our corridor"; "Bobbie," of the same poem, who is "roly-poly as a sperm whale" and "horses at chairs"; Delmore Schwartz's "stuffed duck," which "cranes" toward Harvard; and so on—all animal images, as it happens, and as

Yenser points out.[7] The problem with arguing this technique to be the aspect of the persona who is mentally unbalanced is that the mixed metaphor is an infallible signature of Lowell's technique generally (as we have seen in "Beyond the Alps"). What it expresses, I think, is not so much an unstable perspective as a destabilized metaphysical environment, which a normal perspective would tend automatically to correct. A similar effect is achieved by the way in which ordinary domesticated objects are strangely undomesticated and made to seem sinister and significant in a way that the rational faculty would not apprehend—significant of something never named, but pervasive: the magnolia tree on Marlborough Street hung in winter with "gobbets of porkrind in bowknots of gauze" in "Home after Three Months Away" (Yenser says that this is analogous to Lowell himself at the poem's end—"Cured, I am frizzled, stale and small"—but even this equivalence does not quite make sense, except insofar as it links qualities of the world and of the self); or the magnolia blossoms in "Man and Wife," which "ignite / the morning with their murderous five days' white"; or, in the same poem, the bedposts of his mother's bed, which "shine / abandoned, almost Dionysian"; or the window of the "billiards-room" in "My Last Afternoon with Uncle Devereux Winslow," "lurid in the doldrums of the sunset hour"; or, in "Skunk Hour," the "red fox stain" that "covers Blue Hill." Nothing would seem less likely to be threatening than magnolias or bedposts, sunlit windows, fall leaves; but in these poems they are, and they point us toward a world that has only the shadowy logic of nightmares. The structure of "Skunk Hour" is a model of how this same principle works throughout the volume on a larger scale. Something is clearly wrong in the world of that poem, but what it is we are forbidden to know. Some common denominator, we think, links the "hermit heiress," the "summer millionaire," "the fairy decorator," and the "I," climbing the "hill's skull" to watch "for love-cars"; but however ingeniously we come up with answers that tentatively unify the poem and thus reassure our uneasy intelligence, the poem's inhabitants eventually float eerily away from us and each other into their own preternormal space. When we multiply such examples from *Life Studies*, what we perceive, though never "end up with," is a world that is incomprehensibly awry and not to be set right, and therefore a setting in which—as in "Skunk Hour" specifically—human action seems strangely ritualistic and ineffectual. Freud would call what we do when we impose interpretations, "secondary elaboration"—making inaccurate waking sense of a dream. But the dream itself remains undisclosed and, for Lowell, terrible in implication.

The essay "91 Revere Street" deviously introduces us to the domestic center of this world by assuming the guise of a conventional memoir. But it proceeds on two levels at once: one normal, or at least psychoanalytically explicable, within reach of empirical understanding, and the other preternormal. Commander and Mrs. Lowell are too eccentric to be considered types, but they and their son can be understood on the first level in fairly plain psychoanalytical terms. The conventional Oedipal contest motivates the relationships in the Lowell household. Lowell is all but morbidly insistent upon this aspect of his childhood, and all the principals in the story fare very badly in his recollection. Mrs. Lowell is represented as actively encouraging her son's Oedipal crisis rather than helping him through it, and thereby evading her own sexuality, while warping his: "She ran into my bedroom. She hugged me. She said, 'Oh Bobby, it's such a comfort to have a man in the house.' 'I am not a man,' I said, 'I am a boy'" (*Life Studies*, p. 24). When Commander Lowell is away on sea duty, she all but ritualistically effaces him:

> [She] basked in the refreshing stimulation of dreams in which she imagined Father as suitably sublimed. She used to describe such a sublime man to me over tea and English muffins. He was Siegfried carried lifeless through the shining air by Brunnhilde to Valhalla. . . Or Mother's hero dove through the grottoes of the Rhine and slaughtered the homicidal and vulgar dragon coiled about the golden hoard. (*Life Studies*, p. 18)

In "During Fever," Lowell will recall that as late as his undergraduate years when he barged home late,

> Always by the bannister
> my milk-tooth mug of milk
> was waiting for me on a plate
> of Triskets.
> Often with unadulterated joy,
> Mother, we bent by the fire
> rehashing Father's character. . . .

Commander Lowell does his best to live up to his proper role. He affects military authority, mathematics, manly chromeless automobiles, carving lessons, and, wonderfully, a second-hand "oak and 'rhinocerous hide' armchair...ostentatiously masculine...cracked, hacked, scratched, splintered, gouged, initialed, gunpowder-charred and tumbler-ringed." "I doubt if Father, a considerate man, was responsible for any of the marring" (p. 17). But he is not a very therapeutic adversary for his son. He is vague, ineffectual, uncertain of himself, easily manipulated by stronger wills, inarticulate; and as the memoir proceeds he grows less and less conspicuous, as if he were being wished—or were wishing himself—away. He is too unfinished himself, sexually, to engage in the battle the son needs to win his own sexual maturity and independence. Open conflict does indeed come later, as reported in *Notebook*, but only, obviously, after the psychic damage has been done.

Perhaps more to the point, since so much of "91 Revere Street" pertains to the stifling influence of the invisible Boston hegemony, it is the neurotic isolation from sexual identity, from the self as a biological phenomenon, that Commander and Mrs. Lowell represent. Norman O. Brown would understand them to be classic victims of what he called the Oedipal "project," the psychic drive, motivated unconsciously by the fear of death, away from all implication of being authentically in nature (especially at the early stage away from one's genetic parents who, the mother in particular, are vivid outward embodiments of one's physical source). This neurosis, in Brown's view, is a kind of common psychoanalytical destiny for most people and triggers complex mechanisms of sublimation, specifically the mechanism by which one forges a symbolic (that is, antibiological) self, with, say, a soul, which is apart from nature and thus psychologically breaks the feared connection with life.[8] Lowell's grandparents, we recall, were expert at keeping "nature at a distance" and now are "altogether otherworldly," which is to say, ironically, dead. In "During Fever," Mrs. Lowell's bedroom is said to have "looked away from the ocean," equipped with an "electric blanket" and a "silver [monogrammed] hot water bottle" and a "nuptial bed [to discourage intimacy] big as a bathroom." Commander Lowell is an engineer and mathematician by training and interest. He has made cars into a fetish. "Like a chauffeur, he watched this car, a Hudson, with an informed vigilance, always giving its engine hair-trigger little tinkerings of adjustment or friendship, always fearful lest the black body, unbeautiful as his boiled shirts, should lose its outline and gloss. He drove with flawless, almost instrumental, monotony" ("91 Revere Street," *Life Studies*, p. 23). He approaches meals, food itself, as a challenge to his ceremonial dignity—or is forced to by his wife: "His purpose was to reproduce stroke by stroke his last carving lesson, and he worked with all the formal rightness and particular error of some shaky experiment in remote control" (p. 34). He acquiesces to Admiral De Stahl's command that he sleep each night at his station at the base rather than at home with his wife. He letters his "new galvanized garbage cans: R. T. S. Lowell—U.S.N.," as if some awkward propitiatory act were being performed on behalf of a dead self. This detail is analogous to Mrs. Lowell's coffin in "Sailing Home from Rapallo": "black and gold *Risorgimento*...like Napoleon's at the *Invalides*," while within it her corpse is wrapped in tinfoil to retard decomposition in the Mediterranean heat. On a more demotic level, Commander and Mrs. Lowell in their different ways are victims of the same life-alien, rigidified narcissism that breaks the thwarted characters of *The Mills of the Kavanaughs*—"sinister, bewildered effigies / of kings and queens"—emotional victims of a common psychic tradeoff, one death for another.

In this context Lowell shows that he possessed the good judgment, despite bad models before him, to have at least yearned for contact with vital forces. Much of his otherwise unaccountable and inconsistent behavior in the memoir is attributable to his ragged attempts to achieve— as he later said of his poems in *Life Studies*—a "breakthrough back into life." Even his isolating pettiness, cruelty toward his friends, and violent temper are understandable partially as an unconscious aggression against decorum, just as he comes to idolize Pola Negri as an "anti-Alice." Growing toward manhood for him, he says, meant being "darkly imperiled, like some annual bevy of Athenian youths destined for the Minotaur. And to judge from my father, men between the ages of six and sixty did nothing but meet new challenges, take on heavier responsibilities, and lose all freedom to explode" (*Life Studies*, p. 28). Only his grandfather is a ray of hope, "all I could ever want to be: the bad boy, the problem child, the commodore of his household." (And we might note that this is the same grandfather who is all but excoriated in "In Memory of Arthur Winslow.") Lowell identifies consistently with whatever he perceives as déclassé or renegade.

> On sunny March and April afternoons...our teachers took us for strolls on the polite, landscaped walks of the Public Garden. There I'd loiter by the old iron fence and gape longingly across Charles Street at the historic Boston Common, a now largely wrong-side-of-the-tracks park. On the Common there were mossy bronze reliefs of

Union soldiers, and a captured German tank filled with smelly wads of newspaper. Everywhere there were grit, litter, gangs of Irish, Negroes, Latins. (*Life Studies*, pp. 30–31)

The merest image of a nine-year-old boy on a coerced "afternoon stroll" is enough to evoke the whole pattern of torture inflicted in the name of social regimen. Eventually, in predictable reaction, "Bobby" on his way to becoming "Cal" (for "Caligula") manages to have himself expelled from this elderly Eden, the Public Garden, by its resident archangel, Officer Lever, for bloodying "Bulldog Binney's nose against the pedestal of George Washington's statue" and for pelting "a little enemy ring of third graders with wet fertilizer." Images of ash, blood, sunlight, bodily functions, waste, and flesh recur in Lowell's remembrances with an oddly suggestive and reassuring effect—forbidden symbols, in their reticent way, of organic life. On one memorable occasion at the Brimmer School, the social restraints of the school belle, Elie Norton, dramatically fail, and she is incontinent during class, sending "a great golden puddle spreading toward me" from under her chair. In the resulting confusion Lowell eventually manages to seat himself in her wet, vacated chair and thus to implicate himself ritualistically in Elie's hitherto unthought-of physical being. Later he cannot shake the thought of her from his mind, and talking with her he "felt rich and raw in her nearness" (p. 30). It is on account of Elie that he fights desperately not to be compelled to leave the Brimmer School. It is also leaving Brimmer that he fears will set him on the "darkly imperiled" course toward repressed adulthood.

Randall Jarrell might have observed that a sadly large number of people dwell in a kingdom of necessity of their own making. He might also have offered the suggestion that the poet who wrote the line "Till Christ again turn wanderer and child" is the same poet, fundamentally, who now in this memoir cherishes his remote connection with his great-great-grandfather, Mordecai Myers, a Mediterranean Jew, and follows with rapt attention the ceremoniously boorish tirades of his father's friend, Commander Billy "Battleship Bilgewater" Harkness. Major Myers, as Lowell reconstructs his character from the family portrait, is both voluptuous and patrician, a benign, knowing witness on behalf of acquiescence and happy surrender. "On the joint Mason-Myers bookplate there are two merry and naked mermaids—lovely marshmallowy, boneless, Rubensesque butterballs, all burlesque-show bosoms and Flemish smiles. Their motto [which Lowell, oddly, has either misquoted or mistranslated], *malo frangere quam flectere*, reads 'I prefer to bend than to break.'" At the end of the memoir, as the sun shines "irreverently on our three garbage cans lettered: R. T. S. Lowell—U.S.N.," Major Myers's image returns, "apotheosized, as it were, by the sunlight lighting the blood smear of his scarlet waistcoat," to rebuke gently the misunderstanding of purpose and the rending, displaced fear of life that has thwarted the emotional growth of Lowell's parents.

> Great-great-Grandfather Myers had never frowned down in judgment on a Salem witch. There was no allegory in his eyes, no *Mayflower*. Instead he looked peacefully at his sideboard, his cutglass decanters, his cellaret—the worldly bosom of the Mason-Myers mermaid engraved on a silver-plated urn. If he could have spoken, Mordecai would have said, "My children, my blood, accept graciously the loot of your inheritance. We are all dealers in used furniture."

Even Mordecai's identity, however, is assimilated at this point into that of the essay's other father-surrogate, Commander Billy Harkness, whose vivid presence dominates the last third of the memoir. Commander Billy is Commander Lowell's nautical alter ego, a raucous bourbon drinker (with a Kentucky accent said to sound "like a brass-fed stallion") whose weekly visits to the Lowell household disrupt the tense equilibriums that seem to the boy, and rightly so, far more threatening than the open conflicts. For Lowell, he is a crude and unsentimentalized intrusion of an unregulated life force. In his cups he is the appropriate possessor of "Father's sacred 'rhino' armchair." He proposes toasts to Teddy Roosevelt, or to anything or anyone who comes to mind. He looks on these occasions "like a human ash heap," and his "cigar ashes" bury "the heraldic hedgehog" on the family ashtray. Billy is outraged that Mrs. Lowell, in order to be nearer "the hub of gentility," should have contrived to have her husband transferred from Washington to an inferior duty at the Boston yard (an "impotent field nigger's job of second in command") and that once transferred, Commander Lowell should be required by the admiral to sleep each night at the yard. Commander Billy's character has been developed at such length, we feel, so as to give authority to the common sense and passion with which he denounces all of the absurdly symbolic tyrannies that have deprived Commander Lowell of his inner life.

> Then Commander Harkness would throw up his hands in despair and make a long buffoonish speech. "Would you believe it?" he'd say. "De Stahl, the anile slob, would make Bob Lowell sleep seven

nights a week and twice on Sundays in that venerable twenty-room pile provided for his third in command at the yard. 'Bobby me boy,' the Man says, 'henceforth I will that you sleep wifeless. You're to push your beauteous mug into me boudoir each night at ten-thirty and each morn at six. And don't mind me laying to alongside the Missus De Stahl,' the old boy squeaks; 'we're just two oldsters as weak as babies. But Robbie Boy,' he says, 'don't let me hear of you hanging on your telephone wire and bending off the ear of that forsaken frau of yours sojourning on Revere Street. I might have to phone you in a hurry, if I should happen to have me stroke.'"

Taking hold of the table with both hands, the Commander tilted his chair backwards and gaped down at me with sorrowing Gargantuan wonder: "I know why Young Bob is an only child."

These are the last words of the essay, and by one of those happy mechanical accidents of typesetting, they have the effect on the page of seeming to spill Commander Lowell's son alone out into blank space. The effect is similar to that of the memorable frozen frame at the end of François Truffaut's *Four Hundred Blows*. It is premonitory, too, of a technique that will be common for Lowell from this point forward: that of withheld resolution, a suspension and lack of finality in the poems that formalize both uncertainty and tension.

The ending of "91 Revere Street" directs our attention back to a consideration of what R. P. Blackmur would call the "technical form" of the essay and the disturbing "theoretic form" that it implies. "Technical form," Blackmur said, "is our means of getting at. . . and then making something of, what we feel the form of life itself is: the tensions, the stresses, the deep relations and the terrible disrelations that inhabit them. . . [Theoretic form] underlies the forms we merely practice."[9] If we consider Lowell's memoir simply as a compositional problem, it seems possible that what Lowell had before him as he wrote was much unassimilated material, some of which could be fitted into a thematic pattern and some of which could not, but all of which required unification in some fashion. Like any compulsive observer, he is unwilling to jettison interesting material for the sake of coherence; but like any sophisticated stylist, he is unwilling to resort to a simple catalogue of memories. So what he does instead is something like this:

> I writhed with disappointment on the nights when Mother and Father only lowed harmoniously together like cows, as they criticized Helen Bailey or Admiral De Stahl. Once I heard mother

say, "A *man* must make up his *own* mind. Oh, Bob, if you are going
to resign do it *now* so I can at least plan for your son's *survival* and
education on a single continent."

About this time I was being sent for my *survival* to Dr. Dane, a
Quaker chiropractor with an office on Marlborough Street. Dr.
Dane wore an old-fashioned light tan druggist's smock; he smelled
like a healthy old-fashioned drugstore.(*Life Studies*, pp. 19–20)

That is to say, Lowell frequently forces transitions across the flimsiest of
associations, and manages by this device to subvert or call into question
thematic unity at the same time that he sustains it. A parallel technique is
what might be called the delayed-action topic sentence. The page-and-a-
half-long paragraph that begins, "Physical instruction in the lower school
was irregular, spontaneous, and had nothing of that swept and garnished
barrack-room camaraderie of the older girls' gymnasium exercises" moves
on to report on "botanical hikes through the arboretum" guided by the
"submerged" Mr. Newell and on instructive tours of the city (one of which
is to the Aquarium, where the children are given an "unhealthy, eager,
little lecture on the sewage consumption of the conger eel"); then on to
Miss Manice, the school principal, and her hilarious browbeating of "my
white and sheepish father" on her pet theory that "women are simply not
the equals of men"; then on —returning to the point—to the bewildering
masculinity of the girls in Brimmer's uncoeducational eight upper grades
(they are remembered marching, singing "America," bearing an American
flag *and* a flag of the Commonwealth of Massachusetts *and* the green flag
of the Brimmer School); and then finally, after a fashion, comes home: "I
wished I were an older girl. I wrote Santa Claus for a field hockey stick. To
be a boy at Brimmer [boys were not admitted beyond the fourth grade], was
to be small, denied, and weak" (pp. 26–27). The subject that binds the
elements of this paragraph together is the mystery of sex roles, a theme that
prevails elsewhere in the account of the conflict between Lowell's mother
and father. But even a reasonably attentive reader might never notice this
and might feel only vaguely as if a subject were at hand. Many paragraphs
drift in this way across the submerged possibility of a subject, incorporating
progressively more detail to be made sense of.

The details themselves are an aspect of the overall structural
problem. They are extraordinary for their variety and number. Lowell
seems to have no interest in types, only in particulars. His father's books
include "some American's nationalist sketch of Sir Thomas Lipton's errors

in the Cup Defender races" (p. 32). Billy Harkness "called his wife *Jimmy* or *Jeems*" (p. 33). Lowell's mother "did not have the self-assurance for wide human experience; she needed to feel liked, admired, surrounded by the approved and familiar. Her haughtiness and chilliness came from apprehension. She would start talking like a *grande dame* and then stand back rigid and faltering, as if she feared being crushed by her own massively intimidating offensive" (p. 32). It was "One day when the saucer magnolias were in bloom" that "I bloodied Bulldog Binney's nose against the pedestal of George Washington's statue in full view of Commonwealth Avenue" (p. 31). Cousin Ledyard Atkinson, a temporary admiral, "serene, silver-maned and Spanish-looking, . . . liked full-dress receptions and crowed like a rooster in his cabin crowded with liveried Filipinos, Cuban trophies, and racks of experimental firearms, such as pepper-box pistols and a machine gun worked by electric batteries" (p. 40). His wife, a Christian Scientist, "had a bloodless, euphoric, inexhaustible interest in her own body" and regales the guests at one Sunday dinner party with a story of "how her healer had 'surprised and evaporated a cyst inside a sac' inside her 'major intestine'" (p. 42). Such details float at random in the memoir, this way and that, but then unpredictably make contact with one another and radiate implication, creating a progressively enriched but complex thematic context. At the same time, because they are not overtly coerced by the organization, they seem to escape finally into an unmediated epistemological region of their own, thus both provoking our attention and eluding our understanding.

The cumulative effect of the techniques that complicate Lowell's memoir imposes upon it a strong pressure for unity, while at the same time undermining it. When Billy Harkness speaks his mind so vividly at the end, his words express for him a pattern of cause and effect that for us, and Lowell, is not simple at all, and his words do not have the same reference for us as they do for himself. What is complex is dramatically shown to be so by appearing to be simple. A unity is being imposed, again, that is too elementary to contain the pressure, and it is, for that reason alone, a formal one; the words take on a sinister and premonitory emphasis. "91 Revere Street" enacts a process of making sense of things that nevertheless finally cannot be made sense of, and the world, even this small corner of it, again slips away from signification, having had its invidious effect. When one writes about Commander and Mrs. Lowell from the perspective of one theory, one must omit half of the substance of the essay in order to rationalize, in effect, a corner of a corner. But Lowell's method forbids reduction. Even his authoritative, urbane, and amused tone implies a control that is mainly tonal, or attitudinal. Simply his refusal to make "types" of characters who all but beg for it tells the whole mystifying story. Since the characters are not types, they do not fit into a moral world that is either coherent or immediately recognizable, inhabiting instead the world of a writer's mind in which typology itself is foreign. A world without generic attributes is merely real in the un-Platonic sense, a world of effects without discernible causes. It is too particular not to be believed in, but too unknowable not to be feared. This effect of Lowell's memoir is too vivid, upon reflection at least, to have been inadvertent. The whole essay is, in a sense, a model of the perfectly ludicrous calm with which we manage to face the otherwise terrifying facts of life's contingency. The famous plain surfaces of *Life Studies* are both deceptive and expressive of an attitude of consciousness, and this is nowhere more apparent than in the memoir that disingenuously feigns confinement to the conventional epistemological assumptions of prose.

Part four of *Life Studies*, the "Life Studies" section, is dominated by plain surfaces through which are refracted themes of death and madness, and the style and the themes are brought together in such a way as to suggest a horror indigenous in human life that neither death nor madness can account for adequately. The two subjects of death and madness are metaphorical or, more precisely, synecdochic parts standing for an incomprehensible and invisible whole. And such is the prevalence of these two themes that the title may be taken to mean not only "studies from life," referring to portraits, but studies *of* life, referring to some occult ontological text. One of the truly astonishing moments of this book of plain speech and mystifying juxtapositions comes at the point in "My Last Afternoon with Uncle Devereux Winslow" when Lowell sees himself as a child suffering an abrupt and bizarre metamorphosis:

> I cowered in terror.
> I wasn't a child at all—
> unseen and all-seeing, I was Agrippina
> in the Golden House of Nero. . . .

In the next line he recovers a point of reference in the ordinary world: "Near me was the white measuring door." There is no justification in the phenomenal world of the poem for this histrionic seizure. Uncle Devereux is dying, certainly and irreversibly, and given that this is the first intrusion of human death into the child's experience (that is, apart from that of "Cinder, our Scottie puppy"), fear and confused identification would be the expected response. But nothing or no one else visible has threatened the child, and indeed he has been on the sidelines observing during most of the poem's narrative. And yet, if we take the image of Agrippina seriously, it means not only that the child is threatened to the point of terror in this otherwise "Golden House"* but that he himself is implicated in the sinister power that he fears. It means, too, that he fears himself insane in a setting of insanity, and that a hideous premature omniscience has fallen upon him like a curse.

The lines alluding to Agrippina parallel and intensify another grotesque psychic transformation that has taken place earlier, with even less apparent cause. At one moment, dressed in new "formal pearl gray shorts" like the "models in the imperishable autumn / display windows / of Rogers Peet's boy's store," his perfection and poise are "Olympian." But in the next moment he is deformed:

> Distorting drops of water
> pinpricked my face in the basin's mirror.
> I was a stuffed toucan
> with a bibulous, multicolored beak.

This would appear to have nothing to do with death and dying. Insofar as it is intelligible at all, it juxtaposes felt extremes of the outer and inner life, which are made to seem irreconcilable, and it encourages us to understand that the association with Agrippina has a source that is deeper than that of the external facts alone. Then again, in the section immediately preceding the ones cited above is a passage that seems innocent of mystery until it connects in our minds with the two later ones. It begins in charmed, affectionate reverie—

> What were those sunflowers? Pumpkin floating shoulder high?
> It was sunset, Sadie and Nellie
> bearing pitchers of ice-tea
> oranges, lemons, mint, and peppermints

---

*Lowell is adapting facts here. Agrippina was murdered long before Nero built his Golden House, during his Greek-revival phase after Rome had burned.

and closes abruptly with a freakish omen:

> No one had died there in my lifetime...
> Only Cinder, our Scottie puppy
> paralyzed from gobbling toads.

The faintly absurd quality of this image, the real toads suddenly in the imaginary garden, and the abrasion of the word "paralyzed" against the prevailing verbal texture of the stanza together shake the poem loose from its moorings in empirical experience. An essence of life has been disclosed in the contrast of the beginning of the passage with its end, but we are never to know more about that forbidding quality than the images themselves will show.

Stephen Yenser has exhaustively documented an argument that in almost every image of this poem, "the relationship between life and death is the fundamental subject, but everywhere this relationship is reflected from a slightly different angle so that it has many different forms." He says that the poem enacts the child's seeing "for the first time that his life entails his death, that living and dying can be synonymous."[10] In addition to the obvious details enforcing this pattern—the mixing of earth and lime, the "root cellar" made of it, the young men in Uncle Devereux's poster "being bushwacked on the veldt," the identification by images of clothing and color of the nephew and dying uncle—Yenser cites a number of subtler allusions to the subject: the "shellacked saplings" of grandfather's chaise longue; the paleness of the Huck Finn figurine, linked to Uncle Devereux's anemia; the closing of Uncle Devereux's camp "for the winter"; the oddly inconsistent connection of the half earth, half lime with Grandfather's mixed half shandy gaff and half sarsaparilla and beer, and the duck pond "halved" by "'the Island.'" These references and others that Yenser cites are oblique, and some seem fanciful. The interesting thing about them is that they move us away from abstracted equation as fiercely as they move us toward it. Their very obliqueness creates a thematic texture that is at once unstable and strongly suggestive, so that although the continuity of living and dying becomes the poem's overt subject, there is a frighteningly hidden subject that we and the poet are forbidden to grasp. That hidden subject would be, on this reading, the elusive source of the child's two sinister hallucinations and specifically of his awareness of himself, in the form of Agrippina, as both motivated and threatened—where Cartesian distinctions blur—by dark forces beyond the reach of his understanding or will. He is "all-seeing" and therefore sees more than human intelligence can comprehend. There can be little wonder that he and the adult poet he will become fear madness but are compelled to scorn sanity.

Yenser makes a common mistake, I believe, when he says that the "black earth" and the "white lime," the poems' central symbols, are respectively symbolic of life (the fertile soil), and of death (the caustic substance used to destroy dead bodies). Those indeed would be the conventional associations in a different context; but warmth and coolness are associated with life and death as well, and it is the lime, being caustic, that is warm, and the earth that is cool. Those two sensations—not the abstractions "earth" and "lime"—are what brings the images into the poem in the first place: "One of my hands was cool on a pile / of black earth, the other warm / on a pile of lime." This is oblique indeed. Lowell appears to have gone out of his way to reverse the conventional associations, and in so doing he confuses the issue of the poem while seeming to be clarifying it. The two conflicting directions in which this image moves make it symbolically oxymoronic, and it points toward the two different levels on which the poem as a whole moves, one logical, the other not. The child's disturbing epiphanies are otherwise the only signs of what is going on beneath the surface. Those moments are reminiscent, not so much in form as in meaning, of the occasion in *To the Lighthouse*, Virginia Woolf's own *Life Studies*, when Woolf expresses through Minta Ramsey her perception of the tragic simplicity of human destiny.

> The men (Andrew and Paul at once became manly, and different from usual) took counsel briefly and decided that they would plant Rayley's stick where they had sat and come back at low tide again. There was nothing more that could be done now. If the brooch was there, it would still be there in the morning, they assured her, but Minta still sobbed, all the way up to the top of the cliff. It was her grandmother's brooch; she would rather have lost anything but that, and yet Nancy felt, it might be true that she minded losing her brooch, but she wasn't crying only for that. She was crying for something else. We might all sit down and cry, she felt. But she did not know what for.[11]

The calculated vagueness of "My Last Afternoon with Uncle Devereux Winslow" is important structurally because everything else in part four of *Life Studies* is predicated on a similar experience of ontological

instability. This is particularly true of the poems, which, as Lowell has said
he hoped they would, "seem as open and as single-surfaced as photogra-
phy," for part of the power of the otherwise simple poems of the volume—
"Sailing Home from Rapallo," for instance, or "Commander Lowell"—
derives from our awareness of the latently terrifying context in which the
events of these poems unfold. The single surface is the perceptual illusion
of the characters in this section, who are impatient, as Eliot expressed it,
"to assume the world," while they are relentlessly damaged—maddened,
thwarted, or killed—by forces in life that they cannot hope to understand.
So, for example, when Commander Lowell is said to have "boomed in his
bathtub," "'Anchors aweigh'. . . 'Anchors aweigh,' / when Lever Brothers
offered to pay / him double what the Navy paid" and then "year after
year," failure after failure, to have still "murmured 'Anchors aweigh' in the
tub," the effect is more than simply ironic and sad. He becomes a kind of
absurdist tragic hero, drawn, oblivious, deeper into an incomprehensible
abyss, and warding off awareness with his undying dream of life as a
perpetual postbaccalaureate adventure. There is no solution or rescue for
him, and his desperate faith in mathematics is poignantly irrelevant.

> he grew defiant.
> Night after night,
> *à la clarté déserte de sa lampe,*
> he slid his ivory Annapolis slide rule
> across a pad of graphs. . . .

Hodgkin's disease, which kills Uncle Devereux at age twenty-nine, is
silent and insidious. Commander Lowell suffers two coronaries and is
killed abruptly by a third. His "newly dieted figure was vitally trim" and his
"vision was still twenty-twenty." The single surface of the photograph lies.
If the world is in fact the way Lowell represents it, then the true perspective
will seem like madness, and those who are "sane"—or who, like Lowell's
mother, *strive* to be, in a pathologically futile way—dwell epistemologically in a cruelly false paradise. At Beverly Farms, where Commander
Lowell dies,

> They had no sea-view,
> but sky-blue tracks of the commuters' railroad shone
> like a double-barrelled shotgun
> through the scarlet late August sumac,

multiplying like cancer
at their garden's border.

The "but" here is interesting, suggesting that the sea represents a knowledge from which Lowell's parents are sheltered, like the tracks that resemble a shotgun and the scarlet sumac encroaching like cancer upon the garden. This is what Lowell sees, but Commander and Mrs. Lowell's perspectives are innocent. Commander Lowell smiles "his oval Lowell smile" and dresses for dinner in "his cream gabardine dinner-jacket, / and indigo cummerbund" and is still smiling, though anxiously, when he dies.

Lowell's father's vacant bedroom is a surprise. The pieces of his character never quite fit together; he remains a mystery to the son, lonely in his apartness. So the unexpected oriental-precious decor of his bedroom is all the more touching for the glimpse of a private self it gives us. It would be touching anyway, with its bereft, cherished objects so carefully arranged. But these objects seem especially intimate—

blue threads as thin
as pen-writing on the bedspread,
blue dots on the curtains,
a blue kimono,
Chinese sandals with blue plush straps.
. . . . .
A clear glass bed-lamp
with a white doily shade
. . . . .
resting on volume two
of Lafcadio Hearn's
Glimpses of unfamiliar Japan.

The book had been a gift to Commander Lowell from his mother and is inscribed "To Robbie," and the inscription has been amended, as if to dispel a feminizing stigma, to point out that the book "has had hard usage / on the Yangtze River, China / . . . left under an open / porthole in a storm." That Yangtze River phase has always seemed somewhat bogus in Lowell's accounts of it. Here it is a kind of singular reality principle, seeming surrealistically remote. Otherwise, as an expression of Commander Lowell's view of nature and time, the delicate decor of the bedroom speaks for itself. At the risk of overreaching, we might wonder whether here again it would not be appropriate for the poet to exclaim, "I wasn't a child at all— / . . . I was Agrippina / in the Golden House of Nero."

In the poem about Mrs. Lowell's death, part of the point of the image of her grandiose coffin is that it represents such a predictable evasion of what being dead is. It is a culminating symbol of her evasion of life. In being like Napoleon's tomb it is associated with the "Napoleon book," which we already know (from "Commander Lowell" and "91 Revere Street") to have been the focus for her and her son's dubiously romantic fantasies. The wintry, gothic austerity of the family graveyard at Dunbarton, where the living son and the dead mother are headed, is more to the point, especially as its forbidding tone clashes ironically with the busily oblivious eruptions of spring along the *Golfo di Genova*:

> While the passengers were tanning
> on the Mediterranean in deck-chairs,
> our family cemetery in Dunbarton
> lay under the White Mountains
> in the sub-zero weather.

This laconic juxtaposition has the effect of extending the implication of Mrs. Lowell's life and death, just as it calls attention to the commonness of all human destinations. The same heat that is tanning the passengers in the deck chairs is decomposing Mrs. Lowell's tin-foil-wrapped flesh in the hold.

"'Hardly passionate Marlborough Street'" is an appropriate setting for *Life Studies*, in that it epitomizes the human need to achieve inauthenticity at any cost—

> "hardly passionate Marlborough Street,"
> where even the man
> scavenging filth in the back alley trash cans,
> has two children, a beach wagon, a helpmate,
> and is a "young Republican."
>
>   ("Memories of West Street and Lepke")

The statement "These are the tranquillized *Fifties*" generalizes the idea of there being a pressure toward normality that dissociates people from the undercurrents of their lives. The "young Republican" "scavenging filth" is characteristic. "These are the tranquillized *Fifties*, / and I am forty," Lowell says, in a way that suggests that he is not synchronized, intellectually and emotionally, with the prevailing norm.

When he remembers his "seedtime" in West Street Jail as a criminal among other criminals, even these odd inhabitants of the "Fifties" mode seem surrealistically divided, like the "young Republican," from what they are and do. Abramowitz is a pacifist and a vegetarian; Bioff and Brown, the "Hollywood pimps," wear suburban "chocolate double-breasted suits"; one "fellow jailbird" is a Jehovah's Witness; and Czar Lepke—more respectable than a mere murderer because he is a professional—has such talismanic amenities for his cell as "a portable radio, a dresser, two toy American / flags tied together with a ribbon of Easter palm." In "Waking in the Blue" the attendant of the insane in McLean's Hospital is reading *The Meaning of Meaning*. "Stanley, now sunk in his sixties," hoards "the build of a boy in his twenties" and "thinks only of his figure, / of slimming on sherbet and ginger ale." Stanley is one of the "victorious figures of bravado [who] ossified young." "Victorious," of course, is ironic; "bravado" has the connotation of a foolish rather than affected courage, a hopeless defiance. Stanley is only a caricature of the normal; his fixated withdrawal is different only in degree from anyone else's.

A disquieting *ur*-reality prevails at the beginning of this poem:

Azure day
makes my agonized blue window bleaker.
Crows maunder on the petrified fairway.
Absence! My heart grows tense
as though a harpoon were sparring for the kill.

The dislocation of language in the image of the window, where subject and object are interchanged, may remind us that Ogden and Richards' book, which "our B.U. sophomore" is reading, is about language, a scientific investigation into the "correspondence between word and fact." Lowell's usage not only alludes to two prototypical symbolist poems (Mallarmé's "L'Azur" and "Les Fenêtres"), but it expresses by symbolist grammatical means the perception of a world to which traditional Cartesian distinctions have no access. As far as the mind's reach can carry, that world is a void; and for Lowell to describe the crows' action on the frozen landscape, whether it be their movement or calling out, as "maundering" implies, suggests powerfully that they are as aimless and stranded in that void as the poet himself. Stanley is said to be "more cut off from words than a seal," and in such a context this implies not only withdrawal but the unique, unutterable awareness of the mad. *The Meaning of Meaning* is put before us to begin with as a model of the brave human effort to achieve rational understanding of the relation between the mind and the wordless world. It is affiliated in the poem, therefore, with all of the other more common visible signs of normalcy—being a sophomore in college, Stanley's golf cap (suggestively arrayed against the "petrified fairway"), sherbet and ginger ale, crew haircuts, the poet's French sailor's jersey, "a hearty New England breakfast." The poet is put in touch with this ordinariness by his "sense of humor," and that is its use, which he wonders about. His sense of humor and his breakfast enable him to function in the normal world, suddenly no longer terrified but smug—"cock of the walk." But at the end, Lowell turns the poem ominously back toward its original psychic provenance. "We are all old timers, / each of us holds a locked razor." This about the razors is unlikely to be literally true, so the "locked razor" must be perceived as a metaphor, a reference to something in the minds of all the "old timers" rather than in their hands. One could plausibly say that the image connotes a suppressed suicidal impulse. It seems to me, however, to return us instead to the barely representable dread that falls upon the poet's consciousness at the beginning of the day. That apprehension is temporarily suppressed, but it remains dangerously viable just beneath the surface of consciousness. This is perhaps what is meant by the "locked razor" in the minds of the initiates, the denizens of "the kingdom of the mad." That link seems to be secured by the clear connection between the razor in the mind and the "harpoon. . . sparring for the kill," which patently threatens from some source outside the poet's own will.

If we read "Waking in the Blue" in this way and take what it seems to be saying seriously—that sanity and normalcy are the mind's defenses against itself and what it knows—then it becomes possible, also, to read the ending of "Memories of West Street and Lepke" in a different way from the usual one, by which Lepke becomes an honorary brother of the family of McLean's:

> Flabby, bald, lobotomized,
> he drifted in a sheepish calm,
> where no agonizing reappraisal
> jarred his concentration on the electric chair—

hanging like an oasis in his air
of lost connections. . . .

The conventions of idiomatic English require that we read the participial phrase at the end of the poem as referring to the "electric chair." But it is at least possible to read it as referring to Lepke himself, especially if we account for the dash as a rather clumsy device for breaking up the sentence unit. In this way, "drift[ing] in a sheepish calm" becomes analogous to "hanging. . . in his air" and Lepke himself the oasis in the desolation of his life—not from his point of view but from the observer's, referring to the ordinariness of his appearance and the conventional amenities of his cell. He is not unlike Stanley at McLean's, in other words, and he is like the poet insofar as he has a fearsome, privileged knowledge of the forces that work beneath the surface of human life; his concentration on the electric chair is a cathexis of that knowledge and his own evil implication in it. If the world of *Life Studies*, which terrifies Lowell as a child and imposes chronic dread upon the adult, is the true world, then Lepke is the expression of it; and the vegetarian pacifist Abramovitz or the crewcut Roman Catholic attendants at McLean's, for instance, are aberrations, expressions of the false. Lepke not only has a privileged knowledge of the inexplicable and random cruelty of human life, he is continuous with it, though as seemingly harmless as a senior citizen in a retirement village.

The way Lepke is, or the way he is characterized, is analogous to the way the poems in *Life Studies* are conceived and executed. Just as the title is deceptively bland, the poems concentrate upon surfaces and render those surfaces in a colloquial, unconstraining idiom that gravitates constantly toward the cliché ("they blew their tops and beat him black and blue"). Nothing of very great importance appears to be going on much of the time. But the surfaces and the idiom are controlled so as to produce the illusion of normal experience, against which Lowell can effectively play the dark side of his dualistic obsession. Partly because of the similarity between the way we read the poems and the way we live our daily experience, alternately oblivious and shocked, the effect of this technique is, over the long run, to show how elusively contingent ordinary human life is, subject at every moment to sudden erosion and dread. The impervious insularity of Boston comes ready-made for Lowell's purpose. Boston society is famous for taking itself for granted, and it can only take itself for granted by taking the nicely-arrangedness of the world for granted as well. Even McLean's is made to seem decent, the home only of "thoroughbred mental cases," a model in its won way of normalcy. In this respect the theme of *Life Studies*, coolly under the control of the disingenuous style, is *un-seeing*—what Lowell would later call "the sanity of self-deception."

The calculated effect of indirection and understatement upon this theme in *Life Studies* may be highlighted by introducing into this setting "The Neo-Classical Urn" from *For the Union Dead*, a poem in which the theme is addressed overtly and luridly clarified. The basic materials of the poem are the same as those of the first poems in part four of *Life Studies*. The setting is the Winslow "farm"; Lowell is again a child, and again, all too vividly, Agrippina in the Golden House. That similarity in itself suggests that "The Neo-Classical Urn" might have been composed in the same period but withheld for a later volume because it was incompatible with, and disruptive to, the stylistic norm of *Life Studies*. For besides the subject matter, nothing else is similar. In fact, in terms of the baffled dialectic of all-seeing, the emphasis has been dramatically reversed. I feel it necessary to quote a sizable proportion of the poem in order to give proper stress to that contrast.

> At full run on the curve,
> I left the caste stone statue of a nymph,
> her soaring armpits and her one bare breast,
> gray from the rain and graying in the shade,
> as on, on, in sun, the pathway now a dyke,
> I swerved between two water bogs,
> two seins of moss, and stopped to snatch
> the painted turtles on dead logs.
>
> In that season of joy,
> my turtle catch
> was thirty-three,
> dropped splashing in our garden urn,
> like money in the bank,
> the plop and splash
> of turtle on turtle,
> fed raw gobs of hash. . . .
> Oh neo-classical white urn, Oh nymph,
> Oh lute! The boy was pitiless who strummed

their elegy,
for as the month wore on,
the turtles rose,
and popped up dead on the stale scummed
surface—limp wrinkled heads and legs withdrawn
in pain. What pain? A turtle's nothing. No
grace, no cerebration, less free will
than the mosquito I must kill—
nothings! Turtles! I rub my skull,
that turtle shell,
and breathe their dying smell,
still watch their crippled last survivors pass,
and hobble humpbacked through the grizzled grass.

That the urn is neoclassical implies that it represents an extension of the pervasive innocence of *Life Studies*—extended to include a historical and cultural innocence, committed doggedly through human time to the reassuring ideals of symmetry and order. The decomposing turtles floating to the surface inside are an unsubtle commentary upon that. The burden of the poem is the boy's guilty collusion as he naively abets the inexplicable process by which one innocence mutilates another. That sinister force, which the boy and the adult fear, is perceived as coming from within as well as from without—as it was with the whalemen in "A Quaker Graveyard in Nantucket." The poet reflects on this truth even as he tries to disavow it, and it looms upon him: "I rub my skull, / that turtle shell, / and breathe their dying smell." It is into the present of the poem that the odor of death penetrates, as if in caricature of the timeless moment in Keat's "Ode on a Grecian Urn." The typical curve of *Life Studies* is reenacted here in the middle stanza, where the verbal textures alone transport the theme: "In that season of joy. . . fed raw gobs of hash." Moreover, since the urn connotes art as well, a new dimension of the conflict has been brought into play—the thought of Lowell the poet decomposing within the mocking achievement of his own art, which, in turn, is analogous to the thought of Lowell the nihilist, suffering acutely in his knowledge in the presence of ironic emblems of the shaping spirit. All of these effects are reinforced by the grisly incongruity of the poem's last two lines, an isolated neoclassical couplet that extends the conventional mock-heroic wit toward a radical extreme. The couplet is to the image it contains as the urn is to the turtles, as the poem is to the experience it mitigates by formalizing, as the poet in nature is to his own art. The poem, finally, is a commentary upon the illusion of existential freedom, since the boy free and running in "that season of joy" is collaborating, like Oedipus, in his own destiny and is determined to be moving rapidly through time to the dead end of a morbid anxiety. The difference between this poem and any poem in *Life Studies* may be expressed by saying that the "locked razor" has become unlocked, and that that difference, one of exposed consciousness, will be the difference between *Life Studies* and *For the Union Dead* generally.

It is significant that Lowell is strenuously unwilling to romanticize his own childhood, for his refusal closes off an access through which the illusion of freedom might be achieved, then to be nourished, as it was by Dylan Thomas, as a stay against despair. But Lowell has attended to that matter very early in his career, and his perspective remains basically the same until the end: "The Child is born in blood, O child of blood." That admonition in "New Year's Day" does not, of course, deny the reality of innocence, but it does emphatically deny innocence any power in the face of the prevailing destructive forces in life (described in the earlier poem as "Time and the grindstone and the knife of God"). So it should not be surprising that when Lowell's daughter is brought into the context of *Life Studies*, in three of the last seven poems, her presence is almost symbolically extraneous. In two of the poems she is simply inserted, a point of reference in human meaning. In the third, "Home after Three Months Away," her role is poignantly more prominent, but only, as it turns out, so that what she is or seems to be or to represent is finally rejected. In her first appearance, in "During Fever," she is already a victim and already capable of assuming the guilt for her own visitation:

All night the crib creaks;
home from the healthy country to the sick city,
my daughter in fever
flounders in her chicken-colored sleeping bag.
"Sorry," she mumbles like her dim-bulb father, "sorry."

But though the title alludes to her, this is all that is said about her, and the remainder of the poem, almost forty lines, is devoted to Lowell's cozy Oedipal relationship with his mother and, in turn, to her similar relationship to her father. Harriet, it is implied very obliquely, is to be the latest victim of a chain of baleful parental influences. Her sickness is physical, but she is showing psychological symptoms also in her pitifully baseless apology. She struggles in her sleeping bag as if caught, and the fact that the "sick city" is her home suggests that she has prematurely seen the last of her own particular Fern Hill. In "Memories of West Street and Lepke" she is, oddly, one of the appurtenances, like fresh pajamas or the "young Republican" scavenger with his two children and helpmate, that make Lowell an acceptable resident of Marlborough Street. "I have a nine months' daughter, / young enough to be my granddaughter." She holds her own, briefly, and makes her own little manic statement: "Like the sun she rises in her flame-flamingo infants' wear," but she then recedes, for the foreground is dominated by prisons and by sane madness and mad sanity. She is enveloped, in other words, rather like Christ the wanderer and child.

Harriet's presence in the life of *Life Studies* is only ambiguously a good omen, and in any case it is a bad one for her. In a later poem, "Soft Wood," Lowell, distracted by the sea wind that is buffeting the Maine coast, thinks "sometimes for days here / only children seem fit to handle children," and thus verbalizes his own intellectual distance from childhood and from his own child. (He will return to this theme dramatically in *The Dolphin*.) It is already implicit in *Life Studies* that their association will be distant. When she is born, Lowell is old enough to be her grandfather, and the importance of that fact lies not so much in the difference in years as in the differences in consciousness, which will remain unbridgeable. The tragic human problem is a symbolic one as well, and in "Home after Three Months Away" it becomes the basis for Lowell's strongest assertion, in *Life Studies*, of his will to live only the life that he perceives to be real. On the one hand there is Harriet, "dimpled with exaltation," rubbing noses with her father in the tub, presiding in queenly fashion over the voluptuous rituals of shaving and child's play. On the other hand, down below,

> a choreman tends our coffin's length of soil,
> and seven horizontal tulips blow.
> Just twelve months ago,
> these flowers were pedigreed
> imported Dutchmen; now no one need
> distinguish them from weed.
> Bushed by the late spring snow,
> they cannot meet
> another year's snowballing enervation.

The tulips all too clearly designate the poet and his fated engagement with authentic existence. "Dearest," he says, addressing his child in the lyric language of a child's song, "I cannot loiter here / in lather like a polar bear." That "here" is really nowhere in Lowell's world, and the child, too, in some sense will not exist, since there is no pastoral place for her to inhabit in the landscape of her father's mind. The necessity for this strange psychological rejection is made clear, perhaps, in the poem's last lines: "Cured, I am frizzled, stale and small." To be cured is to be restored to normalcy, with all of the attendant effects that are laid out plainly before us in the other poems. It is better, therefore, to face the destructive element squarely, to be uncured, to affirm nihilism, than to be nothing, or next to it. That is his work ("Recuperating, I neither spin nor toil"), absurd as it is, and choosing it requires him to reject both the child inside himself and the child outside himself as well.

Of course, characteristically leaving the mystery of identity unresolved, Lowell in the last lines of the volume, in "Skunk Hour," gives this theme one more propelling ironic twist. If what happens in "Home after Three Months Away" were all there is, then the Sartrean hero, affirming the authentic, would be the appropriately comparable figure to evoke. But Lowell is no more sentimental about madness than he is about childhood. If sanity is being stale and small, madness is this:

> I hear
> my ill-spirit sob in each blood cell,
> as if my hand were at its throat. . . .
> I myself am hell;
> nobody's here.

These lines mean explicitly what they say—that "I myself am not a person but a hell, and therefore nobody's here." In the last half of "Skunk Hour" the world has become depopulated. The poet is no more real to himself than the lovers in the love-cars had been, and now all that is left is a car with a radio singing a human love song, the chalk-dry spire of a church, and a family of skunks foraging in garbage cans for food. Only "Absence!" prevails, as in "Waking in the Blue." It is a frankly desolated vision, all but unmitigated. Stranded between the church spire and the skunks, the poet has experienced a common human position as an apparition. He is stranded because the two symbols, the spire and the skunks, represent impossible options, the one because intellect refuses it, and the other because intellect precludes it. The mother skunk's regal insouciance is an effect of her being undissociated. The garbage—which has moral qualities projected upon it, absurdly, by the human mind—is, after all, for her merely food. (In this context it is interesting to remember Commander Lowell at Sunday dinner laboring to match his carving lessons stroke for stroke.) But being undissociated in this way is precisely what human beings, by virtue of being human, are forbidden to be. Lowell is as unable to sentimentalize authenticity as he is innocence, and this is unfortunate, since it makes him unable to pretend to have achieved something when he approaches either.

When I say that the desolateness of Lowell's vision in "Skunk Hour" is "all but" unmitigated, the qualification is necessary because of the "rich air" that is cryptically incompatible with the poem's darkening mood. It is identified with survival, of course: breathing it keeps one going. But it is also identified with the ambiguous beauty of the skunks, and as such it becomes another ironic emblem of unmediated nature, which we may know with our instincts and senses but are definitively cut off from by our minds. It is critical to our consideration of the values put forward in Lowell's poem that beginning with the last line of the fifth stanza—"My mind's not right"—it is set in the specific present tense. Breathing "rich air" is not likely to contribute much more regeneration than a pang for one who is a hell to himself and whose ill-spirit is threatened by his own hand. If, as Steven Gould Axelrod argues, the recovery of "the lost self" has brought Lowell new wisdom, it certainly does not follow that wisdom has brought him peace ("a new olive branch to eat").[12] Far from affirming "the value of human experience," *Life Studies* comes close to denying it altogether, and the wisdom Lowell achieves in the process of recovering the lost self will therefore come to be seen as an altogether doubtful return on his emotional investment. This will be the subject of Lowell's next volume, *For the Union Dead*, as its ominously suggestive title portends.

Much of what Lowell writes about in *Life Studies* pointedly involves an effect of double exposure, in which the illusion of being snugly at home—somewhere, whether 91 Revere Street, Marlborough Street, McLean's, the apartment in New York, or the house in Castine—is ironically superimposed upon a more indistinct illusion, like a ghost image, of danger in the unknown and unknowable. We may be reminded by this of Heidegger's apt term, *unheimlich*, from *Being and Time*. It is translated as both "unhomelike" and "uncanny" ("unfamiliar"; "preter-naturally strange"), and in either case is an aspect of anxiety and therefore an aspect of the "primordial" and "direct" disclosure of "the world as world." "Anxiety," Heidegger says, "takes away from Dasein the possibility of understanding itself, as it falls, in terms of the 'world' and the way things have been publicly interpreted. Anxiety throws Dasein back upon that which it is anxious about—its authentic potentiality-for-Being-in-the-world."[13] Anxiety—when allowed to be—is thus a safeguard against Dasein's being absorbed inauthentically into the "everydayness" or the "theyness" of the "world." To experience the world as "unhomelike" is to be forced to become attuned to the openness of possibility, to be forced to allow one's existence to be in question. The "to be forced" parts of this construction are, of course, not Heidegger's language but my own modification in response to the way this occurrence is revealed through Lowell's poems. Heidegger expresses it this way:

> In anxiety one feels 'uncanny.' Here the peculiar indefiniteness of that which Dasein finds itself alongside in anxiety, comes proximally to expression: the "nothing and nowhere." But here "uncanniness" also means "not-being-at-home" [das Nicht-zuhausesein]. . . [As] Dasein falls, anxiety brings it back from its absorption in the 'world.' Everyday familiarity collapses. Dasein has been individualized [that is, set free from "theyness" to choose itself], but individualized *as Being-in-the-world*. Being-in enters into the existential 'mode' of the "not-at-home."[14]

Lowell acknowledges the necessity of anxiety, and in *Life Studies* the autobiographical mode is the instrument by which our essential condition of "not-being-at-home" is ironically revealed. In this respect a small but lovely point is made by Lowell in "Skunk Hour," where he indicates that he stands "on top / of *our* back steps," as the mysteries of being, terrible *and* bracing, swirl in his mind. Heidegger will say finally that all authentic being is being-toward-death, and this means not simply that we all die but that, to be, we must consciously take this finitude upon ourselves. "Dearest, I cannot loiter here / in lather like a polar bear": the choice is very harsh, for, among other reasons, it is alienating and, moreover, unplacating in any terms that the conventional world can understand.

4. The Death of Union

In *For the Union Dead* anxiety is manifested only in its pathological rather than redemptive form, and, as a consequence, the poems of this volume do not transcend their modest ambition of ritualizing living with the truth. Lowell is exposed here in a particularly vicious way to the consequences of his own knowledge. The title, *For the Union Dead*, is, of course, misleading—even read with an imagined comma—to the extent that it signifies a public poetry and a public voice. Nevertheless, it is a title iridescent with implications; the volume's theme is the death of union, private and public, psychological, spiritual, political; and the poems commemorate mainly the will to survive their own threatening awareness. The loss of connections is one of the more ironic consequences of the pursuit of understanding; and knowledge itself, in this volume, is rank with ambiguous consolation.

One of the poet's prototypes in this volume is Eve, desiring knowledge of good and evil and, unfortunately, achieving it.

> He snores in his iron lung,
>
> and hears the voice of Eve,
> beseeching freedom from the Garden's
> perfect and ponderous bubble. No voice
> outsings the serpent's flawed, euphoric hiss.
>
> ("The Drinker")

In this version, Eve is motivated to be the first existential hero, choosing authenticity over the nothingness of perfection. She has, however, shown poor judgment, the poem implies, for the "drinker" of the poem has achieved the bedrock of authentic existence in alcoholic terror. Another of the poet's implied prototypes is God, demoralized by human history.

> But I suppose even God was born
> too late to trust the old religion—
> all those settings out
> that never left the ground,
> beginning in wisdom, dying in doubt.
>
> ("Tenth Muse")

Here Lowell appears, morosely, to encapsulate his own career as well as God's, and he shows his true acedia in the implied, leveling association. So it seems natural that the third prototype in the volume should be Satan, the Satan of Renaissance pride:

> Think of him in the Garden
> that seed of wisdom, Eve's
> seducer, stuffed with man's
> corruption, stuffed with triumph:
> Satan triumphant in
> the Garden! In a moment,
> all that blinding brightness
> changed into a serpent,
> lay grovelling on its gut.
>
> ("Myopia: A Night")

The world changes when knowledge is brought into it, and logically the changer—"the seed of wisdom"—therefore changes, too. He becomes "frizzled, stale and small." Thus, the subject of wisdom is triangulated by Biblical reference, and not only the desire to be "as gods, knowing good and evil" but being God himself, "all-seeing" in *His* Golden House, is perceived to lead only to the subjugation of will and hope and to the dis-apotheosis of Being. Far from being public in scope, *For the Union Dead* is for the most part excruciatingly private and inward, as if the episodic hallucinations of *Life Studies* had metastasized with the effect of obscuring, and therefore estranging the poet from, the objective world.

Lowell's mordant deprecation of wisdom is extended in the high proportion of poems in which consciousness itself is made to seem a prison; and these poems are doubly remote from the common ground shared by reader and poet because they are poems *about* consciousness rather than about what it is conscious of. The memorable lines from "Night Sweat" throw an unusual light on this subject: "always inside me is the child who died, / always inside me is his will to die." The child in this case seems not to be the child as innocent but the child as solipsist, undiscriminating as to the boundaries between the objective and subjective worlds. Significantly, he is dead and yet still inside, prevailing in a way that is markedly different from the visionary child inside Wordsworth or Dylan Thomas. Lowell's child inside is the center of a solipsism that is not innocent, the worst conceivable distortion of possibilities. That child's "will to die" *is* Wordsworthian in the sense that his wish is not for literal death but for maturity, the implications of that being as ironic in Lowell's poem as they are in the "Intimations Ode." It indicates an imperfect transition between childhood and maturity and an arrested suspension between them. The crisis of the poet's knowledge is related to this predicament by reason of their thwarting influences upon each other. The knowledge or wisdom is without utility, even at best, because of the child's fear of, and imperfect access to, the world outside himself; and the world inside is all the more chaotic and exhausting for its being invaded by mature knowledge. Describing what he calls the "combination of solipsism and anomie" that permeates the large middle section of the book, Stephen Yenser points out that the poems of that section are dominated by "images of unbalanced states of one kind or another, of enclosures of various sorts, and of desultory movement."[1] The desultory movement—as, for example, in "Going To and Fro" or "Fall 1961"—is the sign of both the psychic entrapment, having nowhere to go, and of the loss of motivation from the loss of hope. It is the next thing to immobility, paralysis in action. And occasionally, as in "The Lesson," the poet suffers the oppressive realization that in his immobility and incarceration he is expressing a principle of the universe—that nothing really changes or moves forward:

> The green leaf cushions the same dry footprint,
> or the child's boat luffs in the same dry chop,
> and we are what we were

. . . . .
The barberry berry sticks on the small hedge,
cold slits the same crease in the finger,
the same thorn hurts. The leaf repeats the lesson.

Or in "Middle Age," thinking of his father before him:

You never climbed
Mount Sion, yet left
dinosaur
death-steps on the crust,
where I must walk.

To the extent that solipsism represents delimited self-containment
and unregenerativeness, it is not unusual that it should project its own
attributes back upon time and the world and thus reinforce its own lack of
interest in the world. This particular vicious circle will remain operative in
Lowell's work until the end of his career, causing the stylistic and moral
neurasthenia that his most strenuous critics complain of. Yenser, as
obedient to his thesis as I am to mine, argues that the pattern of For the
Union Dead as a whole is a movement "from outwardness to inwardness
and back to outwardness,"[2] and that it thus achieves what Robert Bly
describes as the penetration of the husk of one's own personality in order to
be able to penetrate the husk grown around the psyche of the world. The
outward-inward-outward pattern is perceptibly there, in a considerably
dimmer and more irregular form than Yenser allows, but the poems at the
end of the volume may not encourage us to take quite so sanguine a view of
it. One could also argue that the demoralized gravity of the middle holds
down both ends, whether intentionally so or not, and that the world is not
received gladly in the book at any point. This point can be illustrated by
reference to "Night Sweat," the penultimate poem of the volume. For
Yenser, this poem's second half, expressing "love and reliance upon
another," is part of the light at the end of the tunnel. For Axelrod, it in fact
dramatizes "spiritual recovery," the passage from "sightlessness to vision, . . . isolation to hoped-for connection."[3] If we are speaking simply of
the distilled essence of the poem, these are accurate readings. The poem
does balance in its two halves—two sonnets—darkness and light, isolation
and relation. But the first relation is described this way: "I see my flesh and
bedding washed with light, / my child exploding into dynamite"—in

words that make no sense with reference to the objective world and therefore refer us outward only to deflect us back inward. It is almost as if in that peculiar phrase Lowell were flagging the incompleteness of his return. The reestablished relation to his wife is clearer:

> Poor turtle, tortoise, if I cannot clear
> the surface of these troubled waters here,
> absolve me, help me, Dear Heart, as you bear
> this world's dead weight and cycle on your back.

But here, even as he appeals for grace he also concedes his inability to "clear the surface" of the "troubled waters"—that is, to see clearly what is outside of himself. What is represented in "Night Sweat" in other words, is the will to escape his Cartesian trap, not the escape itself. Almost the same may be said, as I shall try to show, of "For the Union Dead."

The two points about "Night Sweat"—regarding language and the connection with the human world—relate very directly to the crisis of awareness and isolation that prevail in *For the Union Dead* as a whole. "Skunk Hour," as well, has foreshadowed the treatment of these themes, almost schematically. The Trinitarian Church with its "chalk dry spire" may be taken to symbolize, in addition to religious idealism, the human community that is held together by that principle. The skunks embody, on the other hand, undissociated being, uninfluenced by rational consciousness. The poet himself is isolated from both—from the one by choice, in some form, and from the other by necessity; and the quality of that isolation, whether cause or effect, is expressed in language that prefigures the solipsistic humiliation of *For the Union Dead:* "I hear / my ill-spirit sob in each blood cell, / as if my hand were at its throat." Semantically, this is the equivalent of "my daughter exploding into dynamite" in "Night Sweat," except that it has even less intentional and recognizable reference to the objective world. Unlike the later phrase, it overtly describes the isolation in language that, in its illogicality, imitates the nature of the isolation. Prose language, we are told (by Stephen Spender, among others), tends to point away from itself toward objects that exist independently of it; poetic language tends to refer to itself and to states of mind that do not exist apart from the language in which they are expressed.[4] Lowell's surrealistic phrasing is a driven and extreme form of the second part of this principle, and frequently so extreme that it often seems intended to express doubt of the reality of the world in which the first half of the principle applies. The objectivity that was the primary mode for *Life Studies*, in *For the Union Dead* has been turned inside out. The three aspects of isolation predicated in "Skunk Hour" and recurring in "Night Sweat" are all aspects, by definition, of the same problem; and the problem itself is the theme of *For the Union Dead*, and it will remain unresolved.

The problem of the language can be exaggerated, since the language is not often genuinely problematical. But it requires highlighting briefly because it is so obviously, perhaps even deliberately intended to be, symptomatic. Also, the different forms of radical subjectification require sorting out. I discussed versions of the mixed metaphor in the chapter on *Life Studies*. "Exploding into dynamite" is an extension of that effect, a peculiar, stylistic hybrid of symbolism and psychoanalytical self-consciousness. "]Dug[it all out of the dark / unconscious bowels of the nerves" (from "Going To And Fro") mixes so many metaphors at once that the effect is the same—that is, the phrase's identity as metaphor is obscured because tenor and vehicle cannot be separated. Another example of distortion comes in the description of an intense withdrawal in "Myopia: A Night": "my five senses clenched / their teeth, thought stitched to thought, / as through a needle's eye." In "The Drinker," the alcoholic's despair is said to have "the galvanized color / of the mop and water in the galvanized bucket." This makes more sense; it is at least synaesthesia of a sort, but, even at that, it is characteristically labored and self-conscious and solipsistically fixated. Such an image leads us to another principle, which comes into play as the poet's mind tries to negotiate a compromise with the outer world, as in these lines from "Mouth of the Hudson":

> His eyes drop,
> and he drifts with the wild ice
> ticking seaward down the Hudson,
> like the blank sides of a jig-saw puzzle.

"Drifts" and "wild" more or less give the ice its due; through that one line the ice retains its autonomous nature. But "ticking" seaward is a deep subjectification, since the ice pieces from that distance could only be imagined to be making sound, and, in any case, obviously jig-saw puzzle pieces do not "tick." What has happened here is that the world has been sucked almost instantly into the mind. The ice is at one moment itself and in the next a diminished extension of the poet's anxiety. The observer has imposed signification, which issued from the mood he has brought to the scene to begin with; and the outer world, as a consequence, recedes.

On occasions such as this, one wonders whether it isn't mere contingency that most threatens Lowell, so that *any* rule of meaning, even that of impending doom, is better than none at all. At any rate, the effect of psychic imperialism of this kind is inevitably, and ironically, to close up space, picture-space, and thus to reinforce the illusion of the mind's confinement within itself. Lowell's borrowed image in "Florence" of "the Old Palace" piercing "the sky / like a hypodermic needle" does essentially the same thing. This image is representational in a somewhat bizarre and imprecise way, but it is finally its ideational content that prevails and forces our attention away from objective space back to the subjective perceiver, as if the three-dimensional space implied in the verb "pierces" were not really there at all. Curiously, this kind of retrenchment can occur at any point along the emotional spectrum; it is not just anxiety or pain that causes it. In a wistful revery in "July in Washington," he says: "we wish the river had another shore, / some further range of delectable mountains, / distant hills powdered blue as a girl's eyelid." Here, because of the spatial progression in the three lines (unusually musical, structurally, for Lowell—"another shore...delectable mountains...distant hills"), the foreshortening effect of the last simile is even more abrupt. Once more, at any rate, the focus is thrown back upon the mind in such a way as to abridge space and, in this case, to alter and delimit the imagined range of possibility.

Whether calculated or not, it seems inevitable that these instances of language turning in upon itself will remind us at intervals that the principal subject of the volume is the mind's isolating and destructive conflict with itself and with the affiliated resources of the self—will, spirit, and conscience—which in a round world would be expected to work in harmony. When Lowell writes, in "Skunk Hour," "my ill-spirit sob[s] ..., / as if my hand were at its throat," it may be that "hand" is metonymically a symbol for mind or consciousness; "spirit" would thus refer both to the noumenon of the self, which is neither mind nor matter, *and* to moral vigor and will. Certainly the style and tone of the most deeply introverted poems in *For the Union Dead* would support such a reading, and the effect of the surrealistically subjective phrasing is to keep us mindful that even in poems like "For the Union Dead," which seem to be uninvolved with this subject, the crisis remains constant underneath the surface.

In this respect, "Water" and "The Old Flame" make interesting test cases, since, being the first two poems of the book, they are necessarily uninvolved. "Water" ends laconically with a metaphor describing a mutual failure of will. "In the end, / the water was too cold for us." There is no reason given for this. The poem relates—or, to be more accurate, alludes to—a period in the poet's life when he was involved deeply in friendship with a woman (who we learn in *Notebook*, was Elizabeth Bishop), and the anecdote is focused upon the two sitting upon a slab of rock by the sea near a "Maine lobster town." They watch "boatloads of hands" each morning setting off for the "granite / quarries on the islands" leaving behind "bleak / white frame houses stuck / like oyster shells / on a hill of rock." They can see below them "the mazes of a weir" where the bait-fish are trapped. In retrospect, the rock seems "the color of iris" but it was only "the usual gray" at the time, turned "usual green / when drenched by the sea." The sea is remembered tearing the rock away "flake after flake." The "you" dreams she is a mermaid "clinging to a wharf-pile, / and trying to pull / off the barnacles with [her] hands." And that is all, except that they dream that their "two souls might return" one day to the rock, "like gulls." There is no way to know, of course, whether these details are selected by memory because they objectify the failure of the relationship, or whether Lowell is reporting things the way they saw them at the time. That the latter is the case would seem the more likely, since it would *account for* the water's being "too cold"; otherwise the water's being "too cold" is simply the last fateful element in a series of correspondences. This is the respect in which the introverted middle of the volume weighs down both ends. All of the observed objects and events in this poem have a stark, threatening quality—the setting out for granite islands, the houses that are said to be bleak and like oyster shells on rock, the image of the weir that is a trap, the grayness of the "slab" of rock onwhich they sit, only momentarily changed to green by the sea, which at the same time wears it away. The sense of this is that they both shared from the start a perspective upon experience that was cheerless to the point of paralyzing the will, and that each saw signs of the hopelessness of human life in every detail. This we take to be the point of the dream: mermaid against barnacles—and whether the barnacles are on her or on the wharf-pile, it is known that they cannot be torn away. Knowing, in other words, is the enemy of venture and in this case ensures that there will be no escape from its own maze; this in turn ensures defeat of purpose and a sad end. The poem is quite beautiful and extraordinary for its reticent control.

One of the darkest reaches of this impasse is recounted in "Going To and Fro" where the poet addresses himself, or his alter ego, as Lucifer, who is said to have been moved by "The love that moves the stars"—a daring secularization of the ending of *The Divine Comedy*. "[How] often you wanted your fling / with those French girls, Mediterranean / luminaries, Mary, Myrtho, Isis!" But that once-upon-a-time insatiability, it is said, only set him going, and having proved romantic folly now has left him merely going to and fro in the demystified real, which he can "get loose from" only by not thinking of it, "by counting / [his] steps to the noose."

"The Old Flame" relates an occasion on which the poet returns to the house in Maine he once shared with his former wife and where a frenzied, dissolute intensity of conflict and intellectual energy had once blazed:

> how quivering and fierce we were,
> there snowbound together,
> simmering like wasps
> in our tent of books!

But the house has been refurbished by the newest owner and transformed into a picturesque icon of Americana:

> Now a red ear of Indian maize
> was splashed on the door.
> Old Glory with thirteen stripes
> hung on a pole. The clapboard
> was old-red schoolhouse red.
>
> Inside, a new landlord,
> a new wife, a new broom!
> Atlantic seaboard antique shop
> pewter and plunder
> shone in each room.

The restored house, especially as it is an object, all but apotheosizes complacent normality, as opposed to edgy recusance: "No running next door / now to phone the sheriff / for his taxi to Bath / and the State Liquor Store!" The house has become something like the wholly other, and so the poet in this new world seems to himself like a ghost, for in a real psychological sense he cannot exist in it; nor could his wife, "Poor ghost, old love." But, remarkably, his attitude toward the absolute division is ambivalent, and, if anything, more sympathetic toward the new owners than to himself, grimly tightening "the scarf at his throat." He says, point blank, "Everything's changed for the best," and this seems not to be irony. Rather, it is an acknowledgement of his own sickness, or, at any rate, of the appeal for him of the inaccessible alternative to lying "awake all night" under pressure of flaming insight." This new-old world is not one the poet can inhabit, because it is an oblivious world, but its very obliviousness appears to him as mental health; so he says, across the gulf, "Health to the new people, / health to their flag." By the end of the volume, that American complacency will have become a "savage servility" sliding "by on grease." Here he can feel generous toward the new owners' normalcy, and why this should be is hinted at in the noticeably ambivalent quality of his own nostalgia—"simmering like wasps"; "in one bed and apart"—and in the implication at the end that the "old flame" had after all failed. The rationale implied here will be obvious in subsequent poems like "Eye and Tooth" or "Myopia: A Night" or sooner in "Fall 1961," where the mind's aggression against itself will make mere middle-class simplemindedness seem like Nirvana.

"Eye and Tooth," "Myopia: A Night," and "The Drinker," represent the deepest points of estrangement in the volume and they seem all the more cut off from the world for having, as Eliot again would say, no apparent objective correlatives. The suffering is not only "without purgation," as Lowell says in "Going To and Fro," but it is without definable cause. The allusion to the injunction from the Old Testament in "Eye and Tooth" possibly tells us why. Among the images that cannot be dislodged from the poet's memory is that of the eye of a hawk in a bird book remembered from his childhood. The hawk's "one ascetic talon" clasps "the abstract imperial sky," and the eye of the hawk says: "*an eye for an eye, a tooth for a tooth.*" This is a law of the impartial universe. The sky is both abstract and imperial. In the Book of Exodus, where this adjuration originates, it occurs not at all as a rule of vengeance or of draconian punishment but of equity in social justice; the point is that the punishment should fit the crime. Here in Lowell's poem the crime and the punishment have become so finely adjusted to each other that they are indistinguishable. The knowledge of time and death that invades the house of one's childhood gradually fills up all of the space between the inmost self and the outer world. The symbolic pun identifying the "eye" with the "I" of the poem has been exhaustively explicated by other critics, and is obvious enough to begin with. It is worth pointing out, however, that "the boy at the keyhole" watching the "women's white bodies" flash "in the bathroom" is already, as a voyeur, drawing the world into his own safe inner territory, though he is at least looking out to the world; and it is only after this that his "eyes began to fail."

Failing eyes, "the old cut cornea," "seeing things darkly" are the crime and punishment that are universal. The first tooth is "noosed in a knot to the doorknob," signifying in memory the death of the child, and the tooth on the doorknob signifies for the child what the shadow of rot on the roof signifies for the house. These two apparitions are difficult to paraphrase but easy to recognize. And so intense is the pressure upon the speaker of his own dread that the summer rain falling outside, in the present of the poem, seems to the "I" to be "pinpricks," "a simmer of rot and renewal." The passing of innocence has become its own punishment. In the end he says, "I am tired. Everyone's tired of my turmoil," and this seems plain enough (and easy for critics to make irritated jokes from). But it can be read two ways. The other way, besides the plain one, is to think of it as a generalizing of his own private conflict, a neurasthenic version of "Tu le connais. . . / Hypocrite lecteur,—mon semblable,—mon frère!" And though the poet in this poem seems much too alienated from the world to be interested in moral extrapolations, he has also earlier in the poem singularized, as well as vulgarized, a concept that Saint Paul stated in the collective plural: "I saw things darkly, / as through an unwashed goldfish globe." When Saint Paul said, "For now we see through a glass, darkly," he meant that human life is for the mature mind a serious and inexplicable business, not to be dealt with simplistically in the fashion of a child. But for Paul this state of unknowing will prevail only until "that which is perfect is come" and "that which is in part shall be done away" (I Corinthians 13:10–13). Lowell does not share Paul's faith in future revelation, as the belittling image of being trapped in a goldfish globe suggests. Things being "in part," as the poem's structure itself indicates, is a definitive state.

Just how absolute the spiritual prison has become in "Eye and Tooth" is implied by the poet's inability to perceive the summer rain as anything more than pinpricks, or "even new life" as anything but "fuel." Projections from his own despair only strengthen the walls and inhibit his mobility, as the case of "Water" has illustrated as well. He is kin in this respect to Jonathan Edwards, who as a boy delighted in watching "the spiders fly, / basking at their ease, / swimming from tree to tree" but "knew that they would die" and thus twenty-five years later was preaching vehemently of "The God that holds you over the pit of hell, much as one holds a spider or some loathsome insect over the fire." And Lowell himself says in "Fall 1961," "We are like a lot of wild / spiders crying together, / but without tears"—thus perceiving his own sense of dehumanization to be continuous with the world's. In "Myopia: A Night," when the morning star rises on the horizon, instead of presaging rest from the insomniac hallucinations of the night, it merely reminds him that both the morning star and Satan are known as Lucifer, or "light-bearer" (knowledge-bearers), and so another possibility of liberation is abruptly sealed off. It is fitting in this sense that Satan is then contemplated as an analogue of himself, at one moment "triumphant in / the Garden" and in the next a serpent "grovelling on its gut." And when the morning comes, it is by no means as an affirmation, as Yenser and others have called it: the morning says nothing except to point the poet back to the terror and humiliation of his darkness. The anticlimax is exquisite: "Then morning comes, / saying, 'This was a night.' " Of course, "myopia" is as much a pun in Lowell's usage as "eye" is, and symbolizes the same affliction—not being able to see very far, being trapped inside the ego. In "Myopia: A Night," moreover, the poet feels himself betrayed not only by memory and fear but by his "learning" also. His study is said to be a dull and "alien" room, a "cell" of learning. His books become a "departure strip" and "dream-road" only when they and their titles blur, viewed myopically, into "blue hills, browns / greens, fields, or color." He had hoped, he says, that the books, in the austere cell of learning, would "burn away the blur," but instead they have increased the distance between him and the world; and by bringing "wisdom" to the world, he becomes guilty of diminishing it. Wisdom demythologizes. The consequences of his myopia are that he cannot sort out the complexity of human relationships ("What has disturbed this household?"), that even his wife and child to him have no reality of their own ("the familiar faces blur"), and that he himself has become inconsequential, a supernumerary of death ("At fifty we're so fragile, / a feather"). It is consistent that the new morning, as indicated above, should not be much different. Jonathan Edwards had believed in study, too:

> "My defects are well known;
> I have a constitution
> peculiarly unhappy
>
> . . . . .
> I am contemptible
> stiff and dull.

Why should I leave behind

my delight and entertainment
those studies
that have swallowed up my mind?"

This was Edwards's justification for remaining in isolation and exile in his last years. He and Lowell have in common their disposition and their hope—thwarted in Lowell's case—that studies will "swallow up the mind," divert it from itself.

The pessimistic intelligence that is Lowell's bond with Jonathan Edwards binds him also to the mythological monsters of "Florence," and again the connecting link to the other poems is a meditation upon the burden of authentic knowledge. In the opening stanza of "Florence" Lowell establishes clear lines of identification with the fallen and diminished world, the corruptible city where, as he says, "the apple" (of the knowledge of good and evil) "was more human. . . than here."

I long for the black ink,
cuttlefish, April, Communists
and brothels of Florence—
everything, even the British
fairies who haunted the hills,
even the chills and fever
that came once a month
and forced me to think.

What seems merely bohemian here is mythologized in the last half of the poem in the image of the victims of Florence's sculptural "lovely tyrannicides", the pitiable monsters' "tubs of guts / mortifying chunks for the pack." The tyrannicides are too sleek and assured to elicit human interest, but the poet says that for the monster "my heart bleeds black blood." The blackness of his blood implies that he is monstrous as well, as if in a poet-disguise; and if he is, it may well be because of his knowledge of the grotesque and sinister reality of human life. All of the monsters at the poem's end become one in Medusa: "Wall-eyed, staring the despot to stone, / her severed head swung / like a lantern in the victor's hand." The prevailing theme through all of this is that of knowledge through experience of the self, such knowledge as causes monsters to know more than ordinary people (for example, the new owners in "The Old Flame") and especially more than posturing heroes. Their severed heads—where their brains are, where their pain is stored—are incomparably menacing, for exposure to the radiation of what they know is fatal to the innocence of others, particularly of others who, like despots, assume that their power over the world is real. Perhaps the links of the "black blood" and the poet's pity for the monsters are too tenuous to warrant pushing the analogy further, but it does seem that the Gorgon's stare could as well be the poet's baleful introspection turned outward upon an innocent world. This poet, after all, does think of himself as not much more at times than a severed head, and he writes a poem with that image as its title—a poem about himself and his doppelgänger suffocating in a windowless room and wearing a glass cufflink with a butterfly inside. It is an odd psychoanalytical twist to this story that, because in a sense the poet is guilty of conceiving this world, he is in a sense guilty of its effects as well. He is therefore also the "mass of shadows" pursuing the "ocean butterflies" in "The Severed Head," as he is Satan in the Garden in "Myopia: A Night," bringing the wisdom that destroys it.

Lowell's poems of this period resist catharsis as if by an act of will, even when they seem motivated initially by his attempt to achieve a détente with his own unsentimental awareness. The poems end not so much suspended as clenched, at the point of the poet's confronting and considering, but refusing to give in to, the appeal of illusory and usually pointedly momentary gratifications. Such conclusions make a mockery of mere form, imitating resolution while at the same time denying it. It is interesting to consider whether Lowell is not also in this way mocking us and the sentimental expectations we bring to poems—our failure to have observed the distinctions between art and life.

A virtually pure example of this formula and its confusing effect upon readers is the conclusion of "Fall 1961":

> Back and forth!
> Back and forth, back and forth—
> my one point of rest
> is the orange and black
> oriole's swinging nest!

"Fall 1961" is likely to be misread slightly to begin with because of the topicality of the subject matter that commands the foreground—the Cuban missile crisis and the American public's apprehensive response to it:[5] "All autumn, the chafe and jar / of nuclear war." But impending nuclear annihilation seems to be primarily a kind of plot for this poem around which its alternate theme is developed. When we pay attention to the way in which the poem operates as a poem, it becomes evident that it is as much about the illusion of being trapped in time, an oppressively nonlinear time, as it is about global disaster. On the one hand there is the experience of time specifed in the title—historic events in the making on a morbidly grand scale. On the other hand there is the experience of time in the psyche, which is repetitious, nugatory, and tedious. The most lurid historical possibility of the modern world, cultural self-immolation, on the one hand, and something near to pathological boredom on the other. Obviously, the two experiences of time do not coincide. On the outside the moon lifts "radiant with terror"; on the inside where the poet swims "like a minnow" behind his window (and thus back and forth as in a bowl or aquarium) the face of the moon on the clock is "orange, bland, ambassadorial" and it "goes...tock, tock, tock"—nothing so lively as "tick, tock." "It's easy to tick / off the minutes, but the clockhands stick." The phrase "back and forth" is repeated five times, twice in the first stanza, three times in the last. The poem is not about terror but about the inability to feel terror in the face of vividly legitimate reasons for doing so.

If terror indeed were the point, "Fall 1961" would have to be one of the more ineffectual poems in Lowell's canon, for it is monotonously unpressurized in its organization, distracted and paratactic in its sequences:

All autumn, the chafe and jar
of nuclear war;
we have talked our extinction to death.
I swim like a minnow
behind my studio window.

The separation from reality in this case is not the poet's alone but the country's generally, as though people could no longer do more than imperfectly act out being afraid, or being human: "We are like a lot of wild / spiders crying together, / but without tears." Thus, "Nature holds up a mirror" to show the truth of our putative humanness. It is tediously simple: "One swallow makes a summer." So the poet is expressing openly what the world at large cannot admit to: a glum disbelief in his own humanness—loss of affect, as psychologists say. This in turn is registered as a sense that time is static and without scale or purpose, only a force that, unlike our military technology, is wholly outside our comprehension or control. So the ending of the poem—to return to the oriole, or rather the oriole's nest—seems, after all, ironic, and Lowell places the exclamation point where the period would otherwise be, as if to underline the irony. The surprising flash of color alerts us to expect a sudden reprieve, but then we realize that the oriole is only the ghost of an oriole in the mind, not really there at all, and that a swinging, vacated nest in the fall is hardly a reassuring symbol in a poem about what Stevens called the "malady of the quotidian." Lowell is too austerely disintoxicated in this period of his life to respond impulsively to simple dualisms in which there is human life on the one hand and life on the other. (This will change later, but not much.) Whatever is wrong with the world, as Lowell perceives it, is wrong with nature, too. Nature cannot be a source of redemption, in any case, because nature itself is other and inexplicable. Nihilism and solipsism tend to feed upon each other; and the thwarted, comprehensive vision of "Fall 1961" does not leave anything more than an illusory opening for spiritual release.

"The Drinker," coincidentally, is also about time, and follows a similar structural course to a similarly ambiguous resolution. The drinker of the title is said to be "killing time"; what this apears to mean is that he is dissolving his awareness of time in an alcoholic stupor and that, what is more important, he is striving to cut himself off from the level of particular time in which human relationships are conducted, where the self is responsible to other selves. He founders "down / leagues of ocean, gasping whiteness," but "The barbed hooks fester. The lines snap tight." His neighbors' "names blur," though he looks for them; he sees "only glass sky," a sky that encloses. His despair is compared to "the galvanized color / of the mop and the water in the galvanized bucket," and then he thinks of someone once "close to him / as water to the dead metal." This analogy, by association with the preceding one, suggests that the woman at least intended to be a restoring influence, but that the drinker's despair infected her instead, as he "contained" her. But she is now absent— perhaps only figuratively; that is, she is independent of him, and the visible signs of her life in the world of everyday public time, of her separate identity, threaten and indict: "He looks at her engagements inked on her calendar / At the numbers in her thumbed black telephone book. / A quiver full of arrows." He yearns for reification, makes fetishes of metal and glass objects—the galvanized bucket, corroded pipes, an iron lung, car keys, razor blades, an ash tray—as if through them could be found the way back to the "perfect and ponderous bubble" of Edenic time. But outside on the street are further ordinary and familiar signs of ordinary time, which the absent "she" of the poem effectively deals with and inhabits:

> two cops on horseback clop through the April rain
> to check the parking meter violations—
> their oilskins yellow as forsythia.

The cops and the meters and the April rain are clearly and objectively perceived, free of the chaotic inner space of the rest of the poem. They define the world outside the "galvanized bucket" of the self; they participate in an order that is routinely regulated by clocks and seasons—a time, in short, that the protagonist cannot "kill" but also cannot enter. It is this final unresolved paradox that makes the casual allusion to forsythia strike us as more than an afterthought, as if it had come forth unsummoned from some prelapsarian past when self and world were not separate, brought into the mind by an unnoticed residue of innocence rebelling momentarily and ineffectually against both madness and reason. The image can presage nothing for the future, confined as it is to a subordinate clause. It is as forlornly incongruous in context as forsythia, blooming early in late winter, usually is itself. The image is the analogue in this respect of the briefly remembered "orange and black oriole" of "Fall 1961" and a significantly diminished echo of "Till Christ again turn wanderer and child."

The Lowell of *For the Union Dead* is residually nostalgic, but he is defensively skeptical of nostalgia's lyric strategies. Isolated images like that of the forsythia often seem to be a matter primarily of the poet's keeping his hand in, refusing to give up on sensibility altogether. When the cramped tension of the poems relaxes and lyric feeling is permitted to thrive—as it is briefly in "Soft Wood," the single case in this volume—it is easier for us to see what is happening, because the conflict is spread out, but it is no easier to see why. The pain in any poem of this period remains abstracted from specific cause and seems all the more forbidding and demoralizing because of it. Since the poems with their dread and instability are so personal, when there are no personal or particular causes cited we are left with the vague impression that what is wrong is not an individual disorder but a general one, not acute but chronic, and inherent in the structure of life. That this anxiety is made to seem possibly only a symptom of neurosis complicates the issue, of course, because it implies the possibility of a cure;

and that qualification, registered in the subjugated and rare images of affirmation, seems to be the only support against an absolute and suicidal despair. The inability finally to separate subject and object in this respect, to know what is projected from what is introjected, or to know whether both inner and outer worlds simply share the same pathology, is a covert subject of the few public poems of *For the Union Dead*; and simply because it is a subject, never far from the surface of the mind, it imposes restraints upon judgment, and clouds even the idea of political possibility. This problem will be touched upon shortly.

In "Soft Wood" Lowell achieves a clear paradigm of the themes that otherwise appear in the volume only in inchoate and structurally irresolute forms. The poem has the paradoxical role in *For the Union Dead* of being the volume's one indisputable lyric, while at the same time delineating its pessimism with a rational authority that causes the neurasthenic dread of "Eye and Tooth" and "Myopia: A Night" to seem like epistemological plea-bargaining. Whereas the sense of mental instability in those two poems, and others in the volume like them, requires that a margin of error be allowed for their outlook, in "Soft Wood" the same materials are under firm intellectual and aesthetic control, and the poem's fatalism is both elegiac and conclusive. In effect, it commemorates rather than agonizes over a terribly human truth—that knowledge and powers of analysis are as much afflictions as they are resources, and that peace and lyric elation cannot be sustained against their superior force. The momentum of the poem is downward, but only gradually, as if the will to affirm life were being drawn reluctantly into the darkness, as in Stevens's moving image, "on extended wings." The first two stanzas, indeed, virtually apotheosize the elusive quality of "staying" in creatures and things that stay, or seem to, because, without thoughts of death or time or, on the other hand, of a higher order of life, they can face the elements without scruple.

> Sometimes I have supposed seals
> must live as long as the Scholar Gypsy.
> Even in their barred pond at the zoo they are happy,
> and no sunflower turns
> more delicately to the sun
> without a wincing of the will.
>
> Here too in Maine things bend to the wind forever.
> After two years away, one must get used

to the painted soft wood staying bright and clean,
to the air blasting an all-white wall whiter,
as it blows through curtain and screen
touched with salt and evergreen.

With both imagined and objective, inner and outer worlds collaborating, for once productively, this meditated setting is the norm from
which the poem will gradually and painfuly separate. It is a potential mode
of being in a space between the mind and the world, fusing the value of
both, feeling and tangibility. "Without a wincing of the will," plangently
alliterative and resolving a declining syntax, expresses much more,
seemingly, than the words alone would verify: both empathy and
separation. In the second stanza the melopoeic arrangement of vowels
("painted soft wood staying bright and clean") and the three solitary
rhyming words (clean, screen, and evergreen) seem to emerge naturally, as
if from the setting itself. The interesting aspect of these lines is that they
depict a geographical setting that is uniquely austere and yet, in the poem,
is suffused with a voluptuous, almost tropical feeling. It seems proper to lay
stress on the way in which the words and the world they refer to
collaborate, because it is precisely that dialectical result, the intermediate
state, which is the fragile ideal that is about to be disrupted by
introspection. In the third stanza the human and nonhuman elements
begin to separate. The wind, slightly tamed before in the phrase "air
blasting," suddenly returns in earnest as its unmediated self:

Things last, but sometimes for days here
only children seem fit to handle children,
and there is no utility or inspiration
in the wind smashing without direction.

The sound associations in these lines, especially in the third and fourth,
echo the mood of the poem's two earlier sections and convey, more than
fear or menace, a suddenly poignant distraction and isolation. Dissociation
from the credulous life of children is the first observed effect of that state,
and it plainly implies—suddenly for us—a desolate separation from
childhood and from the child's enviable, indiscriminate identification with
the world. The wind without utility is the wind as itself, without purpose
either for the poet or for the white walls—no different, really, from before,
only seen differently, objectively, in a way that sharpens the poet's sense of

his own isolation from this setting with which moments before he had felt euphorically continuous. So the thought of the poem begins to break here through the first of a number of chambers that will lead to his familiar real world in the end. He thinks of the departed grandeur of the old sea captains of this village; and that thought of mutability, added to the harrowing new influence of the wind, forces upon him the realization that "The fresh paint / on the captains' houses hides softer wood," that the wood's softness which keeps it cleansible by the wind also ensures its steadier if imperceptible corruption in time. This leads to the more defeating thought that what gave these houses meaning in the beginning, a life inside other sensibilities and other feelings, is irretrievably lost, and that his own mediatory presence among them is a kind of intrusion and irreverence: "Shed skin will never fit another wearer." Superimposed, then, upon the otherwise conventional theme of mutability in these two stanzas (the fourth and fifth) is the subtler perception, in its way more distressing, of not belonging—here in Castine, where the sea captains harnessed the wind ("their square-riggers used to whiten / the four corners of the globe") and "warped and mothered" their possessions, and where the seals are cheerfully at home in their element. Or perhaps not just in Castine, but anywhere. When the seals of the first stanza return to the poem in the sixth, they mock alienation, and the poet's awareness of this estrangement is intensified by their presence:

> Yet the seal pack will bark past my window
> summer after summer.
> This is the season
> when our friends may and will die daily.
> Surely the lives of the old
> are briefer than the young.

Contemplating the death of one's friends is a reminder that one is of an age when friends begin to die not unexpectedly but in the natural course of things. The dying of friends is one of those agencies of fate that cause one to be even more homeless in the world, and the thought of their death is as alienating as the fact. This is why the last two lines of the stanza transcend mere truism: the brevity of the lives of the old is a function not of time, but of consciousness of time. At this point the separation of the elements of the potential space of the first stanzas of the poem is complete. This shifting of positions at the end, Lowell's readjustment to the world he more habitually knows, perhaps explains why in the last stanza Harriet Winslow, Lowell's cousin, who "owned this house" (the "shed skin" that he is temporarily inhabiting) is referred to first as if she were dead ("*was* more to me than my mother") and then in the next line addressed as "you," as if alive. It is the sort of confusion and reorientation that comes from emerging from a dream or revery, and this emergence becomes painfully emphatic when the thoughts turn, as if jolted, from idyllic Castine to America's urban "land of unlikeness":

> I think of you far off in Washington,
> breathing in the heat wave
> and air-conditioning, knowing
> each drug that numbs alerts another nerve to pain.

This last line simply restates discursively the process that has been enacted obliquely in the poem. The "you" in Washington is oddly almost like the alter ego of the dreaming poet of the first stanzas, who has now stepped out onto the concrete floor of his real, antilyrical world. But even without such magic, the point is essentialy the same—an embellishment of the thought that "each drug that numbs alerts another nerve to pain"; for while the poet has savored the climate of pure being, albeit transitory, another who is close to him has been suffering, *breathing*, with effort, in order to survive. So it is, ironically, that one's own humanity—in its forms as sentience and conscious empathy, by which we transcend the kingdoms of the seal and sunflower—precludes the achievement of a separate peace. Clearly the character of reality has changed radically by the end of the poem, but it is not clear whether this change is for better or worse. Although the poet has achieved a new understanding of his human position in the world, and with it a new depth of seriousness in human relationship, the human position has been defined as consisting of alienation, chronic awareness of death, and pain. These, ironically, are the elements in this poem that make the human community cohesive. In "Soft Wood," Lowell seems to be stating the principle that where the dreamed life fails, as for Lowell it does inevitably, only Pyrrhic victories are posssible. And the pervasively edgy, balked, and deracinated tone of *For the Union Dead* seems to insist that Pyrrhic victories are not enough.

In the end, it seems to be the poet's inability to sustain a faith in the dreamed life that compromises the latent moral fervor of those poems in the volume that address public themes. Where there is no public order or collective moral vision in the world, political or religious, only the individual can supply the predications for judgment out of his own resisting, isolated spirit. Not only does this not happen in the deprived world of *For the Union Dead*, it *cannot* happen, because the poet at the center of the volume is unable to believe it can—is unable to believe in anything that might become a generating source of value, even his own reality. "Sometimes I ask myself if I exist," says the thinly disguised doppelgänger of "The Severed Head." The desire not to exist is born of dread and self-disgust, and carried to its extreme it seems certain to result in the ontological insecurity so baldly stated here. That insecurity has another cause and form as well. If the self of the poet has no means of discriminating between the world's autonomous identity and the identity he projects upon it, then he merges with it and becomes subsumed into it just as surely as it becomes subsumed in him. That is why the problem of the picture space in a poem like "Mouth of the Hudson" seems so much more than merely technical:

> Chemical air
> sweeps in from New Jersey,
> and smells of coffee.
>
> Across the river,
> ledges of suburban factories tan
> in the sulphur-yellow sun. . . .

This is difficult to visualize, because its whole point is the eerie way in which the human and nonhuman aspects of the world have changed places. Since, as a result, it appears that the familiar real world has ceased to exist, the self's existence in it necessarily becomes problematical too. The text of *For the Union Dead* cries out for existential assertion, but that assertion never comes, except once, in vicarious form: "He rejoices in man's lovely, / peculiar power to choose life and die." But this refers to Colonel Shaw, and Colonel Shaw is not the poet, as Lowell is scrupulously careful to indicate; and, moreover, the country that Shaw relinquished everything to serve has plainly gone to hell. Existential integrity is an indispensable condition for the grounding of moral judgment, but that integrity remains only potential and fragmented in *For the Union Dead*. In "The Mouth of the Hudson," the observer is said to stand above the scene "like a bird-watcher," a lonely absurdity to begin with. "He has trouble with his balance" also, as well he might, and in the end he can manage to reject the encroachment of the nonhuman only by thinking of it, effetely, as "unforgivable." Here Lowell has managed skillfully both to affirm and to diminish the idea of "rational man in an irrational universe." Where there is no hope, pronouncements upon the condition of the world seem ludicrous, as Colonel Shaw faintly seems, though no more so than the "giant-finned cars." And in Lowell's case, in this volume, the absurdity is compounded by his own Prufrock-like status in relation to himself and the world: "Do I dare disturb the universe? . . . And how should I presume?"

It is all but axiomatic that in the poems where the zones of private and public experience are continuous, Lowell will remain firmly within the target area of his own better judgment. In such poems, his role as a poet is theoretically generic; that is, the poet in time and history is or should be the embodiment of humanity's collective dream of possiblity. Any poet in this role, whose sensibility does not insulate him from history but makes him more responsive to it, is likely to seem isolated to the extent that the collective dream is receding on the historical scale. The peculiarity of Lowell's position in this regard is that he is at once isolated and implicated, and he makes a point and a moral issue of that saddening ambiguity. Thus it is that in "Buenos Aires" a trivial, self-consciously adolescent gesture becomes a thrust toward existence, and that even this is thwarted, finally, by the combined inner and outer versions of the opposing force.

> Literal commemorative busts
> preserved the frogged coats
> and fussy, furrowed foreheads
> of those soldier bureaucrats.
>
> By their brazen doors
> a hundred marble goddesses
> wept like willows. I found rest
> by cupping a soft palm to each hard breast.

Since the setting here is a graveyard, finding "rest" is more than a little ambiguous, and "rest" in any case seems a marginal achievement, as it does at the end of "Fall 1961." But in the larger setting of the poem— where Buenos Aires is portrayed as a generic, Latin American, unreal city, a monument of torpor, greed, violence, and literally sculptural hypocrisy—the very triviality of the gesture is a matter of some consequence, a modest, ludicrous, and pointedly antiheroic refusal, like the bird watcher's in "The Mouth of the Hudson." It can be understood as wryly empathetic as well, if we take the "soft palm" to be seeking to restore life and warmth to the goddesses, who may be weeping not in mourning but for having been marmorealized against their will. But the poet knows that such spells are not to be broken, especially by one half-bespelled like himself. So the poem concludes:

> I was the worse for wear,
> and my breath whitened the winter air
> next morning, when Buenos Aires filled
> with frowning starch-collared crowds.

Across these last two stanzas of the poem, the rhyming is organized to achieve a deviously rhetorical effect. The two couplets made from "found rest" and "hard breast" and "worse for wear" and "winter air" raise expectations of an elegant couplet closure, but instead the poem collapses, rhymeless, under the weight of its last prosaic vision. Mention of the crowds of (putatively) human beings recalls the image in the poem's opening stanza of the cattle that furnish the poet's new clothes—"the bulky, breathing of the herds." "Frowning" and "starch-collared," by association with the poem's image of ostentatious militarism implicate the Argentine people, somewhat invidiously, in their own fate. No process or circumstance has been or will be affected by the poet's gesture in the graveyard, and the poet himself lounges in the Hotel Continental, idly reading newspapers, sporting a "coat of limp, chestnut-colored suede" and new sharp leather shoes "that hurt my toes." By such axes are the poet, the herds, the dictators, the crowds all identified, all "the worse for wear"; and the poet, to his credit, is fearful for his own inner life because of his association with an outer life whose human attributes by some ghostly process appear to have been destroyed.

Stephen Yenser calls attention to the surprising fact that only when we come to "The Drinker" and the policeman checking parking meters do we first encounter substantial human figures in For the Union Dead, and this is halfway through the volume.[6] Romantic and postromantic poets have not normally been concerned with what Iris Murdoch calls "the reality of persons"; writers who *are* are more likely to be novelists than poets, and Lowell's potential in that respect is fully attested to in *Life Studies*, particularly in its prose memoir. The absence of substantial human figures in *For the Union Dead* seems to involve more than just the poet's world-blurring self-absorption. Humanness actually seems to be in jeopardy on its own terms—as in the fifth stanza of "Skunk Hour"—apart from the poet's intervention one way or the other; and this jeopardy is necessarily extended to the poet, since, as Martin Buber has explained to us, in order for there to be a differentiated "I" there must also be a differentiated "It" and "Thou." So in this respect the poet's continuity with the dehumanized world in "Buenos Aires" paradoxically deepens the ontological insecurity that we infer already from the preceding poems, and in so doing, almost coincidentally, destabilizes all points of moral reference. It is perhaps no accident that the nearest things to "substantial human figures" in "Buenos Aires" and "For the Union Dead" are statues—the goddesses, Shaw and his Negro soldiers, and the "abstract Union soldier[s] / [growing] slimmer and younger each year." In the latter poem, especially, a point is made of the eerie depopulatedness of Boston—the steam shovels have no operators, the cars no drivers—and the only human points of reference are to the past. And, as in "Buenos Aires," the poet is not only isolated but implicated, inhabiting a morally indistinct, and in this case ontologically uncertain, zone between the Is and the Ought.

It is important, as I argued earlier, that we take seriously what Lowell is saying in the opening lines of "For the Union Dead" and not try to convert them into something else more palatable than he himself clearly intended. "I often sigh still / for the dark downward and vegetating kingdom / of the fish and reptile." In the context of the moral issues raised in this poem, it is not even conceivably a worthy ambition to yearn for escape into a "dark" and a "downward" kingdom that is reptilian, with all that "reptilian" connotes, including asociability. That it is a regressive impulse of the most seductive kind, approaching a death wish, seems intended to contrast the poet and his moral will with Colonel Shaw and his. Shaw has "an angry wrenlike vigilance," he seems to "wince at pleasure," and "He rejoices in man's lovely, / peculiar power to choose life and die." These last words are beautifully measured, and they are the moral center of the poem. The power that Shaw rejoices in is peculiarly human, and lovely because of that. It is what raises him above the animal, what would cause him to scorn the nostalgia for uterine, downward kingdoms. He is a grown man. He would prefer to live but he is willing to die, and he is willing to die *for* life, which he believes in, rather than to escape it. The poet of the poem, and of the volume, can neither choose life nor die; and if he is inclined at all, it is toward death, which in "The Flaw," two poems earlier, he calls "the final gift." Shaw would not think of death as the gift, but life. At the end of the poem, after reflecting on the abstractness of Boston's war monument—the Mosler safe, which survived Hiroshima—the poet crouches to his television set. The "to" is remarkably suggestive, as opposed to "before," implying something close to obeisance. He watches "drained faces of Negro school-children rise like balloons." If we are to accept Shaw in the way that Lowell and Saint-Gaudens and Shaw's father saw him, refusing separation even in death from his Negro men, Shaw would not approve of that image either: "faces" like "balloons," almost funny, childlike in perception, dissociated from what is actually happening. Steven Gould Axelrod has pointed out that when William James said at the dedication speech that he "could almost hear the bronze Negroes breathe," he meant that each Negro face was precisely individuated in Saint-Gauden's sculpture, that each Negro was honored not as a class but a specific man who had died bravely.[7] That feature of the monument is strikingly clear even in photographs. The difference between the faces individually rendered by Saint-Gaudens and the collective faces rising like balloons perceived by the poet is a moral difference, and it seems to implicate the poet and his own detachment in the disheveled dehumanization of the city Shaw died to serve. Seeing the suffering faces as balloons, the poet is not much less abstracted from his own humanness than the wholly abstracted drivers of the driverless cars that "nose forward like fish" and "slide by on grease."

It is useful to remember that besides Shaw, the only other "substantial human figure" in "For the Union Dead" is the poet himself. Although they are morally allies at one level, they are poles apart as far as the will to action is concerned, and the will to action is incipiently a will to identity. Shaw still fends off Boston; the poet is becoming subsumed, and his making a point of that painful fact is his way of dramatizing the inexorability of the force. Lowell cannot stand apart from the world like Shaw; he can only be isolated. He makes this role deliberately a symbolic role and a symbolic fate. It is, after all, he who recreates Shaw for this poem and permits him "to stick like a fishbone" not only in the city's throat but in his own volume's throat as well, and the irony of that is strange and courageous. The phrase "nihilist as hero" is not without bleak irony itself, whether Lowell intended it to be or not. For to be a nihilist genuinely—as opposed to affecting nihilism—is to preclude being heroic. That is a dark thought for the moral intelligence, as Lowell well knew, and as, out of the residue of his own resources, he created the figure of Shaw to help us understand. Shaw, as it turns out, as history turns out, is a forlornly symbolic figure, only absurdly grand.

5. The Monotonous Sublime

In *Near the Ocean*, the material that in *For the Union Dead* was introverted is projected outward onto events, nerves flashed in patterns upon the screen of state. Misrule within self strives toward an apotheosis in zeitgeist; but the transformation is awkwardly achieved, for the gyre of Lowell's poetic consciousness, which moves from center to circumference, unpredictably advances, reverses directions, alternately runs both ways. Lowell contrives a new role for this volume, an unstable hybrid of mandarin American prophet and *symboliste* renegade—*Lord Weary's Castle* bred upon by *Imitations*. The times require it, commitment is inescapable; but the times have also ironically introjected and benumbed the will. The poet's jaded pronouncements issue from, and then seem stalled in, the eddies of private despair. The patrician outrage of the earlier war here has given way to cynicism and ennui: "Fierce, fireless mind, running downhill."

> Fire once gone,
> we're done for: we escape the sun,
> rising and setting, a red coal,
> until it cinders like the soul.

The sun, the cindered soul: global and spiritual entropy are the subjects in

Near the Ocean. Society, unjust and pointless, begins to figure as the metaphor of a natural annihilating process, measured in the inch and in the mile and irreversible by any act of individual or collective will. What recourse there is from the pandemic inertia—the love of friends, a wife, a daughter, "blue-ribboned, blue-jeaned" cartwheeling "on the blue"— cannot be sustained against the knowledge that these, too, will yield; the "ironic points of light" do not swell into "affirming flame."[1]

> thumbtacks rattle from white maps,
> food's lost sight of, dinner waits,
> in the cold oven, icy plates
>
> . . . . .
>
> Great ash and sun of freedom, give
> us this day the warmth to live,
> and face the household fire. We turn
> our backs, and feel the whiskey burn.
>
> ("Fourth of July in Maine")

> Sleep, sleep. The ocean grinding stones,
> can only speak the present tense;
> nothing will age, nothing will last,
> or take corruption from the past.
> A hand, your hand then! I'm afraid
> to touch the crisp hair on your head—
> Monster loved for what you are,
> till time, that buries us, lay bare.
>
> ("Near the Ocean")

Lowell's ocean is a desolate expanse of futility, and everywhere in the poems one finds the diminished shade of Juvenal and his inventory of the vanity of human wishes. The translations in this volume converge with the original poems both through the analogue of theme—"Rome, the greatness and horror of her Empire"—and through a common attitude, set firmly by the presence in the volume of Juvenal's Tenth Satire. Juvenal would have his auditor pray for "a healthy body and a healthy soul, / a soul that is not terrified by death / . . . courage that takes whatever comes." The art that Juvenal makes of his own fatalism is in itself a resistance to fortune; Lowell's echo is less elegant and therefore less stout. Juvenal's stoicism is expressed in the clarity of his perception and expression, in what he allows himself to see and say, without what Lowell calls the "sanity of self-deception." Lowell the classicist, the anachronist, has derived sufferance before from his Roman predecessors; in *Near the Ocean* this kinship is more overt because the major poems are more conventionally formal (they are composed in tetrameter couplets) and because that formality declares both a distance from and a disingenuous superiority to the poems' subject matter—their subjects being sprawl, accrual, waste, and cultural detritus. The difference between Juvenal's formalized identity and Lowell's is that the Lowell in the poems is implicated in the subject matter, cannot remain a displaced observer. An element of the action in *Near the Ocean* is the poet's striving to achieve detachment and failing, failing because of an unassimilated and unruly—because faltering—idealism. Yet the stance is there in the form and in the character of the poetic language. In responding to the restraint of his medium, Lowell achieves at least a measure of depersonalization, and this authorizes the subtle rhetorical shading of public utterance. The chronic pain of *For the Union Dead* is alive but it has grown seasoned and stylized.

Conspicuous rhetorical artifice in contemporary poetry suggests a certain traditional role that the poet has determined to project through his style. In "Waking Early Sunday Morning," this role is pronounced: "O to break loose"; "Stop, back off"; "O that the spirit could remain"; "O Bible chopped and crucified"; "Sing softer"; "O to break loose." Since this class of rhetoric is visibly forced onto the poem and awkwardly sustained, especially the biddings (to an unspecified muse?), there would seem to be no purpose for it other than to establish a parodic formal idiom, for this poem and for the volume, which will connect the poet-persona—his voice at any rate—with an earlier point in time: "Far off that time of gentleness, / when man, still licensed to increase, / unfallen and un-mated, heard / only the uncreated Word" ("Fourth of July in Maine"). In "Waking Early Sunday Morning," it is clearly not an ordinary man but a poet-persona suffering, isolated within a vacuum with his poet's values. In the poem's original version this point is most evident in the third and ninth stanzas (later deleted):[2]

> Time to grub up and junk the year's
> output, a dead wood of dry verse:
> dim confession, coy revelation,
> liftings, listless self-imitation,

whole days when I could hardly speak,
came pluming home unshaven, weak
and willing to read anyone,
things done before and better done.

. . . . .

Empty, irresolute, ashamed
when the sacred texts are named,
I lie here on my bed apart,
and when I look into my heart,
I discover none of the great
subjects: death, friendship, love and hate—
only old china doorknobs, sad,
slight, useless things to calm the mad.

With these two stanzas intact, the poem's mixed idiom has a peculiar but demonstrable rhetorical logic. Once they are deleted, or modified for the volume version, the shadow of the theme they focus is visible in the idiom alone; the source and substance of that feeling—the groping toward the "shaping spirit of imagination"—are left unspecified in the content. The poem is left also without effective transitions to and from the third stanza and from the ninth. It is typical of this poem's pronounced stanzaic integrity that two radically revised stanzas can be inserted without requiring revisions in the surrounding areas. "Waking Early Sunday Morning" is also modeled, perversely, on Marvell's "The Garden," tetrameter couplets in eight-line stanzas; but there on the visual surface all comparison virtually ends.* The effect of Lowell's adaptation is the reverse of the cool, meditative authority that carries us from one station to the next in Marvell's pastoral. In place of elegant intellectual pleasure we have the broken rhythm of frustration and monotony motivated by a dreary dissociation.

Pity the planet, all joy gone
from this sweet volcanic cone;
peace to our children when they fall

---

*Jay Martin has pointed out that this stanza form is typical also of New England hymns—possibly a more relevant analogy given the subject matter of this poem and the straining of the rhetorical devices. (*Robert Lowell* [Minneapolis: University of Minnesota Press, 1970], p. 39.)

in small war on the heels of small
war—until the end of time
to police the earth, a ghost
orbiting forever lost
in our monotonous sublime.

"Waking Early Sunday Morning" expresses in its organization an eccentric ambivalence. A unity is imposed by the disconsolate mood and more apparently by the visual regularity of the stanzaic and prosodic form. But that mechanical unity creates only the illusion of a continuous flow of thought; the poem itself is built upon a casual accumulation of thoughts, sometimes radically dissociated from one another. The awkward motion from the ninth stanza to the tenth is the most dramatic example:

When will we see Him face to face?
Each day, He shines through darker glass.
In this small town where everything
is known, I see His vanishing
emblems, His white spire and flagpole sticking out above the fog,
like old white china doorknobs, sad,
slight, useless things to calm the mad.

Hammering military splendor,
top-heavy Goliath in full armor—
little redemption in the mass
liquidations of their brass,
elephant and phalanx moving
with the times and still improving,
when that kingdom hit the crash:
a million foreskins stacked like trash....

It does not help much in bridging the gap of that white space to learn from Lowell through Philip Cooper that the latter stanza alludes to Toynbee's account of the defeat of Assyria at Nineveh in 612 B.C.[3] The relevance, of course, lies in the analogy to American militarism, but this theme has not been introduced previously in the poem and it therefore erupts awkwardly at this point. The intervention is authorized primarily by the ruminative organization, which is driven along across gaps like these by the external energy of meter and rhyme. The rumination has the form not of an articulated logical syntax (as in Marvell) but of a paratactic impressionism. The stanzas are laid upon each other like irregular bricks, and this tenth one appears simply and arbitrarily as one more item in a dismal personal and cultural inventory. The formal order of the poem is an illusion that seems intended to correct for the lack of vigorous intellection within the syntax of the poem itself. Lowell's tendency to work in fragments chafes against formal design, and the rigors of the spare four-stress line clearly inhibit his gift for taut, charged phrasing in a line's interior regions.

When "Waking Early Sunday Morning" is examined closely, its fragmentings and dislocations and jagged enjambments seem to be as much the deliberate norm as the metrical model itself:

> O to break loose. All life's grandeur
> is something with a girl in summer. . . .
> elated as the President
> girdled by his establishment
> this Sunday morning, free to chaff
> his own thoughts with his bear-cuffed staff,
> swimming nude, unbuttoned, sick
> of his ghost-written rhetoric.

"Elated" in this construction has nothing to modify and therefore forms only a pseudosyntactical link between the two images that delimit life's "grandeur"—the evanescence of a summer romance and a brief interlude of reprieve for a political man imprisoned by his public role. The association is a strangely unbalanced one because of the portentous topicality of the second image, but it has the force of a sad truth perceived suddenly for the first time, appropriate for the poem and for the moment— the truth that as selves we are all helplessly caught in the process of history, over which we have no control. The affective poles of this image are enormously distant from each other, and the distance seems to be both emphasized and abridged by the elliptical grammatical formation across the second into the third line. If the transition were less taut and more logical and direct, the quality of surrealistic tension in the total image would be lost. Again, the pronounced rhythm has a binding effect upon the otherwise displaced coordination. The two norms, the prosodic and the syntactic, work together and against each other in oddly unsettled ways.*

Lowell is uncomfortable with the sparseness of the octosyllabic couplet, and the poise inherent in this theoretical norm is therefore disrupted throughout the poem by crude enjambment—a reversion, in a way, to his earlier style, but considerably less powerful in effect in this new four-stress prosodic setting. Fully one-fifth of the lines in "Waking Early Sunday Morning" are disintegrated at the end by ungainly leaps from adjective to noun, pronoun to noun, noun to verb, verb to direct object, preposition to object; and of course, in metrical procedure the total effect is much greater than the sum of the parts. The first stanza sets this pattern vividly:

> O to break loose, like the chinook
> salmon jumping and falling back,
> nosing up to the impossible
> stone and bone-crushing waterfall—
> raw-jawed, weak-fleshed there, stopped by ten
> steps of the roaring ladder, and then
> to clear the top on the last try,
> alive enough to spawn and die.

In this case the effect of the "suspended upbeat" (Hayden Carruth's phrase) in the first, third, and fifth lines is a forceful mimetic laboring, which is resolved and released beautifully in the last three lines. But in another stanza exhibiting a high degree of enjambment, the ninth, quoted earlier ("When will we see them face to face?. . .") the effect is one of an awkward and apparently pointless sprawl. In the middle couplets the rhythm collapses virtually into prose:

---

*Since this stanza has been consistently misread by Lowell commentators, it seems appropriate to point out here that the portrait of President Johnson is basically sympathetic, or at least empathetic. He is seen in a moment when he is free, insulated ("girdled") by his establishment—free *with* "his own thoughts" *from* "his ghost-written rhetoric." "Sick" in the last couplet is unavoidably ambiguous because of its strong substantive position at the end of the line and, seemingly, at the end of a three-part catalogue, and because it is separated from the prepositional phrase that modifies it and makes the critical difference. But the intended force of the phrase intact ("sick of his ghost-written rhetoric") is unmistakable. The ambiguity seems unintentional and unfruitful. This is one of the points where the formal exigencies cause difficulty. (It is also difficult to see how the president can be both nude and unbuttoned, but the basic sense again, is clear enough.)

In this small town where everything
is known, I see His vanishing
emblems, His white spire and flagpole sticking out above the fog. . . .

They are, in another view, like iambic pentameter lines chopped up by a paper cutter. The penultimate and last stanzas have the same tortured quality. On the other hand, the fourth through the eighth stanzas are almost symmetrical, so the norm is really highly irregular, and that fluctuation from an achieved to a broken poise cannot help reflecting the character of mind of the new Lowell persona.

The theme that links the disparate parts of "Waking Early Sunday Morning" becomes clear only in the poem's last stanza, where it is condensed in the phrase "our monotonous sublime." The phrase is intentionally oxymoronic. "Sublime" refers to the scale of the subject, and its usage here is accurately explained by a consensus definition: that which arouses "a sense of vastness and power outreaching human comprehension," exceeding *"grandeur"* in magnitude "in its immeasurability and its suggestion of indefinite power."[4] In effect, the world universalizes the monotony of pointless activity and endeavor. What is true of the field mouse rolling the marble in the third stanza is true of the earth "orbiting forever lost" in the last, and true of all of the activities and historical events in between, whatever their scale: "business as usual in eclipse" going "down to the sea in ships"; the tropistic assembling of the faithful at church (the electric bells chime, the congregation gathers); ancient wars and modern wars, indistinguishable from one another—"Wars / flicker," earth licks its open sores, but there is "no advance." Distinctions between events within one class wear away to the point that there are no longer even distinctions between classes. The stubborn, incomprehensible courage of the spawning salmon simply makes one small circle of repetitive futility among larger ones—he is "alive enough to spawn and die" so that other salmon will be alive enough to spawn and die. And where spawning thrives in the human species, Malthusian principles immediately take command: "Only man thinning out his kind / sounds through the Sabbath noon, the blind / swipe of the pruner and his knife / busy about the tree of life." The "tree of life" sounds halfway mystical, but it is not. It is simply a sign of the reducibility of all ideological differentiations to the simple biological necessities of survival, an end in itself. In this process, symbolic objects lose their significance to the extent that they previously signified purpose, or a call to purpose. God's "vanishing emblems," a "white spire" and "flagpole" rising above the fog, are relegated to the status of the "old white china doorknobs," which their tips resemble—"sad, / slight useless things to calm the mad." Why they might calm the mad is not altogether clear; we can only guess that they are like artifacts, as the doorknob is, suggestive of a possible surviving viability of purpose in life—palliatives to anxiety, stabilizing points of contact with the idea of *use*. Doorknobs once opened doors. Separated from that function, they imply, without disclosing, a utility or meaning. In I Corinthians 13, Paul urges that we not be discouraged by the imperfections of the world, for God's plan will be eventually revealed and we shall "understand fully." In "Waking Early Sunday Morning," this process is reversed: "When will we see Him face to face? / Each day, He shines through darker glass." God's imagined role in this context is not redemptive but teleological, and therefore the farther He recedes, the more pointless the repetitious cycles of life and time become. Thus it is that when the poet in the original stanzas comes to inventory his output for the year, he finds only "dead wood" and "listless self-imitation"; everything has been "done before and better done." He is "empty" and "irresolute" and can discover "none of the great / subjects" in his heart, only the "old china doorknobs," which are perhaps also displaced projections of himself. The great themes are not in his heart because he cannot transcend the pessimism of his world view. To achieve expression of any of the great themes would be to earn surcease, albeit temporary, from the dreary and leveling futility of the daily round. As things stand, the poet can neither transcend nor ignore the "monotonous sublime," and the progressively clarifying process of "waking" through the poems only broadens and deepens his despair. Lowell seems to intend "waking" to indicate the process of becoming more aware, and of the mind's being drawn into and becoming implicated in time. In the few moments before dawn comes, he is "squatting like a dragon on / time's hoard," but this mock transcendence is not to last for long, as the other ironic image of the stanza ("no rainbow smashing a dry fly / in the white run is free as I") portends. At the end of the poem, the "criminal leisure of a boy" that he feels in the beginning is ironically modernized in the image of "our children" falling "in small war on the heels of small / war"—responsibly policing the earth forever. Childhood is gone as joy is gone, and with joy gone the earth is merely a ghost, "orbiting forever lost." The president, then, in the twelfth stanza, is clearly an odd alter ego for the poet. He, too, enjoys the "criminal leisure of a boy," for a moment free of the wheel, "swimming nude," bear-cuffing his staff, insulated, and, like the poet, sick of his own rhetoric, though it be ghost-written for him. The emphasis in both cases is upon the envisioned freedom of the self from the general, relentlessly repetitious tendency of things. The president in the pool is "free to chaff / his own thoughts"; in his rhetoric he is a slave to events, and it is "ghost-written," then, in another sense, obedient to and determined by the same aimless, invisible authority that moves the "ghost" of the earth. The nihilistic fatigue of "Waking Early Sunday Morning" is unmitigated, and it sets the tone for two of the other three long poems of the volume, "Central Park" and "Near the Ocean."

In "Central Park," human life is hideously bound and finite. The lion in the zoo cage is the poem's central symbolic figure: he is said to serve his "life-term in jail," the implication being that one's life is a sentence to be endured whether it be served in jail or not. The lion, like the other life-termers of the poem, rebels—inwardly, existentially, but pointlessly: "glaring, grinding, on his heel, / with tingling step and testicle." The poet's need to escape, "to break loose," is evident ironically in his role here again (recalling "Skunk Hour") as a voyeur, scaling rocks, "gasping at game scents like a dog" for a glimpse of lovers. His erotic quest is not only humiliating but fruitless. It is his perspective as observer that denies him the release of forbidden pleasure, for unlike the pairs of lovers, he is compelled to see a hopelessly generalized and abstract rather than intimate event, as the lovers seem to multiply before him in their uniformity, to fill up all of space.

> one figure of geometry,
> multiplied to infinity,
> straps down, and sunning openly. . .
> each precious, public, pubic tangle
> an equilateral triangle,
> lost in the park. . . .

This is a characteristic dilemma for the Lowell persona. Ontologically insecure himself ("nobody's here"), he is driven to feed off those who at least seem to have an assured identity, only to lose the specific once more in the general. The lovers, who have become triangles here and "lost in the park," are the same as the lovers who have become their cars in "Skunk Hour." It is also well to remember in this case that "Central Park" is a poem of the middle sixties, when making love had become as much a political as an erotic activity and thus forced into an abstract and uniform region that did indeed conflict with intimacy. In any case, "anatomy"—as the bodies and selves here are abstractly seen—is "trapped" and stained by "fear and poverty."

> All wished to leave this drying crust,
> borne on the delicate wings of lust. . . .

The poet's privileged foreknowledge is all but invidiously expressed in the meaningful clash of word textures: the gravitational frankness of "lust" nicely qualifies, and dooms, the spirit of "delicate wings." The subtle message of that phrase is restated in terms that bring the stanza back around to the discouraged fatalism of "Waking Early Sunday Morning." Whatever the individual innocent ambitions may be, they all come out the same in the end, absorbed into time; they "cast their fertile drop / into the overwhelming cup." The "overwhelming cup" in this poem is the cognate of the ocean in the title poem: both reduce individual distinctions to nothingness, and both are aspects of the "monotonous sublime." This theme is restated again a few lines from the end of the poem, where Lowell abruptly invokes the old pharaohs and the ironic defeat of their pride and fear: "all your embalming left you mortal, / glazed, black, and hideously eternal." By this time it is night in the park, and in the shadows, associations flourish. The rich in their "slit-windowed" towers are like the pharaohs, whose "plunder and gold leaf / only served to draw the thief." But the rich are prisoners in their towers and thus "trapped" like the lovers in the park and caged like the lion, which in turn has a familiar relation to, and shares a destiny with, the "one-day kitten" found in the park, left to die with food out of reach. A balloon is snagged in an elm, a kite sails into darkness. The rich, who are like thieves by virtue of their plunder, also "draw the thief," and in the poem's last, Juvenalian twist, even the police and thieves have become one:

> We beg delinquents for our life.
> Behind each bush, perhaps a knife;
> each landscaped crag, each flowering shrub
> hides a policeman with a club.

This is finally no political poem in any conventional, utilitarian sense. There is no rationale for what has happened in its model of a world, and therefore no implied possibility of change through political means. Begging delinquents for our life is ironic at two levels, the second one inviting us to wonder why one should beg life from anyone, if, living, we are thus indentured to this "drying crust."

In "Near the Ocean," the brutal fatalism of "Waking Early Sunday Morning" and "Central Park" is pressed to an extreme so final that it has the paradoxical effect of producing, as with people who are faced with the sudden fact of imminent death, a sense of freedom or release. Whatever else may be obscure about "Near the Ocean," that much, it seems, is clear—that in the poem's last lines a cruelly Pyrrhic victory is wrested from defeat:

> Sleep, sleep. The ocean, grinding stones,
> can only speak the present tense;
> nothing will age, nothing will last,
> or take corruption from the past.
> A hand, your hand then! I'm afraid
> to touch the crisp hair on your head—
> Monster loved for what you are
> till time, that buries us, lay bare.

There is a quality of exhausted horror in this passage. The dehumanizing ferocity of marital and sexual conflict that has been the subject of the poem is finally subdued only by the cold realization that the expanse of time makes everything, including one's own terrors and one's attempts at love, meaningless. As the poet has said earlier:

> Older seas
> and deserts give asylum, peace
> to each abortion and mistake.
> Lost in the Near Eastern dreck,
> the tyrant and tyrannicide
> lie like the bridegroom and the bride.

A life that counts for nothing is no more worth fighting over than begging for. The vague echo of Marvell does indeed evoke, as Stephen Yenser unironically proposes, the tradition of the *carpe diem* theme,[5] but it is surely being parodied here in the most bleakly nihilistic way. There should be no equivocating over what the poem's next-to-last line means.

Steven Gould Axelrod makes the plausible suggestion that in addressing the woman (he says "wife") of the poem as "Monster," the poet is declaring his acceptance of her *"as she really is,* in all her foreignness," thus moving "from Martin Buber's I-it to I-thou" and "creating in human communion the value, the reason for living."[6] But what the lines seem actually to say is that the woman is loved for being *monstrous,* and Lowell's capitalizing the noun emphasizes that fact. Far from *carpe diem* pragmatism or "I-thou" harmony (this is not what "I-thou" means in Buber, anyway), the utterance is an expression of the darkest and most unsentimental psychic realities at work in the attraction-repulsion pattern of sexual relations: the hand is needed, the hair is feared, and the union between the two partners is life-supplying, it appears, only because it is violent. The epiphany of the end, sober as it is, comes only in the blank clarity of exhaustion ("Their eyes worn white / as moons from hitting bottom"), which has its parallel in the eroded effects of the ocean's action and the sand of the shore. The allusion to Atlantis in the penultimate stanza ("Sand built the lost Atlantis. . . sand, / Atlantic ocean, condoms, sand") seems meant as one of the poem's several mythic parallels that attempt to define the sexual relationship. Clearly the story of Atlantis as Critias relates it in Plato's *Dialogues* is analogous, since it didactically traces the decline of that kingdom from divine wisdom into barbarism, and hence, we infer from the Critias fragment, its sinking back into the sea from which it was created. The ocean can speak only the present tense, and that is some consolation: time is a continuing present. But this also means that what happens in the past will be repeated in the present, eternally, and that one story of a life is only an allotropic form of the continuous "monotonous sublime." This, at least, has the merit of deterministically erasing individual guilt and— probably more important in the emotional context of this poem—shame.

The poet's role in each of these three poems has been different, and in "Near the Ocean" Lowell is frankly implicated in the world's irrational violence, which in the other two he has wearily deplored. That makes a new moral context and, of course, reinforces the volume's primary theme of the reductive, cyclical sameness of human life. Other than its being psychosexual and squalid, the exact nature of the violence is never explicit in the poem because it is not clear to the poet himself. (To whom is it ever clear?) This confusion perhaps accounts for his being unable in the beginning to choose the appropriate myth for (falsely) aggrandizing his own conflict: Perseus and Medusa or Orestes and Clytemnestra. Each contains elements of the other, as the real story in the poem no doubt contains

elements of both. One would have to be as obsessedly exegetical as Freud
to sort out all of the possible themes. But what with all the severing and
decapitation alluded to in the first two stanzas (in the second stanza the
snakes of Medusa's head appear to be not only "uncoiled" but themselves
"beheaded"), the fear of symbolic castration and impotence flourishes, and
this is associated with a mother figure who is at once desired and feared.
"He knows," the poet says; and what he knows is that even if he destroys
the terrible mother, he will seek her out again, thus caught in a
psychoanalytically repetitious pattern of his own.

> And if she's killed

> his treadmill heart will never rest—
> his wet mouth pressed to some slack breast,
> or shifting over on his back. . . .

This last fragmented image implies a passive and therefore—in the
context—childlike sexual position; and thus recurs suddenly "the severed
radiance" of Medusa's head, the sight of which, Freud argued, terrifies
because it threatens by association with both castration and female
genitalia. And so the cycle would resume. The theater in the beginning of
the poem can only be the theater of the poet's mind, wherein he achieves
fancied (and temporary) stature and earns his own applause as the hero
who has defeated the "monster." It is obviously much to the benefit of his
threatened ego to mythicize his adversary. With all of this as preparation,
the real-life events opaquely recounted in the stanzas that follow seem,
perhaps intentionally, tame by comparison, certainly diminished and
ordinary, making a point of the folly of fancied self-aggrandizement. And it
is also clear, because of this, that the "Monster" loved at the end is not
monstrous "as she really is" but, instead, is monstrous because of the
psychosexual disturbances that the poet has projected upon her. The truth
of the matter is touchingly registered in the poem's dedication: "For
E.H.L."

　　Although it is the second poem of the volume—and thus breaks up
the consistent bleakness of "Waking Early Sunday Morning," "Central
Park," and "Near the Ocean"—"Fourth of July in Maine" comes last in
my discussion here because an understanding of the poet's role and attitude
in the other three poems is essential to our understanding of how that role
is significantly compromised in the setting of this lighter poem's compara-

tively optimistic tone. Despite the public setting implied in the title, by the end of the poem we have been carried again into the interior regions of personal pain. We are carried there across a deceptively rolling topography only to return to a source in exposed awareness and isolation. Several of Lowell's commentators have observed the parallels between this poem and Yeats's "Prayer for My Daughter"—citing mainly the stanzas devoted to Harriet Winslow and to Lowell's daughter as the heir of Harriet's "tireless sedentary love." But the analogy holds for the mood and subject of the entire poem, and most firmly at the point where the scene darkens:

> And now the frosted summer night-dew
> brightens, the north wind rushes through
> your ailing cedars, finds the gaps. . . .

Yeats and Lowell are in the wind, tower and cherished home notwith-standing; their daughters are "half-hid / Under this cradlehood and coverlid" and "cartwheel[ing] on the blue." Yeats's majesty of feeling is not available to Lowell, but it is affecting nevertheless to see the two beleaguered father-poets touching across time in this tentative way. The point of contact is radical innocence, which is the subject of both men's poems. In this respect "Fourth of July in Maine" is radical innocence revisited, half a century later, in a new dispensation of "the murderous innocence of the sea." The poet in this case cherishes most the values and the gifts of life that he is dispossessed of, which are accessible to him only in the experience of others, and only then in the secondary elaboration of a poem. The combination of formality and intimacy of tone is very significant, making an odd split image of intellect and emotion. Castine's Independence Day parade and her stubborn citizens, "scions of the good old strain," are characterized in the opening stanzas as celebrating the pageant vision of America, which is divorced utterly from the realities of our history. Yet that vision does seem in some ironic and oblivious way to uphold the American dream: "all innocence / of children's costumes, helps resist / the communist and socialist." That innocence is of a sort that has survived the militant zeal and seriousness of purpose of New England's theocracy, which

> drove in its stakes here to command
> the infinite, and gave this land
> a ministry that would have made

short work of Christ, the Son of God,
and then exchanged His crucifix,
hardly our sign, for politics.

It is not a vision of things the poet can share, or even wishes to share. We understand this from his wry characterization of "our. . .dandyish Union Soldier"—a fellow witness of the spectacle—as a willing "convert to old age." And it has little more relevance to the real world than do the guinea pigs later in the poem. But that vision, because it is childlike, because it is irrelevant, expresses a faith only in a quality of life, preserves a connection that is mercifully separate from and therefore uncontaminated by time and mission:

This white Colonial frame house,
willed downward, Dear, from you to us,
still matters—the Americas'
best artifact produced en masse.
The founders' faith was in decay,
and yet their building seems to say:
"Every time I take a breath,
my God you are the air I breathe."

This is one of Lowell's moving stanzas—full in conception, finely resolved in design, and central to the subtle ambivalences of the poem. The house is the poet's legacy, and so also should be the spirit in which it was built, a lost harmony of craft and work and religious feeling and joy in life; but the second part of the legacy will not be assured. The "bright thing[s] thinner than a cobweb" in the following stanza have survived almost as if by accident—"old letters" crumbling "from the Book,"

one more line
unravelling from the dark design
spun by God and Cotton Mather. . . .

"Unravelling" is the main conceit in this text, carrying with it the implication of a carefree, untidy liberation from an oppressive order. Harriet Winslow herself is one of those unravelled lines, having lived cheerfully in cherished decor of her own choosing, in "one dear perpetual place," as Yeats put it—radically innocent, one of the free in the kingdom of necessity. It is that "proportion," a strong and spacious life,—which the poet wishes upon his cartwheeling child—that she like the older Harriet may possess

> friends, independence, and a house,
> herself God's plenty, mistress of
> your tireless sedentary love.

But the solemn thought concealed in this reverie is that the poet and his own generation have been passed over by Harriet Winslow's peculiar saving grace. He is in the house where that grace is present, but he is not of it.

The transition to himself from the brief image of his daughter is achieved pointedly in the two charmed stanzas devoted to the young Harriet's guinea pigs. The unstipulated logic of that transition is the logic that controls the poem—the accumulating finality of the poet's alienation. Associated with the daughter and nearer to her than to the poet, the guinea pigs nevertheless inhabit the world of this poem as irreducibly themselves:

> giving, idle and sensitive,
> few animals will let them live,
> and only a vegetarian God
> could look on them and call them good.

The implication in this last couplet refers back to the characterization of God earlier in the poem—in league with Cotton Mather and his "dark design," in no sense a vegetarian God:

> Man's poorest cousins, harmonies
> of lust and appetite and ease,
> little pacific things, who graze
> the grass about their box, they praise
> whatever stupor gave them breath
> to multiply before their death. . . .

The use of the concept of harmony here depicts the guinea pigs as complacently self-contained systems and focuses their irreducibility as well. They are comic kin of the skunks in "Skunk Hour" and of the striving salmon of "Waking Early Sunday Morning," and they emerge at this point in the meditation as the lowest common denominators of radical innocence. In that role they and (more expressly) what they stand for are impossibly remote from the moral realities of the world of the poet's mind. Innocences of many forms have been cherished in the poem and are here discharged.

The poem thus narrows to converge upon its psychic provenance, the poet in the wind, in the house, in his unique isolation, and a single abrasive image impels us into the natural habitat of his consciousness: "thumbtacks rattle from the white maps." No defined relationship between tenor and vehicle in this image could make it more grimly effective than it is as it stands—or as it abrades against the uniform bucolic surface of what has gone before. What was a bright unravelling in the one context is here disintegration and terror:

> food's lost sight of, dinner waits,
> in the cold oven, icy plates—
> repeating and repeating, one
> Joan Baez on the gramophone.

"Joan Baez" and "gramophone" are disjunctive, especially since during Harriet Winslow's tenure the gramophone had been more at home with Nadia Boulanger. The effect is vaguely one of anomie. Things have not worked out right. Harriet, lying in Washington, paralyzed and half-blind, could still name on the telephone each object in its place; but what she had held in order in her mind has fallen asunder outside it. We discover that, all along, the center of this poem's vision has been remorse, as well as an exhaustion that is the more wasting for being both metaphysical and neurasthenic. Both the logs (fuel of the household fire) and the logos fall. The wordplay itself is cynical and nugatory, confirming the mood:

> And here in your converted barn,
> we burn our hands a moment, borne
> by energies that never tire
> of piling fuel on the fire;
>
> monologue that will not hear,
> logic turning its deaf ear,
> wild spirits and old sores in league
> with inexhaustible fatigue.

Far off that time of gentleness,
when man, still licensed to increase,
unfallen and unmated, heard
only the uncreated Word—
when God the Logos still had wit
to hide his bloody hands, and sit
in silence, while his peace was sung.
Then the universe was young.

We watch the logs fall. Fire once gone,
we're done for: we escape the sun,
rising and setting, a red coal,
until it cinders like the soul.
Great ash and sun of freedom, give
us this day the warmth to live,
and face the household fire. We turn
our backs, and feel the whiskey burn.

The extraordinary theological concept expressed in the two last stanzas is Lowell's familiar private heresy. For the various celebrants brought together in this poem on the day of independence—the paraders, the loving builders of Harriet Winslow's house, Harriet Winslow herself, the poet's exuberant child, her nibbling guinea pigs, complacent tenants of Eden—living unravelled from the dark design is itself praise of the uncreated word, in a mythical time before God disclosed Himself and intervened. The poet who gathers them lives on another side of time altogether, a time that God has entered and is burning out. Both visions are true, in the poem; the burden of the poem is that only the poet's is accessible to the poet. The burned-out center of experience is reached through concentric circles of radical innocence. The burning whiskey is its characteristic sign, heat without warmth. Facing the household fire seems to imply taking up the challenge of Harriet Winslow's legacy, the fire of the hearth being almost a primitive symbol of the unity of cave dwellers against the darkness of the fearful universe. It is a powerful paradox in this poem that facing that fire, rather than the ash of the sun, and achieving the "warmth to live"—measures that everyone else appears to be able to take for granted—for Lowell requires an impossible exertion of will. It would be as easy to become a guinea pig. It is impossible for him to take that communion affirming life ordered by love, and whoever it is who turns away with him is alone with him in a terrible, chosen void. A nihilism so deeply entrenched as that is beyond irony and too powerful for utterance.

In one way or another, the sun as it appears in these poems is always either in eclipse or exhausted; and, in a bleak parody of the romantic vision, the poet is one with nature. Finally, that is what it means to be near the ocean, where "the battering ram" lies "abandoned, prone, / beside the apeman's phallic stone." "All discussions / End in the mud-flat detritus of death"—but here there is no saving kingfisher fire to dive upon the heart. The condition is not unique to poets, but it may seem more ironic for the poet, if he has cherished life and in some way given life in his poems. That particular irony is underscored by the volume's elegy for Theodore Roethke—Roethke standing for the poet who is one stage farther along:

> All night you wallowed through my sleep,
> then in the morning you were lost
> in the Maine sky—close, cold and gray,
> smoke and smoke-colored cloud.
>
> Sheeplike, unsociable reptilian, two
> hell-divers splattered squawking on the water,
> loons devolving to a monochrome.
> You honored nature,
>
> helpless elemental creature.
> The black stump of your hand
> just touched the waters under the earth,
> and left them quickened with your name....
>
> Now, you honor the mother.
> Omnipresent,
> she made you nonexistent,
> the ocean's anchor, our high tide.

Roethke, a struggling, bereft redeemer, dissolves into the cold sky. The loony hell-divers dive into and become quietly one with the cold, monochromatic water. Roethke had given human beauty to inhuman nature, but he is recalled nevertheless in the end as being—like the rest of us—helpless and elemental, a "high tide" of the human dream drawn finally down to honor the real inhuman mother, ironically, in nothingness.

6. THE GROUND OF BEING

The Roethke elegy from *Near the Ocean* reappears revised in *Notebook* with three initial lines added:

> At Yaddo, you shared a bathroom with a bag
> tree-painter whose boobs bounced in the basin,
> your blues basin where you wished to plunge your head....
> All night, my friend, no friend, you swam my sleep;
> this morning you are lost in the Maine sky,
> close, cold and gray, smoke, smoke-colored cloud.
> Sheeplike, unsociable, reptilian, the shags
> fling in straight lines like duck in a shooting booth,
> divers devolving to a monochrome.
> You honored nature, helpless, elemental
> creature, and touched the waters of the offing;
> you left them quickened with your name: Ted Roethke....
> Omnipresent, the Mother made you nonexistent,
> you, the ocean's anchor, our high tide.
>
> (*Notebook*, pp. 202–203)

As Philip Cooper observes, the new lines wedge Roethke's character and the poem more firmly into the common clay:

The principal difference between the *Notebook* version of "For Theodore Roethke" and the version that appeared in *Near the Ocean*, aside from modifications to conform to the semi-sonnet pattern, is the addition of the anecdote about Yaddo. The culminating image is the same: Ted Roethke dead, become the earth itself, the solid globe, concave at ocean bottom, is the "ocean's anchor, our high tide"; but now the pull of gravity makes itself felt by the movement of the earth-mother boobs, as well as by the waters of the ocean. The boobs at the beginning of the poem and the tide at the end respond to each other as alternate reflections of the anchor's mortal gravity.[1]

If the sense of Cooper's "gravity" here can be slightly calibrated, it might be said to be the force that draws Roethke out of what he called "the realm of pure song" downward to death, and along that journey through the sphere of desymbolized existence wholly in the physical world.

> The indignity of it!—
> With everything blooming above me,
> Lilies, pale-pink cyclamen, roses,
> Whole fields lovely and inviolate,—
> Me down in that fetor of weeds,
> Crawling on all fours,
> Alive, in a slippery grave.[2]

The region is the realm of being where time and nature press back against the imagination, where (to modify Stevens) the violence from without challenges the violence within; *Notebook* at its simplest level may be understood as a field for this encounter. A poem called "White" from the same group as the Roethke elegy just as candidly consigns all symbolist and Platonic idealism to this naturalistic dimension:

> Genghis and Attila killed fewer of their kind.
> This kind is only expelled by prayer and fasting;
> yet we were no kinder when we had the Faith,
> and thought the massacred could be reformed,
> and move like angels in the unwithering white,
> file upon file, the beds of long-neck clams,
> blue-white and hard and sharp and stiff and pure—
> the clam-shell cunted in the ground of being.
>
> (*Notebook*, p. 200)

The grammatical transaction in this last phrase—and, once focused by the phrase, *Notebook* itself—gives no indication and yet leaves no doubt as to what Lowell takes the ground of being to be. As he himself might say elsewhere, in one of the neurasthenically redundant gestures that become a mannerism of the *Notebook* style, the ground of being is the ground of being. Being cunted there with the rest of us—"hard and sharp and stiff and pure," all of these things at once—is *Notebook*'s primary subject. The image itself is a parody of Mallarmé's ice-locked swan, a transposing of the same quality of suffering from an idiom of the high mimetic into that of an ironic stylistic mode. That effect has been achieved partially already in Lowell's rendering of "Le Cygne," the fifth, sixth, and seventh lines of which express Lowell more precisely even than Mallarmé:

> The virgin, the blind, the beautiful today,
> dares it break the mirror of this lake,
> hard, neglectful, hoarding under ice
> a great glacier of flights that never fly?
> The swan worsens, remembers it is he,
> the magnificence that gives itself no hope,
> the fortitude that finds no *raison d'être*—
> the great boredoms blaze in the sterile winter.
> The whole neck shakes in this white agony
> inflicted by the space the swan denies....
>
> (*Notebook*, p. 133)

But the new image in "White"—yoking and therefore identifying "cunted" and "ground of being"—asserts a negation that Lowell's "Le Cygne" only implies. *Notebook* everywhere proclaims a rejection, even a loss of interest in, the *symboliste*'s faith in or vision of *l'azur*, and the renunciation is expressed both implicitly in the book's form and explicitly in its declarations. The renegade Catholic has become a renegade *poète maudit*. *Notebook*'s persona is fixed in time and nature, and Lowell's vision of possibility is foreshortened cruelly by the subduing of idealism to the decomposing matter of fact: "A nihilist has to live in the world as is, / gazing the impossible summit to rubble." The influence of gravity, in effect, has grown irresistible.

> Kneedeep in the cowpond,
> far from this cockfight, cattle stop and watch us,

then, having had their fill, go back to lapping
soiled water indistinguishable from heaven. . . .

(*Notebook*, p. 27)

With a bull's watery eye,
dewlap and misty phallus, Cuyp caught the farthest glisten,
tonnage and rumination of the sod. . . .
. . . . .
—only the lovely,
the good, the wealthy served the Venetian, whose art
knew nothing yet of husbandry and cattle. . . .

(p. 131)

The Republic! But it never was,
except in the sky-ether of Plato's thought,
steam from the ordure of his city-state. . . .

(p. 151)

Albert Cuyp's cows with their massive, complacent beauty command the foreground of otherwise delicate landscapes. When one remembers them from galleries or art texts, they command memory and ideas in the same way—more vividly than the "sky-ether of Plato's thought"—looking out upon the human observer as if to say, "Enjoy well the loot of your inheritance. We are all dealers in used furniture."

In one aspect, *Notebook* is in a body of poetry written against poetry and art and the associated forms of idealism on behalf of the ground of being in phenomenal reality.

And here on this wavy earth, we, like the others,
too thoughtful clods, may learn from those we walk on:
Star-nosed moles, their catatonic tunnels
and barrows . . . only in touch with what they touch. . . .

(*Notebook*, p. 259)

At other points the poet is not so much arguing on behalf of this ground of being as struggling in its grip and learning to live with it and extort from it whatever share of remission and well-being it can be trusted to afford. The alternative, symbolic mode of existence supplied by the imagination's rage for order, and by the self's fear of time, is understood to be at worst an insidious and mocking fiction and at best no longer a viable environment for the whole, "green and dying" self: "I am learning to live in history, / What is history? What you cannot touch" (p.103). Living in history is perhaps the reverse of comprehending it, a centripetal motion into time rather than a centrifugal one outward and beyond it—"On my great days of sickness, I was God" (p.223)— and being unable to touch it means not being able to transcend it. Paradoxically, for a New England brahmin like Lowell, this desymbolizing process requires the patience, commitment, and discipline of a craft.

Craft in the conventional sense and the life dedicated to its service are characterized in *Notebook* as hopelessly dissociated and contingent, very nearly as a wasteful expense of spirit, a demanding loyalty to a truth in form that steadily gives way in aging to the truth of time. Of Flaubert, and thinking perhaps of himself in retrospect, Lowell says:

> Is it refusal of error breaks a life—
> the supreme artist, Flaubert, was a boy before
> the mania for phrases dried his heart.
>
> (*Notebook*, p. 38)

"Refusal of error": the obsession with form here is represented as a negation that conceals a specific, insidious pathology. That idea is surrounded, shaded, reconsidered, asserted, and implied throughout *Notebook* to make the volume dense with what Hugh Kenner calls subject rhyme. The theme supports the logic of *Notebook* and also supplies a unity for its contrived, inchoate form. Virginia Woolf's Professor Ramsey finds himself saying in imaginary argument that "the arts are merely a decoration imposed on the top of human life; they do not express it."[3] The poems of *Notebook* work toward *expressing* in this sense, Lowell perhaps having considered that art's being long is cold consolation for life's being short.

Writers and artists introduced in *Notebook* by allusion or in profile seem enlisted to substantiate Lowell's own ambiguous fatalism. Most are caught at some point, including the terminal one, along the downside of the curve of their careers or in moments of anguish and self-recrimination, and these images accumulate to express a tragic, humanized view of visionary idealism. The point is sharpened to a poignant irony in the poem recounting a visit with Ezra Pound:

> He showed us his blotched, bent hands, saying "Worms.
> When I talked that nonsense about Jews on the Rome
> wireless, she knew it was shit, and still loved me."
> And I, "Who else has been in Purgatory?"
> And he, "To begin with a swelled head and end with
>   swelled feet."
>
> (*Notebook*, p. 120)[4]

We would expect Pound to savor with wry detachment the parallel implied in the allusion to Oedipus. Lowell hangs it laconically above a void.

Two related poems focusing first upon Margaret Fuller, and then upon Emerson and Thoreau, isolate a specific tragic quality indigenous to the American imagination. Margaret Fuller expresses for the volume its classic existential ambivalence:

> "Ourselves . . . are all we know of heaven.
> With the intellect, I always can
> and always shall make out, but that's not half—
> the life, the life, O my God, will life never be sweet?"
>
> (*Notebook*, p. 90)

In "Henry and Waldo," Emerson's austere armor of character is set as a foil against the more susceptible, exposed, and receptive spirit of Thoreau, who is connected with Margaret Fuller across the page by the comment that "Thoreau, like Mallarmé and many another, / found life too brief for perfection and too long for comfort." The poem goes on to conceive that the language of living nature to which Thoreau was attuned—despite Hawthorne's sense of him as indifferent to the society of men—eventually was baffled by the encroachment of a new language in the same order of experience, prefigurations in shadings and signs, perhaps of our own experience now, but in any case death for Thoreau's. The texture of Lowell's own language and the curve of its rhythms cohere beautifully to evoke romantic euphoria suddenly dispersed by anxiety:

> he easily heard voices on the river,
> wood groans from the banksand gliding of bark canoes,

> twilight flaking through the manes of trees;
> the color that killed him was perhaps a mouse,
> zinc eating at the moonstalk, or the starlings
> flocking and lighting, a dash of poisonous metal.
>
> (*Notebook*, p. 91)

Nothing is more typical of Lowell's style than the elusive relationship in these last three lines between tenor and vehicle: vehicle concrete and tenor vague, with the result that implication radiates strongly outward and recovers definition only in the vehicular language itself. At best, the effect is to contain an extensive reach of implication within a maximum density of concrete verbal texture. Tenor and vehicle remain indivisible. Paradoxically it is because of this effect that isolated lines and images in *Notebook* seem so easily to separate from their context to move into other regions of implication. Hence, it does not seem at all gratuitous to speak of Lowell's characterization of Thoreau as being simultaneously prototypical and irreducibly individuated or, for example, to perceive a suggestive articulation between Thoreau's "starlings flocking and lighting" and the image of Margaret Fuller going down with the *Elizabeth*, preferring to die with her husband and child than to save herself—

> in a white nightgown, hair fallen long
> at the foot of the foremast, Margaret Fuller
> forty, Angelo thirty, Angelino one—
> drowned with brief anguish, together, and your firecall.
>
> (*Notebook*, p. 90)[5]

Drowning has carried forward an ironic metaphoric connotation from the poem, set in the present, that immediately precedes the one for Margaret Fuller:

> your girl, she's nine still, comes wisely, inopportunely
> reappearing—you standing on your bed
> in your Emily Dickinson nightgown, purely marveling
> whether to be sensible or drown.
>
> (*Notebook*, p. 89)

Set over against "being sensible," "drowning" is a risk that is calculated when the imagination presses out into and against reality: " 'Ourselves. . . .

are all we know of heaven but . . . / the life, the life, O my God, will life never be sweet?"

Lowell's unconsoled secular magi, appearing and disappearing in the depths of his ground of being, seem to echo with different inflections Margaret Fuller's generic despair; the nineteenth-century American transcendentalist in this way becomes a prototype for the poet living in the twentieth century through the twilight of a double vision. Images and fragments of conversations recur and attach to this central preoccupation like iron filings to a magnet: Pound's "To begin with a swelled head and end with swelled feet"; William Carlos Williams saying, of his mother, "The old bitches / live into their hundreds, while I'll kick off / tomorrow . . . / I am sixty-seven, and more / attractive to girls than when I was seventeen" (p.122); Kokoschka saying, "If you last, / you'll see your reputation die three times, / and even three cultures; young girls are always here" (pp. 27–28); Frost saying, "When I am too full of joy, I think / how little good my health did anyone near me" (p. 122); Elizabeth Bishop writing that her situation in life begins to seem like exploring a cave: "Finally after hours of stumbling along, / one sees daylight ahead, a faint blue glimmer. / Air never looked so beautiful before. / That's what I feel I'm waiting for now" (p. 235); I. A. Richards saying, "My vanity won't let me believe my death . . . / A suicide takes chances. I'd choose the ocean, / who knows, I might reach the other side" (p. 125); a priest in Cuernavaca asking Lowell, "Will you die, when the book is done?" (p. 129); Melville saying, "There's a wisdom that is woe, / but there is a woe that is madness" (p. 153); Mary McCarthy (apparently) saying, "The real motive for my trip is dentistry, / a descending scale: long ago, I used to drive / to New York to see a lover, next the analyst, / then an editor, then a lawyer, last . . . / I can't quite make this the Seven Ages of Man / Faith is in labor" (p. 190); Louis MacNeice saying, "It's better / to die at fifty than lose my pleasure in terror" (p. 202); Jarrell appearing in a dream to ask, "But tell me, / Cal, why did we live? Why do we die?" (p. 116); or F. O. Matthiessen, mutely expressive in death, "frozen meat," his "fast colors lost to lust and prosecution" and when alive, "torn / between the homosexual's terrible love / for forms, and his anarchic love of man" (p. 172). Lowell's crisp characterization of Matthiessen's conflict seems at least to include the terms of his own, and it is readily generalizable as a theme of *Notebook*. Otherwise, there is a calculated directness in Lowell's presentation of this material ("why did we live? Why do we die?"), as if to stipulate that the truth as anyone sees it and all really final questions find their true mimetic form only in banalities, "the terrible love for forms," homosexual or otherwise, notwithstanding. Gift, talent, love of the beautiful and good, of the best that has been known and thought, the life of the imagination do not avail here against the steady encroachment of the random, misshapen, unpredictable, and grotesque:

> I stand between tides; quickly bit by bit
> the old crap and white plastic jugs lodge on the shore,
> the ocean draws out the river to no end:
> most things worth doing are worth doing badly.
>
> (*Notebook*, pp. 25–26)

Debris piles up in *Notebook*, burying or snagging and unraveling both private and community dreams of the reasonable and ordered life; and in this setting, Lowell portrays his two principal culture heroes, Allen Tate and Randall Jarrell, with a cutting and epitomizing poignancy. Tate is rendered once in a reminiscence: "On your enormous, cannonball head of a snowman, / is a ripped red tissuepaper birthday hat." The primary conceptual textures in this image—cannonball, snowman, tissue paper— seem to be doing several things at once: they objectify paradoxical feelings about Tate the man; at the same time they trace a delicate curve from the sublime to the frivolous and a somber one from power to fragility, the course of mortality. By the poem's end the two old friends have reached the point of friendly conflict, having grown "too much the soldier from Sourmash," and Pickett's columns at Gettysburg—fittingly for the wistful *ubi sunt* motif, which is the real blood-flow of the moment—have become "Ashtrays and icecubes." "There," says Tate, pointing, "if Longstreet had *moved*, we would have *broke* you" (p. 121). Lowell's style is such that at times his experience seems to consist almost exclusively of detail; but his facts are selected and surreptitiously arranged to create the effect of an artless symbolic integration. Hence, in a book-consciousness burdened by images and implications of detritus and junk it is not merely reportorial accuracy that causes Lowell to record that Michael Tate, less than a year old, dies "gagging" on a "plastic telephone"—or to have prepared us for that image by juxtaposing the world we dream and the world we live in with the simple observation: "Things no longer usable for our faith / go on routinely possible in nature." In characterizing the Tates' response to that death, he obliquely affirms another of *Notebook*'s covert realizations, that the process of growing older is a process of moving farther and farther out and away from the sphere of our expectations: "They are no longer / young enough to understand what happened" (p. 251). This extraordinarily thoughtful paradox seems central somehow to Notebook's saturation in demoralized anxiety. The two poems about the Tate twins are called "Father and Sons," as though it were in the order of living that one should have two sons, one living and one dead. The second of the two is devoted to Tate himself, still "magisterial and cocky," still hewn on the grand scale ("Who else would sire twin sons at sixty-eight?"), living quietly in retirement with a young wife and the surviving twin, captor and source of joy—yet still required to hold strength for the resolving irony, "I shall not live long enough to 'see him through'" (p. 252).

In the first of the two paired poems for Jarrell, Lowell represents their past together at Kenyon College in an ironic compression of two experiences of time, "students waiting for Europe and spring term to end," then crystallizes that feeling sharply, reporting to his dead friend that what remains of that landscape (at Kenyon) is time itself: "Randall, the same fall lunges on the windshield, / the same apples ripen on the whiplash bough." In the second poem the scene shifts slightly forward to the point in time of "our first intoxicating disenchantments"—the epithet describing a remote and callow phase of disenchantment—then abruptly forward to "the night of the caged squirrel on its wheel" (an allusion here to Jarrell's "Well Water" from Lost World)[6] and then on to the end of Jarrell's unrequited life—

> you plod out stubbornly,
> as if asleep, Child Randall, as if in chainstep,
> meeting the cars, and approving; a harsh luminosity,
> as you clasp the blank coin at the foot of the tunnel.
>
> (Notebook, p. 51)

The point at the end of the tunnel calls attention to the fact that across the two poems we have been drawn through progressively constricting settings. The "harsh luminosity" is Jarrell's (from Lowell's memorial essay for Jarrell: "He had the harsh luminosity of a Shelley"),[7] meeting and defying the headlights; the "blank coin" is his and ours, currency only in the lost world, or in a nonexistent one. Calling Jarrell "Child Randall" not only brings an echo from the ballad—"For I'm sick at the heart, and I fain wald lie down"—but summons in a single etymology the two Jarrells, the innocent and the patrician, who were one as enfant terrible. "Who wouldn't rather be his indexed correspondents / than the boy Keats spitting out blood for time to breathe?" (p. 87): we come across this elsewhere, and seem expected to remember Jarrell. And still farther on we find this, of an image:

> smoke-dust the Chinese draftsman made eternal.
> His drawing wears; the hand decayed. A hand
>   does—
> we can have faith, at least, the hand decayed.
>
> <div align="right">(<i>Notebook</i>, p. 247)</div>

Clearly in *Notebook* the burden upon Lowell's conscience—a conscience habitually alert to irony and, moreover, to the kind of irony that engages us with life rather than detaching us from it—is the mocking phantom of art and the artist as a shaping spirit. That value of art is the predication, for instance, of Thomas Parkinson's judgment of what he calls Lowell's passivity before experience: "Art can be judged, perhaps must finally be so judged, by what it asks its audience to become, and pop art and confessional poetry coerce their audience into postures that I find not at all edifying."[8] Lowell might respond that some art asks the audience to understand itself, whether the result be edifying or not, and goes further to ask how art's visions and illusions are and are not measures of that reality— how the characters of the poetic and empirical selves are intertwined. Lowell's life, mismanaged like anyone else's, is given full exposure here and in *The Dolphin* and in *Day by Day* not despite his being an artist but because of it, with undiverted ethical understanding a principal objective. William Meredith has written that Lowell's "readings carry always a slight tone of complaint, as though he would make some disappointment heard beyond that of man's tragic predicament. This disappointment, half modest, half the reverse, seems to express: although I am the man of remarkable vision who has seen and said this, am I not sadly unremarkable?"[9] The authority for that ironic self-consciousness, the awareness that Parkinson would have more firmly shaped, accrues from the *Notebook* poet's appraisal and reconstruction of other lives as well as from his own, and the reach through history is vast.

> In his dark day, Dante made the mistake of treating
> politics as if it belonged to life,
> not ideology. In Purgatory,
> the poor souls eclipse the black and white of God.
> Likeness to exile warms the sun in Hell—

the man running for his life never tires:
Ser Brunetto, running like one of those
who ran for the green cloth through the green fields
at Verona, looks like the one who won
the roll of cloth, not like those who lose....
All comes from a girl met at the wrong time:
God and her love that called him forth to exile
in midwintertime cold and lengthening days,
when the brief field frost mimics her sister, snow.

(Notebook, p. 233)

Here Lowell's theme is recast. The subject of the opening lines is difficult
to ascertain. The first three sentences seem both stubbornly paratactic and
idiosyncratically allusive. The contemporary occasion from which they
arise, however, is clearly Chicago, 1968, represented in the ten poems
given to that subject in the sequence—called "The Races"—immediately
preceding the poem on Dante. The subject of Dante's exile by this
association is given a special focus: his exile is both a hell, and, as the last
two lines seem to imply, an enforced freedom from which grew his greatest
work. Purgatory may be understood as the fierce political conflict in
Florence and Dante's equally fierce commitment to it, which obscured the
vision of his ultimate mission as a poet. His "mistake"then emerges as
something like a fortunate fall. The *Divine Comedy* begins:

Midway the journey of this life I was 'ware
That I had strayed into a dark forest,
And the right path appeared not anywhere....[10]

But mid-life in the dark wood for Dante turns out to be the spiritual winter
solstice before the ultimate revelation, which the *Divine Comedy* leads us
toward from the point of these opening lines. And Lowell appears to allude
to that issue in paraphrasing for the last two lines of "Winter" half of the
busy epic simile that opens *Inferno*, Canto 24:

In that part of the young year when the Sun
Beneath Aquarius warms his beaming locks
And toward the South the nights begin to run,
And then upon the ground the hoar-frost mocks
With likeness her white sister's effigy,
But soon are blurred that limner's pencilled strokes,

The peasant, who hath nothing now laid by,
   Rises and looks and sees the fields and lanes
   All whitened; and thereat he beats his thigh,
Returns to his house and to and fro complains,
   Like a starved wretch who knows not what to do,
   Then again comes out and his hope regains,
Seeing what the world has changed its face into
   So briefly, and takes his crook and out of door
   Goes driving forth his lambs to pastures new. . . .

The resolution of "Winter" is therefore reticently sanguine, the element of hope in it being all but invisible, as it were, to the naked eye. But even that restrained optimism seems discounted beforehand by the image of Brunetto Latini that is wedged into the poem's center. Dante's revered teacher looks to Dante like one who ran for the green cloth and won, but the point is that he is not—he is in Hell for eternity and running eternally from pursuing flame:

whoe'er
the instant stops, an hundred years must lie
Helpless against the fire a hand to stir. . . .

The equivalence seems to be this: the poet in the world (and this one, Robert Lowell, later calls his book a honeycomb, which "proves its maker is alive") *looks* like one who won the green cloth, but that is because he never tires, and he never tires because he is running for his life. We return to the theme of the artist as shaper by the stern way of *realpolitik*—perhaps by association with Brunetto Latini, as one of the early academic masters of the science of politics—and the brutal treatment of both Lowell's and Dante's political fantasies once transposed from the insular realm of ideology into the arena of authentic power. We return to the theme of exile and isolation by contact between this poem and a dream related in a poem in "The Races":

a kind of camp army, not altogether
anything from Chicago, has barbwired off
my house. I wake up shouting, "No, don't, don't!"
               (*Notebook*, p. 230)

Lowell's "Dates" at the end of *Notebook* include: "The Vietnam War, 1967; the Pentagon March, 1967; the McCarthy Campaign, 1967–68;

Martin Luther King's Murder, 1968; the Columbia Demonstrations, 1968; Robert Kennedy's Murder, 1968; Chicago, 1968; the Vietnam War, 1968, 1969, 1970." In this dark and pathless wood, it is difficult to sustain faith in the liberal imagination or in art as a shaping spirit; the dark may be the point of the winter solstice, but the generic poet in time, here understood and represented by Robert Lowell, has come to the point of wondering out loud whether the imagination has not overplayed its hand.

Commemorating New year's Eve, 1968, he writes:

> This year runs out in the movies, it must be written
> in bad, straightforward, unscanning sentences—
> mine were downtrodden, branded on backs of
>   carbons,
> lines, words, letters nailed to letters, words, lines. . . .
>
> (Notebook, p. 172)

Technical form and theoretic form in this way come together. Yvor Winters would pronounce this "the heresy of expressive form," but it would be heresy only to one who subscribes to the Winters dogma to begin with. Poetry here swerves vividly from its fidelity to the mystery of logos toward a simpler human determination not to lie. How not to lie and at the same time cherish poetry and remain a poet is one of Notebook's most exposed and excruciating dilemmas. Kierkegaard is worth quoting again, on the temptation of aestheticism: "[Every] man can live poetically who in truth desires to"; but "if we . . . inquire what poetry is, we might answer with the general characterization that poetry is a victory over the world. It is through a negation of the imperfect actuality that poetry opens up a higher actuality, expands and transfigures the imperfect into the perfect, and thereby softens and mitigates that deep pain which would darken and obscure all things."[11]

Against his own expressed ambivalence, Lowell poses a conservative order of rhetoric which he bluntly represents as both inhumane and, as a Heideggerian would say, ontologically opaque. The setting for this poem is May, 1968 (the month of the Columbia riots) and its target is Irving Howe.[12]

> How often was this last salute recast?
> Did Irving really want three hundred words,
> such tact and tough, ascetic resonance,

> the preposition *for*, five times in parallel,
> to find himself a "beleaguered minority,
> without fantasies of martyrdom,"
> facing the graves of the New York Intellectuals,
> "without joy, but neither with dismay"?
> This art was needed for his final sentence;
> others see the entombment with dismay.
> How often one would choose the poorman's provincial
> out of town West Side intellectual
> for the great brazen rhetorician serpent,
> swimming the current with his iron smile!
>
> (*Notebook*, p. 187)

"Serpent" may be unnecessarily choleric, but "brazen" is precisely right for the context, implying as it does a sculptured detachment from the organic complexities of experience and a fraudulent, disciplined organization of feeling. (Lowell's phrase "brazen rhetorician serpent" is itself a handsome model of aural invective.) In any case, the point takes on a more than topical relevance in the larger context of *Notebook*'s gloomy transvaluation of the shaping spirit. Just after this, a fragment of conversation is recorded—"'Williams . . . / could never learn the King's English of the New Yorker'"—and we understand it as praise: "'Dr. Williams / saw the germ on every flower, and knew / the snake is a petty, rather pathetic creature'" (p. 188). Earlier, an encounter with Paul Claudel is recalled to indict a seamy hypocrisy always implicit in the poised style:

> He's near me now, declaiming:
> "*L'Académie Groton, eh, c'est une école admirable,*"
> soaring from hobbled English to a basic French,
> a vocabulary poorer than Racine's . . .
> minotaur steaming in a maze of eloquence.
>
> (*Notebook*, p. 80)

These lines, and particularly their acerbic peroration, are situated in the poem so as to comment not only upon Claudel but upon the poet himself, eating out alone and glumly warding off loneliness with erotic fantasies.

Still another recorded conversation rearranges essentially the same point, the contrast between the straining authentic self in time and the fictional persona remodeled in language:

> "Even if such a one indiscreetly writes
> the perfect sentence, he knows it isn't English;
> he goes to bed Lord Byron, but wakes up bald."
>
> (*Notebook*, p. 154)

Finally there is this compressed resolution of the theme, a synthesis and an extension of it toward its inescapable implication:

> Christ's first portrait is a donkey's head,
> the simple truth is in his simple word,
> lies buried in a random, haggard sentence,
> cutting ten ways to nothing clearly carried.
>
> (*Notebook*, p. 129)

In the spirit of Wittgenstein—and of the Eliot of *Four Quartets*—the poet here concedes the inevitable failure of language and affirms the existence, but not the accessibility, of truth.

Evaluating the achievement of *Notebook* is primarily a matter of determining whether in some coherent way the work surmounts and expresses Lowell's wavering faith in art, or whether it simply represents the collected, remorseful gestures of a broken spirit. Wherever sympathies lie in this regard, it seems clear that Lowell has chosen *Notebook*'s course consciously and that its form is the contrived expression of a deliberated ontology. A rationale for that form—for *Notebook* as a whole, its plan as a structure, as well as for the individual poems and their groupings within it—has been supplied, inappropriately enough, by Donald Davie, commenting upon Ezra Pound, specifically upon the controversy over *Homage to Sextus Propertius*. Davie cites Yeats as having said that one gets the impression from Pound's poems "that he has got all the wine into the bowl." Davie then goes on to say that

> a poet might contrive this effect because he wants *not* to seem to have "got all the wine into the bowl," because "deliberate nobility" is the last thing he is after. If he is sure that there is more to his subject

(more perhaps to any subject) than he got out of it or ever could get out of it, if he believes that all the wine never can be got into the bowl or into any bowl, then, like Michelangelo leaving some portion of the stone unworked in his sculptures, the poet will deliberately seek an effect of improvisation, of haste and rough edges. For only in this way can he be true to his sense of the inexhaustibility of the human and non-human nature he is working with, a sense which makes him feel not noble but humble. And the same reason will make him use rhythms which seem or are uncontrollable, not to be measured. . . in order to compass the unforseen which inexhaustible nature necessarily and continually provides.[13]

Commenting in a review upon Davie's remarks, Michael Wood adds this:

Thomas Mann's Adrian Leverkühn thought a modern work imposs-ible because its closure would be an infidelity not so much to the world's inexhaustibility as to its inherent, encroaching chaos, and Pound himself wrote, . . . "Art very possibly *ought* to be the supreme achievement, the 'Accomplished'; but there is the other satisfactory effect, that of a man hurling himself at an indomitable chaos and yanking and hauling as much of it as possible into some sort of order (or beauty) aware of it both as chaos and as potential."[14]

"Inexhaustible nature" and "encroaching chaos" are mirror-image perceptions of the same phenomenon, and Notebook enriches the potential confusion by confronting and expressing both. The difference between the two and the negotiation between them in the process of living is one of Notebook's implied themes. "The slush-ice on the east water of the Hudson / is rose-heather this New Year sunset; the open channel, / bright sky, bright sky, carbon scarred with ciphers" (p. 173). Art in Notebook voluntarily yields its privilege to the authority of both inexhaustible nature and encroaching chaos, and bears witness to the authentic power of the world against which and out of which the poet strives to make a separated, human way. One aspect of that concession is the poet's openly portraying his resistance, in defense of the self and the shaping spirit, as a "yanking and hauling" and his eschewing altogether the more shapely effects of poetic decorum. The effect is the opposite of the one achieved in the method of, say, Richard Wilbur, where what Wilbur calls the "conflict with disorder" appears to be resolved and chastened by the time it enters the made poem. Even in its most obvious structural aspects, Notebook expresses this precarious relationship between the poet and the undirected flux of his experience: it is a journal that moves with the years and seasons but also in the most unpredictable and erratic currents of the time stream, open at both ends, and yet all of that flow is harnessed to the rigorous structural model of the sonnet—the sonnet paradigm itself declaring "some sort of order" even as it is being consumed. Yeats might have been less austere regarding Pound's improvidence had he thought the problem through, since this concept of form is finally no more or less than a radical extension of the journey from Byzantium toward the rag-and-bone shop of the heart. In Lowell's case the rag-and-bone shop of the heart is continuous with the rag-and-bone shop of our history. The poet "hurling himself at an indomitable chaos" in this way becomes the "nihilist as hero."

Paraphrasing T. W. Adorno, Fredric Jameson sets forth in *Marxism and Form* the argument that the violin, with its "newly soulful tone," was one of the great—and inevitable—"innovations of the age of Descartes."

> Throughout its long ascendancy, indeed, the violin preserves this close identification with the emergence of individual subjectivity on the stage of philosophical thought. It remains a privileged medium for the expression of the emotions and demands of the lyrical subject, and the violin concerto... stands as the vehicle for individual lyric heroics... [When] composers begin to suppress the singing violin tone and to orchestrate without strings or to transform the stringed instrument into a plucked, almost percussion device, ... what happens to the violin is to be taken as a sign of the determination to express what crushes the individual, to pass from the sentimentalization of individual distress to a new postindividualistic framework.

In this "postindividualistic framework" individual subjectivity is expressed, in other words, as it is apparently subsumed with the expressed "necessities of the objective universe."[15] In this respect, the sonnet and the violin share a sufficiently similar history for it to be possible to say that Lowell manipulates the sonnet and its classical tradition—and the expectations we bring from it—in order to register, by transforming it from a singing to a percussion device, precisely the death of the illusion of the beauty and the viability of the inner life.

Another way of representing this issue is to focus the openly disordered conflict in *Notebook* between subject and object—a conflict that in its overtness reminds us again of Wallace Stevens and also of the tide of reality that has risen ominously against poetry since Stevens first essayed to contain it. The character of this conflict is most apparent in *Notebook*, as it frequently is in Stevens, where the poet encounters the new myth of the city ("The Mouth of the Hudson" is a prefiguration of this theme).

> Somewhere a white wall faces a white wall,
> one wakes the other, the other wakes the first,
> each burning in the other's borrowed splendor—
> the walls, once woken, are forced to go on talking,
> their color looks much alike, two shadings of white,
> each living in the shadow of the other.
> How fine these distinctions when we cannot choose!
> Don Giovanni must have drawn sword on such an avenger,
> two contracting, white stone walls—their pursuit
> of happiness and his, coincident . . .
>
> (*Notebook*, p. 146)

Don Giovanni is a figure who recurs often in *Notebook*, portrayed more or less sympathetically, and here explicitly as the poet's surrogate—an image of self-assertion, resisting void. For Lowell the city, like nature for other poets, discloses, when attended, a hidden secret of existence. That secret is blankness—the autonomy, neutrality, and indifference of the universe, the awareness of which closes in remorselessly to suffocate the self. This poem ("Two Walls") ends in self-effacement: "I lie here, heavily breathing, the soul of New York." The identification of the "I," the poet, as "the *soul* of New York" is of course ironic, and all the more so for the contrast with Don Giovanni, for the momentary savoring of death, the lying passively, the labored breathing. As Alan Williamson has observed, "The poems in *Notebook* make us feel nature retreating before our eyes like a mirage." The city, he has said earlier, paraphrasing Norman O. Brown, "is man's most perfect sublimation; in it he flees both the body and death by identifying himself with pure geometries, with indestructible, ethereally beautiful metals and stones."[16] Williamson implies that this is Lowell's criticism of culture; but if it is, it is criticism from a standpoint that is not detached but continuous, implicated, and threatened. Certainly Lowell is nowhere represented as an uninhibited protégé of Norman O. Brown. His sexual life in *Notebook* is markedly labored and willed—his Don Giovanni, in other words, is existential rather than erotic.

In any case, Lowell's city grows more imposing as his work progresses. In *Notebook* this world beyond the self gathers nightmarish dimension and volume: massive anonymous structures, their menace intensified by stark lighting, loom above a prospect of cars, bridges, superhighways, polluted rivers. Stone, steel, and concrete—the epic inertia of matter—aggrandize the external world's sheer bulk, which in turn seems to usurp the authority of the poems that strive to contain it. What is left of nature, in paradigm of the diminished self, may appear as a leaf, the veins of a leaf, a flower breaking through the crack of a sidewalk:

> The rain falls down, the soil swims up to breathe,
> the squatter sumac, shafted in cement,
> flirts its wet leaves to heaven like the Firebird.
> Two girls clasp hands in a clamshell courtyard to watch
> the weed of sumac aging visibly. . .
>
> *(Notebook*, p. 65)

> We open the window, and there is no view,
> no green meadow pointing to *the* green meadow,
> to dogs, to deer, Diana in her war-skirt. . . .
> Heaven must be paved with terra-cotta tile.
>
> (p. 63)

In *Notebook*, as earlier, Lowell's art is to characterize this environment as both implacably autonomous, external to the self and consciousness—the dissociation which is the source of its power—and also malevolently animated by the threatened subject's perception of it: either way it is beyond control. *Notebook*'s vision is that of a modern anachronist whose notions of identity are rooted in the past, fearing and resisting what some futurists have professed to cherish and embrace: the deformalization of consciousness and, in that sense at least, the dehumanization of art. Yeats pronounced in 1931 that the long era of romanticism "with its turbulent heroism, its self-assertion, is over, superseded by a new naturalism that leaves man helpless before the contents of his own mind."[17] A generation later, Alain Robbe-Grillet proposed a new phenomenology of art for taking up that slack. The chief theoretician of the "new novel" has described the obsolete tradition that Yeats was commemorating as one in which "the word functioned as a trap in which the writer captured the universe in order to hand it over to society"; the appeal of conventional narrative to those who continue to cherish the tradition is that "it represents an order."

> This order, which we may in effect qualify as natural, is linked to an entire rationalistic and organizing system . . . In that first half of the nineteenth century which saw the apogee of a narrative form which understandably remains for many a kind of paradise lost of the novel, certain important certainties were in circulation: in particular the confidence in a logic of things that was just and universal.
>
> All of the technical elements of the narrative . . . tended to impose the image of a stable, coherent, continuous, unequivocal, entirely decipherable universe. Since the intelligibility of the world was not even questioned, to tell a story did not raise a problem.[18]

The idea of character in fiction, Robbe-Grillet argues, always involves an implicit and innocent declaration of faith in the worth of individual self-assertion, and he represents this subject in a way that is clearly pertinent to Lowell's sense of his own life.

> Perhaps this is not an advance, but it is evident that the present period is rather one of administrative numbers. The world's destiny has ceased, for us, to be identified with the rise or fall of certain men, of certain families. The world itself is no longer our private property, hereditary and convertible into cash, a prey which it is not so much a matter of knowing as of conquering. To have a name was doubtless very important in the days of Balzac's bourgeoisie. A character was important—all the more important for being the weapon in a hand-to-hand struggle, the hope of a success, the exercise of a domination. It was something to have a face in a universe where personality represented both the means and the end of all exploration.
>
> Our world, today, is less sure of itself, more modest perhaps, since it has renounced the omnipotence of the person, but more ambitious too, since it looks beyond. The exclusive cult of the "human" has given way to a larger consciousness, one that is less anthropocentric. The novel seems to stagger, having lost what was once its best prop, the hero. If it does not manage to right itself, it is because its life was linked to that of a society now past. If it does manage, on the contrary, a new course lies open to it, with the promise of new discoveries.[19]

If we adjust for the differences between poetry and fiction and then imagine Yeats situated at one pole in this century and Robbe-Grillet at another, it becomes evident that the Lowell of *Notebook*, as hero and nihilist, scion and nobody, is stranded in between, the worst place to be. It becomes apparent as well that he has moved poetry not only close to the experiential provenance of prose fiction but also closer to the ultimate discontinuity that has been latent in fiction's realist tradition from the beginning—a potential that seems fully realized in the austere epistemology of Robbe-Grillet.* That development as represented by Notebook, and in it as well, registers an uneasy détente in the engagement between the maker and his materials, a conceding of the world's decisive autonomy, a realignment of the border between self and its environment, a recession of form into the substance of its perceptions. If, as Robbe-Grillet says, objects and the world suffer under the "tyranny of significations," the compulsion to create signification can be a far more serious tyranny, which human consciousness imposes upon itself. For obvious reasons this crisis is a constant occupational hazard for poets, and it becomes critical to the degree that there is margin left in the mind through which the presence of the authentic world may intrude. For some poets, whatever goes on outside what Yeats called "pure mind" is immaterial. Lowell is not among those, and in fact the persona of Notebook appears to be inhabiting the worst of both possible worlds.

Again, looking back, we can see that the method of Notebook was inherent in the method of Lord Weary's Castle, and in this context their similarities and differences are instructive. Eliminate from "New Year's Day" or "Christmas in Black Rock" the tenuous connective tissues—pronouns, prepositions, and the dramatically transitive verbs, which create more the illusion than the substance of syntactic logic—and what is left is a set of arranged but discrete images and perceptions, disposed as the discontinuous syntax of Notebook. Reinstate them and what is gained is the famous Lowell torque and pressure, the baroque energy, an image in form of aggressive self-assertion. Self-assertion in form is precisely what is missing in Notebook's style, suggesting in the comparison that the poet has concluded that the rational will and the illusion of rational continuity are not identical. The Notebook poems individually, like those of Lord Weary's Castle, are built from fragments, but they remain fragments. They operate without structural momentum or the fluid, guided convolution of Life Studies, lurching from one instant to the next across frequently incomprehensible discontinuities. The poems give the appearance of functioning

---

*How close may be seen in Notebook's representation of time. Technically the volume is chronologically linear, but its real time is the atemporal phenomenology of the poet's consciousness. The irregular notation of dates and seasons only calls attention to the illusory transcendence that recorded time affords.

without benefit of internal memory, as if recording the experience of a minutely differentiated multiple personality. The important difference between this and Lowell's early style is not so much the loss of control as the recession of formal identity—an expression in the form of that consequence of modern history, the loss of self, which is pervasive enough by this point to be characterized as a traditional modern theme. The relationship between this pronounced discontinuity and the focus through-out *Notebook* upon the discontinuity between art, the artist, and the empirical self seems obvious. The wholly absorbed vision of Davie's "inexhaustible nature" or Wood's "encroaching chaos" is the motivating influence. The ambiguities of that vision implied in the mirror-image phrases create the volume's tension, and the exhausting conflict with encroachment is the cause of its pervasively demoralized and mordant tone. The ground of being exacts tribute from both art and the self at once.

Lowell's abstract city and associated object-symbols portend unwilled self-annihilation.

> Roads on three levels parallel the river,
> roads pace the river in a losing struggle,
> forces of nature trying to breathe beneath
> the jacket of lava. We lie parallel,
> parallel to the river, parallel
> to six roads—unmoving and awake...
>
> (*Notebook*, pp. 69–70)

Affective liberation in the experience of sexual love—Don Giovanni's means of resistance—is invariably threatened or thwarted in this way by the implacable autonomy of the objective world, by some intruding, often monumental, image of inertia.:

> I tasted first love gazing through your narrow
> bay window at the hideous concrete dome
> of M.I.T., the last blanched, hectic glow
> sunset-blackened on the bay of the Esplanade:
> an imperial shrine in a landscape by Claude Lorrain....
>
> (p. 68)

or by a grotesque premonition, here through a torpor reviving sufficiently to perceive its own state objectified (we walk "downhill" into "this"):

As if we chewed dry twigs and salt grasses,
filling our mouths with dust and bits of adobe,
lizards, rats and worms, we walk downhill

. . . . .

Six stone lions, hard drinkers, more like frogs,
guarding the fountain; their rusted arc-lights, rusting;
four stone inkfish, thrice stepped on, lifting the spout—
not starred in any guidebook. . . this city of the plain,
where the water turns red, as if it were dyed. . .

(p. 104)

or by a coldly lucid detail that cuts across a poem's euphoric feeling like an incision:

a silk stocking, blown thin as smog, coils in a twig-fork,
dangling a wire coathanger, rapier-bright—
a long throw for a hard cold day. . . wind lifting
the stocking like the lecherous lost leg.

. . . . .

Each hour the stocking thins, the hanger dulls;
cold makes the school's green copper cupola
greener over the defoliated playground:
clouds lie in cotton wads on the Dutch sky,
an end to the epic lays of dwarf and giant,
the dirt of students and the doctor's pearls.
My mind can't hold the focus for a minute

. . . . .

my *Absence* is present. . . .

(p. 79)

Each of these fragments expresses in Lowell's unmistakably personal idiom a characteristically modern experience of dread: that the mind set loose from its tether to explore freely in the field of perception will range dangerously, to be surrounded, enveloped, and consumed. Only the self's absence is then present, and *any* resistance to this encroachment, to the eventuality of blankness, is salvation for the self even where (as with Don Giovanni) salvation of the soul is not yet a moot point.

I've lived to the vibration of fulfilment;
the bash is a light sentence for my plunge

past galleried windows of the neighbor house,
this shadow built between the sun and me
gagging on the eaten air in the wellshaft.

(p. 182)

   Notebook seems fundamentally antiteleological both in viewpoint
and in design, and its illusion of random accumulation of unsorted debris
is an essential and even formal component of that vision. "What
distinguishes *Notebook*," Helen Vendler says, "is not particularly a modern
form but rather a modern mind. The mind is in thrall to history and
current politics; it reads newspapers, notices its surroundings, remembers
its private and public past, knows an immense number of people, and
thinks restlessly in eddies without any fixed center."[20] The fact that the
volume through its progressive stages continues to accommodate rather
than eliminate material seems to support this point. Its final reorganization
as *History*, all symmetry and linear arrangement, perhaps implies a
recovered equilibrium; but *History* is even more inclusive, and its
comprehensively erratic style remains the same. Lowell's calling *Notebook*
a "poem," rather than a collection of poems, focuses our attention upon
the larger hierarchy of its cumulative effect. On the other hand, if the
book's random inclusiveness has the point of subduing the rage for order,
the psychic and moral experience that it records may be described more
precisely as that of a renegade teleologist—the documented ambivalence
of a man who has been compelled by his self-destructive integrity to live his
way out of an old and attractive but unpersuasive world view into the
frightening but cogent implications of a new one. This would account for
the fact that the emphasis in *Notebook*'s idiom *and* structure is as much
upon the living of that experience as it is upon the shaping of it. Once a
poet commits himself to writing about his own life (a perilous undertaking
from the outset), if he is honest with himself he will continually be faced
with the possibility that he is dissembling, performing cosmetic surgery
upon the disfigured shape and form of the actual quality of his existence.
Whether he chooses to lie in this modest way or not (or perhaps lie less)
will obviously depend upon where his allegiance is attracted in the
theoretically opposed claims of life and art. Even taking *History* and its
form into account, it has become progressively clearer since *Life Studies*
which choice Lowell has made and what that choice implies.
   Once human life is considered to be without design, two alternatives
make themselves apparent: to remove oneself from it altogether in one way

or another, or to reconceive the relationship between the self and experience, to relinquish as far as possible the design-models within the mind by which the self is delimited and known—the "self-born mockers of man's enterprise"—in order to converge with the flow of "inexhaustible nature." Something like this full exposure is what Leonard Meyer has described as "radical empiricism" or, more confusingly, "transcendental particularism":

> According to transcendentalism, the constructs of analytical formalism—whether in the arts or in the sciences—misrepresent and distort our understanding of the world. What are truly real, and really true, are concrete, particular sense experiences. These are what we know. The rest is inference. Theories and hypotheses, hierarchies and relationships, are abstract, artificial extrapolations which come between man and the unique, existent facts of the universe. When perception is ordered in terms of such abstract categories, the primordial, concrete immediacy of things is obscured. We see a circle rather than *this* incomparable red roundness; we hear this chord as, say, a dominant-seventh, functionally related to the chord which follows, rather than as a singular combination of sounds valuable in themselves; and we feel emotions in terms of the classificatory arrangements institutionalized by our culture rather than as unique, incomparable responses. "At every instant," writes Robbe-Grillet, "a continuous fringe of culture (psychology, ethics, metaphysics, etc.) is being added to things, disguising their real strangeness, making them more comprehensible, more reassuring." To experience the poignant, deep-down freshness of things, we must get rid of preconceived categories, including those arising from personal goals and private desires. The world should be perceived and experienced, not in terms of self-interest, but objectively and disinterestedly; and art should be created in the same way.[21]

Of course, what is wrong with this argument is that it naively absolutizes empiricism. It is not possible to function in the world without abstracting principles and categories from experience, by which we predict behavior and events. The "continuous fringe of culture" that disguises "the real strangeness" of things is, at its least, the *quid pro quo* for daily survival. The experience recorded in Lowell's *Notebook*—"learning to live in history"—approximates Meyer's "radical empiricism," but the intelligently ambivalent character of his version of it supplies a cautionary implication: to choose to enter "inexhaustible nature" is to face the clear risk of being consumed by "encroaching chaos." Lowell can understand this for us because he is not properly conditioned for the role, because his is a traditonal, rational consciousness forced into a metaphysical environment where traditional modes of perception have become suspect. The poems remain sonnets, the lines iambic pentameter. The poet whom Allen Tate once sponsored as the exponent "of the spiritual dignity of man" rubs shoulders only uncomfortably with Alain Robbe-Grillet. Because he is never more than partially deprogrammed, he can never fully achieve a naive transcendence; and because his pain threshold is chronically low, quiescence is out of the question. Yet once the premise is considered, choice seems inescapable even where the dangers on both sides are fully understood and faced. This ambivalence continuously churns *Notebook*'s feeling and style.

Meyer also argues that a culture that either is or perceives itself to be static, a culture not dominated by "notions of progress and teleology, *Zeitgeist* and cultural coherence, necessity and organic development," will produce not a uniform or dominant style in the various arts but a "pluralism of styles" coexisting in a "fluctuating stasis, a sort of dynamic steadystate."[22] In short, once prevailing ideas of evolution and historical progression recede, a culture will proceed to explore and express richer and more complex dimensions of its own "manifest diversity." For Meyer, it follows from this reasoning that what is true of the culture as a whole in this state may also prove true of the individual artist, depending upon the range of his ability and the breadth and fluidity of his field of perception. Lowell's career would seem to express something of this same pluralistic character, especially considering the seemingly retrograde classical formality of *Near the Ocean*, and what is more important at this point is that *Notebook* itself is vividly pluralistic in both idiom and subject matter. One reason that Lowell can even attempt a genre such as *Notebook*, which for most poets would be a disaster from the start, is that his mind is extraordinarily capacious and richly eccentric in its operations.

In an interview, Lowell said that he had "hoped in *Life Studies*—it was a limitation—that each poem might seem as open and single-surfaced as a photograph. *Notebook* is more jagged and imagined than was desirable in *Life Studies*." Looking back from *Notebook*, one can see immediately what Lowell means to point to in the contrast: that *Life Studies* achieves its subtle power from a carefully managed uniform style at the expense of dimension and idiomatic range. For him to associate *jaggedness* with *imaginedness* speaks to that point directly. Elsewhere in the same interview

he speaks (echoing Williams) of trying in *Notebook* for the effect of speed—
"rhetoric, formal construction, and quick breaks"—the quick breaks being
essential for gratifying the book's and each poem's omnivorous appetite for
detail. "Much of *Life Studies* is recollection; *Notebook* mixed the day-to-
day with the history—the lamp by a tree out this window on Redcliffe
Square . . . or maybe the rain, but always the instant, sometimes changing
to the lost . . . I wished to describe the immediate instant." Still further on,
he says of *Notebook*'s style and structure: "I hoped to steal from the novel—
even from our new novel—because I think poetry must escape from its
glass. It might be better for a long poem to be drawn from *Madame Bovary*
than the *Cantos*. The *Cantos* did this; after Tennyson's *Idylls* or *The Ring
and the Book*, they look for transcendence in contemporary abundance.
The novel is the great form. . . little since Mann and Faulkner."[23] These
remarks easily thread into an informal poetics for *Notebook*, and what they
collectively depict is the work's effort to represent experience comprehensively, at all psychic, moral, and, therefore, idiomatic levels. Lowell is
expressing here lessons learned from both Williams and Pound: that
certain kinds of formality must be denied the poems if the objective is to
somehow compass "contemporary abundance." The quick breaks make
the poems "jagged"; they are normally executed in defiance of syntactic
logic; and they forgo altogether the available force of construction and what
Donald Davie calls "articulate energy." But the method is fundamentally
one of rigorous economy; its achievement at best is an illusion of density of
thought and image and (paradoxically) monumental, even sculptural
volume.

At the theoretical level of poetics, where getting all the wine into the
bowl becomes a serious issue, the most difficult feature of *Notebook* is to
come to terms with this scrupulously erratic idiom. A poet who will chance
an "image" such as this one—"Four windows, five feet tall, soar up like
windows"—and let it remain intact through two stages of revision is clearly
being scrupulous in a perverse way at the expense of the bowl on behalf of
not so much the wine as its sediment. Such, the line's presence in the
volume says, is the uncertain fate of afflatus, and thus the poetic spirit
registers its own neurasthenic exhaustion and permits objects to retain their
indifferent, unmodified presence. The completed statement in the next
line makes this intention ironically plain: "rinsing their stained-glass angels
in the void." The first line's banality is, in other words, its own statement,
tracing a moment's mood or tone, which expands to become the poem's
subject: "Time stops here too—Flesh of my Flesh / elastic past the mind's

agility"—a state of mental evacuation clarified by the neutral space between night and "uncreating dawn" (p. 188). One may therefore say of the line "Four windows, five feet tall, soar up like windows" that its idiom is too plainly flaccid for poetry, which must be firm and shaped (as Donald Hall has argued of *Day by Day*);[24] or one may say that the idiom of poetry in English has once more been extended—precariously—into the limitless reservoir of human consciousness. If one is unwilling to impeach, one strategy is to invoke Eliot on Donne and the subject of metaphysical poetry in general:

> When a poet's mind is perfectly equipped for its work, it is constantly amalgamating disparate experience; the ordinary man's experience is chaotic, irregular, fragmentary. The latter falls in love, or reads Spinoza, and these two experiences have nothing to do with each other, or with the noise of the typewriter or the smell of cooking; in the mind of the poet these experiences are always forming new wholes.[25]

F. O. Mathiessen characterizes that phenomenology more precisely:

> What [Donne] strove to devise was a medium of expression that would correspond to the felt intricacy of his existence, that would suggest by sudden contrasts, by harsh dissonances as well as by harmonies, the actual sensation of life as he had himself experienced it...[He] knew that no part of life should be barred as "unpoetic," that nothing in mature experience was too subtly refined or too sordid, too remote or too commonplace to serve as material for poetry. His great achievement lay in his ability to convey "his genuine whole of tangled feelings."[26]

It seems reasonable to assume that a poet who pursues Donne's course into the "actual sensation of life" is clearly in danger of becoming, in Eliot's terms, an ordinary man and of ceasing to be a poet "amalgamating disparate experience" and "forming new wholes." Clearly the Robert Lowell in Lowell's poems is becoming more ordinary than most criteria can tolerate, even in this post-Eliot era. But this crisis in an explicit subject of *Notebook*, and the very "ordinariness" of the poet's presence suggests that his crisis could be the crisis of any responsible being in this time, beset by its unpredictable and defeating contingencies. Had Lowell objectified himself, disingenuously as, say, a new Prufrock or Leopold Bloom, the mainly technical difference would have eliminated the scandal altogether. As it is, Lowell's *Notebook* pushes at the outer limits of Eliot and Matthiessen's theory of language as no volume before it has done.

I should make clear that I am understanding idiom to be expressive of mental activity as an object in itself, and therefore only ambiguously accountable to even the most liberal canons of poetic decorum. An analogy in kind, though of course not in degree (or range), would be the idiom of the Pound-persona in the *Cantos*. Perhaps more than anything else, Lowell's style in *Notebook* is remarkable for the willing self-exposure achieved in what might be called expressionist bathos: tired redundancies ("It's certain that we burned the grass, the grass is burning..."); inept forgeries ("for laws imprison as much as they protect"); brave assertions that trail off abruptly with the equivalent of a shrug or a wave of the hand ("The muse, a loser, she is sort of sad dirty—"). But to isolate stylistic characteristics of any kind from the gestalt of the whole volume is to misrepresent the nature of the project entirely.[27] For that total configuration is distinguished for being rich in expressive resource:

> our generation bred to drink the ocean
> in the all-possible before Repeal;
> all girls then under twenty, and the boys
> unearthly with the white blond hair of girls,
> crawling the swimming pool's robin's-egg sky;
> safe and in reach. The fall warms vine and wire,
> the ant's cool, amber, hyperthyroid eye,
> grapes tanning on these tried entanglements.
>
> (*Notebook*, pp. 26–27)

The last image here is so exacting in its implication and yet secures tenor and vehicle so firmly that it might be ranked alongside Eliot's "pair of ragged claws" as a model of imagistic economy. Part of its force is owed to the contrast with the limpid, picturable simplicity of remembered youth, and part to the image of the ant that intervenes grotesquely and inexplicably to break up the implied and expected linearity of movement. This dense. eidetic mode, or flaccid locutions like those cited above, may as suddenly be counterpointed by a sweep of traditional rhetoric such as this couplet from "Romanoffs": "Arrogance gives the mighty solitude / to study the desolation of their thought"(p. 72); or this one from "Napoleon": "The price was paltry ... three million soldiers dead, / grand opera fixed like morphine in their veins" (p. 77); or by the hybridized antirhetoric that is uniquely a product of Lowell's constant ambivalence: "Tragedy means to die . . . / for that vacant parsonage, Posterity, / tabloid stamped in bronze, our deeds in dust" (p. 167). Insofar as any principle could be said to account for this diversified range of styles, it could be defined as an attempt to reproduce the continuous turbulent activity of projection and introjection as the mind erratically relaxes, holds firm, and fights its way back against encroachment.

This whole matter may be argued by use of an analogy that comes to hand from *Notebook* itself. In a curiously consistent way, the *Notebook* poems are densely populated with swallows. Swallows are clearly creatures that can be represented in imagery along widely different points of a hypothetical mimetic scale, depending upon the convention adopted and upon the perspective. Unvisualized, the swallow may be vaguely a harbinger; observed in flight, it may represent grace and alertness of action—stylized by the distance, but still concrete and to that degree "real"; or, studied at close hand, in its habits and specific features it may seem nervously compulsive and predatory, even menacing. Its character, and with it the idiom in which it is characterized, will alter radically to the degree that it approximates the observer's full and attentive consciousness. This would be true for the swallow, and for virtually any other creature, one might add, except for the fact that the swallow has a specific literary history by association with its extreme mythic subjectification in the Procne-Philomela myths. The existence of the myths alone extends the expressive possibilities of the image, since the poet may either incorporate their symbology into his own system or, on the other hand, assume its viability in the mind of the reader and play against it. The former method has been employed in poetry from as early as *Pervigilium Veneris* to as recently as Swinburne's "Itylus" and Eliot's *Waste Land*; partly because of that, perhaps, Lowell's method is the latter. The swallows of *Notebook* are fiercely naturalized to the point of embodying an antimythological myth:

> Men find dates
> whenever summer is on, these nights of the swallow
> clashing in heat, storm signal to stay home.
> We will each breath, and make our peace with war,
> yearning to swoop with the swallow's brute joy,
> indestructible as mercy. . . .

Lowell's use of swallows as an image inescapably evokes the idea of the specific Ovidian myth and of the mythic mode in general, and then proceeds down the scale of stylization from the point of the swallow in flight to the point of the swallow nesting and grounded. That process indirectly shows the volume's deliberate saturation in demythologized nature. An anguished question poised in the poem about Robert Kennedy's death epitomizes the entire process of desymbolization:

> Who can believe the nesting, sexing tree swallow
> would dive for an eye or brain...this handbreadth insect,
> Navy butterfly, the harbinger of rain,
> change to danger in this twilight?
>
> (*Notebook*, p. 198)

What is true of Lowell's image of the swallow is true of his idiom; each admits of a wide range of perspectives upon experience, and *extends* experience; each is identified irreversibly with the viscous texture of *Notebook*'s ground of being.

> Our going generation; there are days
> of pardon...perhaps to go on living in
> the old United States of William James,
> its plaintive, now arthritic optimism—
> hear the swallow's coloratura cheep and cluck
> shrilling underneath its racket, *fuck*....
>
> (p. 241)

> Serfs with a finer body and tinier brain—
> who asks the swallows to do drudgery,
> clean, cook, peck up their ton of dust per diem?
> Knock on their homes, they go up tight with fear,
> farting about all morning past their young,
> small as wasps fuming in their ash-leaf ball.
> Nature lives off the life that comes to hand....
>
> (p. 216)

The first of these passages seems self-explanatory. It advances a nihilistic knowingness against the naive pragmatism of James; hearing the "fuck" in the swallows' coloratura is as significant as its being there. The second passage prepares the way for an acerbic ironic reversal: "Yet if we knew and softly felt their being, / wasp, bee and bird might live with us on air." The full antiromantic thrust of this poem is propelled by the title from *Faust*, "Das ewig Weibliche"—"The eternal feminine draws us up and on." The fanciful notion of the poet as myth-maker, redeeming nature and womankind, and preternatural himself, is affected here ironically, only to be clearly mocked by the larger content of the volume in which it appears.

> Now I can tan on my belly
> without impatience, almost hear out old people,
> live off the family chronicle—the swallow
> scents out the kinship, dares swoop me from her nest.
>
> (p. 217)

> When I show my head by your birdhouse you dive me,
> graceful, higher, quicker. . .unsteady swallow. . . .
> Who will uproot the truth that cannot change?
>
> (p. 215)

Lowell's swallows are graceful, alert, musical, but more often nervous, predatory, and ominous. The swallows that stop in flight "to see your beauty / and my good fortune. . .as if they knew our names," it is said, will not come back; the dark ones will, "killing / the injudicious nightflies with a clack of the beak"(p.210); and they are the same birds, we guess, manifest in different aspects to different moods. It may be too much to say that Lowell's swallow has shed Procne's grief but retained her savagery, since there is no use made of allusion in the text; but it seems useful for understanding Lowell's method to point out that his more naturalistic idiom extorts from the image some of the same qualities as the mythic and stylized one (especially Swinburne's in "Itylus") and that the prior existence of the myth is essential to the arresting effect that Lowell achieves from his radically expressive variation. *Notebook* either withstands scrutiny at the level of its total range and volume—as a poem—or it does not withstand scrutiny at all.

Lowell's allowing his imagination full range—the open-ended structure, the technique of discontinuous arrangement within that struc-ture, of the poems and within the poems, the prodigality of material and modes of expression—involves obvious dangers. The most predictable effect is the pervasive and stupefying drift toward inertia, both as a subject and as a formal characteristic. Against that, however, works the counter-force, the illusion of an almost continuous creative commitment, productivity, and alert intellectual attention. Both illusions are efforts of the same method, and their coexistence and the tension between them is the source of *Notebook*'s total illusion of a fathomless and harrowing authenticity. In playing to his strength, Lowell simultaneously plays to his weakness. Discord, banality, and opaqueness are the costs paid for the eccentric and somehow Byzantine ambience that Lowell's unique vision imposes upon ordinary, lived experience, and for the arresting rear-rangements of perception that has rapid juxtapositions and dislocations continually force us to undergo.

The activity of consciousness in *Notebook* is similar in form and effect to that of *The Waste Land*. It is less anonymous and therefore more consistent and visible, but it is in no way more coherent or systematic in its operations or less sweeping in its range of available associations. Since, as in *The Waste Land*, the uncertain dynamics of consciousness are as much a subject as a model for technique, in *Notebook* any given set of lines can accommodate the interpolation of virtually any image that currents underneath force to the surface. In a crude sense, the technique is cinematic: from some level below the normal flow of action comes an abrupt flash onto the screen, there and gone before it can be fully absorbed. In this way, *The Waste Land*'s disintegrated persona is haunted and baffled by the archetypal code language that intermittently breaks into his field of perception: "(Those are pearls that were his eyes. Look!)." All such interruptions in Eliot's poem are regulated by its theme. In *Notebook* there is no such control system to underwrite anything so uniform and unifying as a code. Insofar as there is a system at all, it is one of drawing abruptly together the past and the present, the trivial and the momentous, the grotesque and the beautiful, the personal and the historic to create a perpetually changing and turbulent mental environment that is alternately centripetal and centrifugal in relation to time and place—in Pound's words, "yanking and hauling," or in Eliot's "amalgamating disparate experience."

A modest illustration of this technique in action is the poem "Returning Turtle":

A week slogging the road, one fasting in the bathtub,
raw hamburger mossing in the watery stoppage,
the room drenched with musk like kerosene—

no one shaved, and only the turtle washed.
He was so beautiful when we flipped him over:
greens, reds, yellows, fringe of the shadowy savage,
the last Sioux grown old and wise, saying with weariness,
"Why doesn't the Great White Father put his red
children on wheels, and move us as he will?"
We drove to the Orland River, and watched the turtle
rush for water like rushing into marriage,
swimming his uncontaminated joy,
lovely the flies that fed the sleazy surface,
a turtle looking back at us, and blinking.

(*Notebook*, pp. 242–243)

The connection between the turtle and the last Sioux is easy enough to specify in analogical terms, despite the remoteness of the association and the elliptical syntax. But as soon as that logic is sewn together, one becomes vaguely conscious of a tear in it. In the space of that tear lives what John Bayley would call the "ghost" of the poem. Concepts emerge and circulate—displacement, the mysteries of symbiosis, the shared identity of simple and complex systems (Roethke's "Moss-Gathering" and Lawrence's "Snake" come to mind)—but none of this is organized or required to be; the texture sustains its own meaning. The fact that the phrase "swimming his uncontaminated joy" only makes it to the edge of sense would appear in itself to be part of the point: the turtle's final inaccessibility to our separated understanding. That separation is heightened by the anthropomorphic similitude in the previous line. If this poem were to be dismantled (as some others are for *History*), the three lines devoted to the last Sioux might well be transported, such is Lowell's method, into an altogether different context—for example, into one of the city poems, "A Second Plunge" or "Alba" or "For Norman Mailer"—and not seem much more or less arbitrary in effect. There are perhaps a dozen or more poems in the volume where the lines could serve as effectively as they do here. This means, of course, that the poems of *Notebook* do not have structural integrity of a conventional kind, and that they do not affect to. But it also means that the total volume has structural integrity of recapitulated moods and themes that lends itself to an infinite process of rearrangement and permutation, while remaining absorbed in and contained by the same central concerns. In this respect, the protean shape of experience is both the book's subject and its model. On the other hand, it is also apparent at many points throughout this text that the portability of fragments is a convenient feature for bailing out otherwise underdeveloped "sonnets"; where a *donnée* does not lend itself to a full fourteen-line development without thinning out, fragments from other settings can be called in almost at will to shore up the illusion of tension and density of effect. The tension available from this manner or organization is likely to be more static than it is productive, but since, as Hayden Carruth has observed, Lowell's tendency is to work in fragments in the manner of mosaic, this procedure serves the poem as often as it subverts it, and it may be cited as one more illustration of the bizarre ways in which Lowell's strengths and weaknesses remain intertwined.

Even at their most surrealistic, Lowell's "arrangements" give the paradoxical appearance of being firmly directed by some obscure intellectual process, as if ordinary human experience were being shared and reported upon by an extraterrestrial intelligence; and it is from this often baffling counteraction that his poems frequently achieve their most arresting effects.

> Humble in victory, chivalrous in defeat,
> almost, almost. . . I bow and watch the ashes
> blush, crash reflect: an age less privileged,
> burdened with its nobles, serfs and Faith.
> Posessors. The fires men build live after them,
> this night, this night, I elfin, I stonefoot,
> walking the wildfire wildrose of those lawns,
> filling this cottage window with the same
> alluring emptiness, hearing the simmer
> of the moon's mildew on the same pile of shells,
> fruits of the banquet. . . boiled a brittle lobster-
> shell-red, the hollow foreclaw, cracked, sucked dry,
> flung on the ash-heap of a soggy carton—
> two burnt-out, pinhead, black and popping eyes.
>
> (*Notebook*, pp. 24–25)

This poem is rich in ideas, although that aspect of its character can be obscured by the vivid concreteness of its texture and by the seemingly discontinuous form of the meditative process itself. But up to the point of the ellipsis in the eleventh line, which signals a pause and a turn, image and idea coexist in a secure ecological balance to conduct the mind through several variations on a ruling concept; an earlier age *less* privileged than ours because burdened by *noblesse* and possession, an age that, like the fire, radiates grandly while collapsing of its own weight; that fire (associated with Mark Antony's "evil" by the allusion in line five to *Julius Caesar*) surviving in the imagination of the poet; the paradoxically fierce and delicate character of the age's transience and mutability ("wildfire wildrose"); the poet's walking that setting in his mind, both diminished and clumsy in contrast; the insubstantial allure of that distant prospect signified in its reflection (in *History* it is "my lust's / alluring emptiness"—basically the same thought); then back to the tepid present (simmer of the moon—as much heard as seen; mildew; a pile of shells); a faint curve back to the heraldic past ("fruits of the banquet"); then dramatically the irreducibly concrete image of the fleshless sea creature, a grim focus for the converging themes of past, present, and the poet's self—a consumed lobster, brittle, sucked-dry, burned out, "flung on the ash-heap of a soggy carton." In a later poem addressed to Elizabeth Hardwick, Lowell remarks wanly: "We were sort of religious—we thought in images." Thinking in images is one of the definitive characteristics of Lowell's style. His mental powers are magnetized by the substance and detail of lived experience, and yet the poems that result appear to move firmly and freely under the weight. Hence, again, the disconcerting cuts from one context to the next, which appear nevertheless to be controlled by some intellectual process moving surreptitiously beneath the surface.

A poem that is parallel in method and theme with the one reproduced above (Poem 2 from "Long Summer") is the sixth poem in the sequence called "Charles River":

> Longer ago than we had lived till then,
> before the *Anschluss*, the thirty or forty million
> war-dead...but who knows now off hand how many?
> I tasted first love gazing through your narrow
> bay window at the hideous concrete dome
> of M.I.T., the last blanched, hectic glow
> sunset-blackened on the bay of the Esplanade:
> an imperial shrine in a landscape by Claude Lorrain,
> an artist out of fashion, like Nero, his Empire
> of heaven-vaulting aqueducts, baths, arches,
> roads, legions, plowshares beaten down to swords,

the blood of the spirit lost in veins of brickdust—
Christ also, our only king without a sword,
turning the word forgiveness to a sword.

(Notebook, pp. 68–69)

On first reading, partly because of its extraordinarily phrasal construction, this poem appears to consist primarily of flotsam drifting about arbitrarily in in the eddy of memory. When the apparent flotsam is sorted and integrated, the composition gradually reveals itself as a series of linked but fragmented meditations on another of Lowell's obsessive themes: trajectories and transitions. The opening line implies the downward curve of a life span. The *Anschluss* yields to carnage, which in turn evaporates into statistics lost in the thinning atmosphere of the remote past. First love deflects against the "hideous concrete dome," and by this implication seems headed in the direction of a portended fate. This portent is reinforced by the image of Claude's decaying monuments brooding over the backdrop of idyllic landscapes (a sense lost in the revision for *History*, which specifies a painting of Claude's that does not feature "an imperial shrine"). Nero the putative artist and empire builder is transformed, in part by the influence of a zealous passion, into a maddened and suicidal tyrant: "The blood of the spirit lost in the veins of brickdust"—subject yields to object. The spirit of Christ becomes an implement of agression—a thought that has affinities with the trajectory between first love and the sunset-blackened dome. In these ways, Nero is now more in fashion than Claude, his vision in a sense that of Claude's turned inside out. By spreading his association out over different realms of experience—ancient and recent history, art, sexual love, the *agape* of religious vision—Lowell portrays the pattern as inherent universally in existence, but only elusively visible because of its manifestation in allotropic forms. This is technique as discovery, and Lowell's trust in it continues to be the source of his originality. What the poems discover by remaining open gives strange shapes to experience and revised perceptions of its character.

Other versions of this method at work may be cited to indicate the extent to which a form of discursive imagism emerges as *Notebook*'s principal formal activity. Poem 4 of the sequence called "Harvard" describes a declining sexual relationship in which the margin for freedom (the "leeway") sought from it has been supplanted by the simpler, bedrock value of existential assertion. The last six lines transmute the thought, the

setting, and the situation by introducing an abrupt and arresting shift in
focus:

> still this is something, something we can both
> take hold of willingly, go smash on, if we will
> all flesh is grass, and like the flower in the field;
> no! lips, breasts, eyes, hands, lips, hair;
> as the overworked central heating bangs the frame,
> as a milkhorse in childhood, would crash the morning milk-can.
>
> (Notebook, pp. 80–81)

The relationship between the statement in the first pair of lines and the two
images in the last pair—more suggested than secured by the two
conjunctions—is basically the conventional interaction of abstract and
concrete: the two images give texture to the idea. But rather than clarifying
the thought, the images complicate it by shifting attention off to a different
space and then hanging it there over a suggested silence. We are left, then,
thinking on silence, which by aural association with the concepts of void
and emptiness becomes a condition to be resisted, to be broken. Hence,
the simple phrase "go smash on" assumes an odd metaphysical character
and reaches further into thought than at first seems possible. "I've lived to
the vibration of fulfilment," he says later in "A Second Plunge, A Dream";
"the bash is a light sentence for my plunge" (p. 182).

In "Dalliance," a similar effect is achieved by more overt means.
The dalliance of the title is again a sexual encounter that has hovered
tantalizingly on the verge of fruition; it is compared with the relationship of
Cassio and Desdemona and then associated with the comforting allure of
the "Macbeth murk of Manhattan." Manhattan brings to the poet's mind
Melville and his years of obscurity, and that association, in turn, calls up
Melville's own vivid image of the will, the self, on the edge of subversion:

> "I must not give me up then to the fire,
> lest it invert my fire; it blinded me,
> so did it me. . . . There's a wisdom that is woe,
> but there is a woe that is madness."
>
> (Notebook, pp. 152–153)[28]

Here there are two quantum progressions—the second, at the point of the
ellipsis, more vivid than the first. Up to this point, the thought process has

advanced fairly securely across the broken terrain and seems both enlarged and resolved on the expressed fear of the inversion of the inner fire, clearly the issue of the artist's brooding upon "dalliance." But Melville's paradox in the last line and a half has a separate interest and appears as a comment upon everything that has preceded, a sudden uncertainty rising to obscure the decisive articulations of that process: How may one understand whether the pain of resisting the inversion of the inner fire, or any grief, is an effect of wisdom or of madness?

The meditation called "Wind" is broken up by two images that simply float into the poet's field of perception:

> The girl has been rowing her boat since early morning,
> her jewelry is twenty wolf teeth pendant.
> The snail, a dewdrop, stumbles like the blind,
> puts out her little horns to test the sun—
> hard riding has never blistered her agile thigh.
>
> (p. 159)

Without this interruption, the meditation is uniformly focused: upon the winds that drive Paolo and Francesca in Hell ("the folly of Christendom that loathed her flesh"); upon the seed winds of an earlier, undissociated, classical time "when each progression of our carnal pleasure / was a firm extension of the soul" (reminiscent of the "pagan quality" Faulkner attributed to Lena Grove and her association with a "luminosity older than our Christian civilization");[29] and finally, after the interruption, upon the whirlwind of these winds mixed, "this delirium of Eros— / winds fed the fire, a wind can blow it out." The image of the girl rowing and the delicate image of the snail with her agile "thigh" appear to function in this context as suggestions of chasteness, of stasis and calm, and in that character bear a structural similarity to the Walsingham passage that briefly subdues the violence of "A Quaker Graveyard in Nantucket."

The paratactic arranging that Lowell executes within poems is frequently achieved in the groupings of the poems as well, and alertness to this stratagem can have a crucial influence upon our formal perception. The poem entitled "Fame" is an illustration of both principles in action.

> We bleed for people, so independent and selfsuspicious,
> if the door is locked, they just come back, instead of knocking—
> hearts scarred by complaints they would not advance;

it was not their good fortune to meet their love;
however long they lived, they would still be waiting.
We believed you, they said, by believing you were lying. . . .
Timur saying something like: "The drop of water
that fails to become a river is food for the dust.
The eye that cannot size up the whole of the Tigris
in a drop is an acorn, not the eye of a man. . . ."
His face in the mirror was like the sun on a dewdrop;
the path to death was always underfoot;
this the sum of the world's scattered elements—
fame, a bouquet in the niche of forgetfulness!

(Notebook, p. 139)

Here we have two substantially independent blocks of subject matter;
each is potentially material for a full poem, but instead they are cemented
together by contrast. Then in the last couplet, or in the last line alone (the
punctuation makes it difficult to know which way the pronoun "this"
refers), they are made into one poem, and the contrast is depressurized by
the effect of dividing both sections by the common denominator, which is
always death. But although "Fame" appears in a group of twenty-five
poems ("February and March"), it is more precisely situated, because of
thematic relation, in an undelineated subgroup of four: "Under the
Dentist"; "Sense of Reality"; "Fame"; "Growing in Favor." In "Under the
Dentist," the poet (as "Bob") is cautioned by his dentist against thinking
too much:

"Thinking burns out nerve;
that's why you cub professors calcify.
You got brains, why do you smoke? I dropped smoking, drinking,
not pussy. . . it's not vice. I drill here 8 to 5,
make New York in the sunrise—I've got nerves."

(Notebook, p. 138)

This character in the prologue of this group is a comically demotic parody of
Tamurlane, and the poem ricochets smartly against "Fame" across the page:
"The drop of water / that fails to become a river is food for the dust." "Sense
of Reality," following "Under the Dentist," has the attributes of an imitation
of "The Wild Swans at Coole," transposed to an urban setting. Erosion of
the body, of belief, of relationships, of joy is contrasted with the bleakly

unaltered survival from childhood of an asphalt playground. Then, two poems further on, the effect of *déja vu*—for both reader and poet—is reinforced by a concluding apostrophe that grimly echoes both Prufrock and the last lines of "The Wild Swans at Coole":

> My pinch of dust lies on the eternal dust-tray
> . . . . .
> Who will call for me, call girl, when I start awake,
> all my diminishment retarded, wake
> to sing the dawnless alba of the gerontoi?
>
> (*Notebook*, p. 140)

Feeling "the city jangling" in the nerves ("a professor might even feel the cosmos jangling"); time, aging and death; being a pinch of dust or a drop of water; remorse: these subjects adhere to the matter of "Fame" and the contrasting figure of Tamurlane because of their common magnetic field— the perception of the self wizening under the continual influence of external and internal forces. Retroactively the other shoe has already been dropped, even for Tamurlane: in Marlowe's play he says, "Shall sickness prove me now to be a man, that have been termed the terror of the world?" Each of the four poems is intensified and strengthened by contact with the others; critical mass is the source of energy.

Lowell's *Notebook* is inconsistent and multidimensisonal, but its organization is not haphazard, despite the occasional span of poems that are linked by nothing more than a common chronological or geographical setting. There appear to be as many principles at work in the groupings— structural and thematic—as there are within the poems themselves. The group called "Symbols" (pp. 60–63) is built around a common subject: congestion, crowding, and madness. The section opens on a clearly sym- bolic image of a well, standing alone with "no dwelling near and four square miles of flatness, / pale grass diversified by wounds of sand." The well appears to will its own solitude and rootedness and yet is understood to be, in its isolation, vulnerable to abuse and contamination. "It's not the crowds, but crowding kills the soul"; the soul may be crowded into extinction by the "scuttled gear" of other generations, other lives. "Hell" is a modification of Glenn Gray's description of a ghetto, which gruesomely echoes both Dante and Father Arnall's sermon in *A Portrait of the Artist as a Young Man*. "Rats" recalls, from the period in Danbury Jail, a Black Muslim's sweeping his hand "over the postcard Connecticut / landscape"—nature uncrowded and at peace—and saying *"only man is miserable"*; but the poet sees the Muslim's pessimism as simplistic, sanguine: "he forgot the rats. A pair / in an enclosure kills the rest, then breeds a clan." These laboratory rats murdered all foreign rats introduced into "the enclosure"; then, trained to identify an electric lever that could cause an orgasm, they "died of starvation in a litter of food." "In the Cage" is imported from *Lord Weary's Castle* to render for this setting the regimented hysteria of prison life and, by extension, imprisoned man: the "lifers" file in "twos of laundered denim," and "Fear, / the yellow chirper beaks its cage." "The River God" reports— by analogy with Aztec sacrifice—Mao's "final solution" for the problem of the leper population ("each family had a leper, fed it like a pig"):

> Mao announced the people's plan for leprosy,
> the lepers came bounding from the filth of hiding,
> . . . . .
> Then doped like kings, the boatride colorful,
> launched on the Yangtze with a thousand flowers—
> the river god caught them in his arms when they drowned.
>
> (*Notebook*, p. 62)

Following this, the setting constricts suddenly to the inhibiting, tiled quarters of the city-dwellers' more common enclosure. The leak from a faucet opens through an apparition to a tantalizingly buried image in the mind: "I hear their water torture, running rivers: / *Let us cross over the river and rest under the trees.*" The image is Hemingway's, but the method is Eliot's in *The Waste Land*. By fateful stages in meditation, an insignificant detail in the field of perception becomes isolated, becomes synecdoche, and leads to the ambiguous promise of an archetypal source. The poem and the entire section conclude in defeat, the imagination—especially the Platonic one—blunted by the poverty of its objective correlatives; even heaven ends up urbanized.

> We open the window, and there is no view,
> no green meadow pointing to *the* green meadow,
> to dogs, to deer, Diana in her war-skirt. . . .
> Heaven must be paved with terra-cotta tile.

To the extent that the imagination and the soul can be identified, this resolving image extends to a point of ultimate frustration the postulate of the section's initial poem—"it's not the crowds, but crowding kills the soul." In the continual engagement between subject and object, objectivity, whatever is external and opposed to the self, contains and converges to claim its most esteemed casualty.

The four poems in the group preceding "Symbols," called "Autumn in the Abstract" (pp. 57–59), are orchestrated in a way that makes analogies to music indispensable, even literal. The thematic contact between the four poems is tenuous; and yet, with this minimal unity, the poems develop from one to the next a remarkable progression and intensification which then resolves upon an ironic two-line coda, the idiomatic equivalent of an abruptly diminished chord. "Alba" initiates the progression with an image of New York on a dead Sunday embodying a monstrous blankness and void; the only animated object is a Harvard blazer ("a replica / of the one I wear") blowing in the fall air. With "In Sickness," the sequence gathers intensity and dimension:

> Sometimes, my mind is a rocked and dangerous bell,
> I climb the spiral steps to my own music;
> a friend drops in the street and no one stirs.
> Pavlov's dogs, when tortured, turned neurotics. . . .

The focus then shifts suddenly to the cultural mania of "Deutschland über Alles"; Hitler's and Il Duce's forces ("knights corrupted by their purity") on the march for *lebensraum*, "spaces enough to bury what they left, / the six million Jews gassed in the space to breathe"; and from that to "End of the Saga"—Kriemhild's barbarous revenge upon the Burgundians:

> "If they get to the air,
> and cool their coats of mail, we are all lost."
> Then the great hall was fired; we saw them kneel
> beside their corpses, and drink the flowing blood—
> unaccustomed to such drink they thought it good. . . .

After this grisly climax the final couplet is both a release or a depressurizing, and in its laconic dispassion a strange loop back to the tonal origins in "Alba" of the entire sequence: "The king is laughing, all his men are killed, / he is shaken by the news, as well he might be." A bizarre psychic pattern flows through this sequence—as though the mind, in retreat from boredom and then from the fear that boredom opens into, is impelled toward images of violence and bloodletting as a positive escape. In this dimension, the orchestration of the grouping is a form of musical statement.

The sequence called "Through the Night" (pp. 44–47) is a small chronicle tracing the mood of an affair in Cambridge, an internal monologue that analyzes from one stage to the next—from the point of meeting, through the night, to the point of the emergence of clarifying dawn—the sensations and implications of such an event as this, in which flesh and consciousness strive, ineffectually, to make a marriage. The sequence is controlled by chronology, and by a movement toward generalization in the seventh and final poem. But at the point of the sixth poem, this unity is broken abruptly by an extraneous historical anecdote and the only poem in the sequence with an independent title, "The Duc de Guise":

> The grip gets puffy, and water wears the stones—
> O to be always young among our friends,
> as one of the countless peers who graced the world
> with their murders and *joie de vivre*, made good
> in a hundred aimless amorous bondages...
> As some great hero, Henri, Duc de Guise,
> forge and Achilles of the Holy League
> whose canopy and cell we saw at Blois,
> just before he died, at the moment of orgasm,
> his round eyes, hysterical and wistful,
> a drugged bull's breathing, a cool, well-pastured brain,
> muscular slack of his stomach swelling
> as if he were pregnant...before he sprang, his sword
> unable to encircle the circle of his killers.

The interruption is astonishing and disconcerting, a wedge driven crudely and deliberately into an otherwise delicately constructed sequence. But just as clearly, this poem has erupted from another setting at some point during the process of shaping the sequence, and has been allowed to stand as a mordant commentary upon the experience recorded in the poems that surround it. By introducing the image of sexual potency striving against the course of physical decay (from "Achilles of the Holy League" to "muscular slack of...stomach swelling") and against death, the poem supplies a

response to the dispirited question that concludes the preceding poem:
"Why was it ever worth my while?" At the same time, this extremely
private interlude is ironically generalized by the new association, and is
anchored as well in the substance of history. The method of this
organization is analogous to Lowell's technique of interweaving dissimilar
idioms: here one discrete compartment of experience breaks open into
another, at the expense of the poet and his sexual ambition; the two are not
allowed to remain harmlessly autonomous.

The two poems that constitute the grouping called "My Death" (p.
129–130) bear so little apparent relation to each other that they seem to
have been brought together arbitrarily under an equally arbitrary title.
However, the title turns out to be the clue to and the focal point for the
generic subject that each of the poems addresses from a different angle: the
relationship between the poet in his role as a poet and the poet himself. In
the first, he is asked by the Monsignor of the monastery at Cuernavaca,
"Will you die, when the book is done?" In a related vein later in the
volume, the poet broods upon the limited nature of his own achievement:
"I memorized tricks to set the river on fire, / . . . and earned a pass to the
minor slopes of Parnassus."

> No honeycomb is built without a bee
> adding circle to circle, cell to cell,
> the wax and honey of a mausoleum—
> this round dome proves its maker is alive. . . .
>
> (Notebook, p. 213)

The living, continuing book is identified in both poems with the poet's life;
and by the same reasoning, life for the poet is identified with the creation
and publication of poetry. The last four lines of the first poem of "My
Death" raise another, opposing hypothesis: that the truth of the self is even
simpler but lies buried in the "random haggard sentence" of the poem,
"cutting ten ways to nothing clearly carried"—"Christ's first portrait is a
donkey's head." The second poem of the pair may then be understood as
an extension of the second hypothesis of the first. In the form of a
recounted dream, it considers possibilities that would issue from dying, as a
poet, into life as an ordinary man.

> The dream is changing costume, set and cast,
> all working more in character than life—

It is a sort of Harvard of the arts,
though none I met were artists, only people.
At the top of hightable, I heighten my jokes, and shake
salt on the winespots, till I sit alone,
talking to someone presently my father.
His hair, grown richer, peacocks out in bangs;
"I do it," he says, "to look manlier and younger.
I have had to sink all my spare money in courses:
calc and singing, and my trusty math."
We were joined in the arts, though old. Then I,
"I have never loved you so much in all our lives."
And he, "Doesn't it begin at the beginning?"

The people met here *are* artists, and the trick of the dream is to cause them to be seen divested, as the ordinary people that in fact they are. By implication, the same reverse apotheosis has transformed the poet-dreamer as well. Hence, he and his father can meet for the first time at eye level, so to speak; although they are joined in the arts (his father's being "calc and singing," and his "trusty math"), they meet not as artists—as artist and father or even as father and son—but as man and man. At this level, love is freely given and taken; the death of the poet is the birth of the man. Thus, beginning at the beginning in the second poem is the anologue of Christ's first portrait in the first, and each poem by an unexpected contact gives a life and dimension to the other that neither would have alone. As in "Sailing Home from Rapallo," an earlier experience of contact through humility, subtle intellection has awakened and motivated feeling; and the feeling implicit in the second poem of "My Death" is all the more poignant for being (except in dreams) beyond the reach of realization.

   Notebook's last full sequence, "Half a Century Gone" (pp. 258–260), is unique structurally in that it advances firmly through convolutions and digressions a single meditation. Models that immediately come to mind are "Among School Children" and "The Tower," both occasions of introspection, both commanded by the living present and yet evolving toward understanding through reflection upon the past. Like "The Tower," Lowell's meditation grows from a specific setting and its intimately familiar detail. And like "Among School Children," it conveys the articulating activity of the mind in the form, without its bullying either the syntax or the organization; the transitions between "stanzas" are more felt than seen. Unlike either of these two poems, "Half A Century Gone" concludes without affirmation or resolve except that of its own being, the mute affirmation that is the poem's existence. The setting is Lowell's West Side apartment in Manhattan, and the details of its character—the bust given Lowell by Elizabeth Hardwick for his fiftieth birthday; the circlet of laurel, now dead, crowning it, presented on the same occasion by a waggish friend; portraits of ancestors; other pictures not identifiable from the text; the massive windows—ground the feeling and tone of the sequence and become centers for the expanding and overlapping circles of meditation.[30] The poet's mind ranges widely through disparate associations, but the subject through all five poems remains clearly in view. This unity is symbolized by the delicate points of contact provided in the first lines of each new "poem," each of which in this sequence is more like a paragraph in an essay than a stanza in a poem: "*Those* serfs with the pageboy bob of Shakespeare's kings"; "*And* here on this very earth, *we*, like the others"; "We will remember *then* our tougher roots"; and, as the poem returns to its present, "On the rainy outlook, the great shade is drawn"—a line that because of the clustered stresses at the end is a striking rhythmic echo of Yeats. The integrity of this sequence may derive partly from the fact that it serves as a confluence of two major themes that have circulated freely and erratically through the volume's terrain up to this point: the peculiar continual imminence of death for the man of fifty, and the cruel frustration of a life's reach perpetually and eternally exceeding its grasp. Joined here in the synthesizing activity of meditation, the two themes issue at one point in what seems to be a resolution: how to want less in order to have more—or, as the volume's final poem, "Obit," expresses it, "the rest / of all transcendence in a mode of being, stopping / all becoming." But even that resolution remains unclear and infirm, for at the center of this entire reflection is the painfully realized identity of the life and death forces, the Dionysian paradox—

> I feel the woven cycles of His pain,
> reticulations of His spawning cells,
> the intimations of my family cancer.

In the first poem of the sequence, the horses of the poet's ancestors are "the gods of the city." In the last poem, their "dead sounds" and the "fertile stench" of their droppings ascend from the "war-year of our birth": "hear it, hear the clopping / of the hundreds of horses unstopping-. . . / each hauls a coffin." From these thematic stations, the poems hold a steady course through complex associations. The intimations of the family cancer (life-forces run amok to accelerate death), literal in the first instance, become figurative in the next, where the poet coolly epitomizes his ancestral heritage: husbands who could never sit out a marriage because "they lacked staying power" but "not the will to live"—obviously a dangerous combination. This reflection leads to the second poem, where the poet's own dying marriage is characterized as a loyal union of "professional sparring partners" debased only (a critical exception in context) by the "impossible love" for Beatrice who "always met me too early or too late, / piercing the firelit hollow of the marriage." It is instructive, then, the third poem asserts, in the uneven ("wavy") course of human life on this earth, to study the creature subdued to its element and function, the mole only in touch with what he touches or a half-fledged robin (aggrandized through field glasses) whose form and function are perceived as an "invincible syllogism." But here the reflection takes an ironic turn into a deeper past inhabited by older, generic ancestors: our "tougher roots," serfs and tillers of the desert, branded with another's identity, "the coin of Alexander," now laid waste beneath the sand drifts of Cleopatra, their own identities "simplified / to a single, indignant collusive grin." When time in the mind is given an ample span toward past or future, overreaching and underreaching reduce finally to the same leveled desolation and anonymity. Hence, in the concluding poem the poet's vision is once again blocked. The outlook is rainy, the shade is drawn, and what view there is left is "blanked out by blind brick." The only prophecy appropriate in this setting is the conventional admonition against false pride. The dwelling itself, "this same building, the last gasp of true / Nineteenth Century Capitalistic Gothic," by remaining, mocks the vanity of ancestral ambition, saying with Shelley's Ozymandias, long past irony's point of no return, "Look on my works ye Mighty and despair."

"Half a Century Gone" is unified in another way by a continuous subliminal contact with the language of the first three chapters of the Book of Isaiah: "And the strong shall become tow and his work a spark, / and both of them shall burn together, with none to quench them" (1:31); "and they shall beat their swords into plowshares, / and their spears into pruning hooks" (2:4); "Their land is filled with silver and gold, / and there is no end to their treasures; / their land is filled with horses, / and there is no end to their chariots" (2:7); "and the idols shall utterly pass away. / And men shall enter the caves of the rocks / and the holes of the ground, / from before the terror of the Lord, / and from the glory of his majesty" (2:18–19); "and their corpses were as refuse / in the midst of the streets" (5:25). Black snow grilling "on the fire-escape's blacker iron," the poet writes, inexplicably, is "Isaiah's living coal." Neither the tone nor the rhetoric of the sequence is public or prophetic; the echoes of Isaiah and Isaiah's Jahweh are wholly subdued to the mood and texture of meditation. The echoes suggest faintly, however, that time and nature remain as the sole executors of a vanished God, and in doing so the echoes loop the faltering pessimism of this sequence deeper into the poet's consciousness of history and time. The tone of the sequence is unmistakably valedictory, addressed to some invisible point midway between the poet and his wife, to the better selves perhaps, paradoxically, at the "firelit hollow of the marriage." "Half a Century Gone" is not a seamless web, but it seems so by contrast with the volume's other sequences, and the unpredictably formal resolution that it brings to the volume's otherwise inchoate development—especially as it yields to the elegiac simplicity of "Obit"—is a striking example of the authority of organized feeling.[31]

Notebook is a death-haunted and therefore ambiguously life-cherishing volume. More than by any other single preoccupation, the poems of this volume are bonded together by the poet's awareness of aging and, in the grip of that issue of process, by his recognition of time and nature as the true and only ground of being. He concedes the meager limitations of human existence and strives to salvage and consolidate what is left, while remaining fully conscious of the psychic, moral, and artistic risks involved in such a commitment, cherishing the ensuing returns from this dangerous investment (being in touch with what we touch) even when "we are firemen smashing holes in our own house" (p. 47), learning to live into history by risking—perhaps even ensuring—failure, but knowing as Lowell's Flaubert did not that it is refusal of error that breaks a life. Taken together, this is the principle of "the round green weed / slipping free from the disappointment of the flower" (p. 47). Generically the experience recalls the restoring fatalism of William Carlos Williams: "something which occurred once when I was about twenty, a sudden resignation to existence, a despair—if you wish to call it that but a despair which made everything a unit and at the same time a part of myself. I suppose it might be called a sort of nameless religious experience. I resigned, I gave up."[32] J. Hillis Miller cites this passage in connection with a reference to the resolution of Williams's early poem "The Wanderer" by way of characterizing Williams's decisive closure with nature, his rejection of the isolated ego of romanticism. Williams's wanderer is a kind of anti-Endymion; he finds identity by immersing himself in "the filthy Passaic":

> Then the river began to enter my heart,
> Eddying back cool and limpid
> Into the crystal beginnings of its days.
> But with the rebound it leaped forward:
> Muddy, then black and shrunken
> Till I felt the utter depth of its rottenness
> the vile breadth of its degradation
> and dropped down knowing this was me now....
> And so, backward and forward,
> it tortured itself within me
> Until time had been washed finally under,
> And the river had found its level
> And its last motion had ceased
> And I knew all—it became me.[33]

But the surrender that for Williams yielded freedom, for Lowell—classicist, historian, and American brahmin by birth and temperament—can only deepen a crisis of identity and further reduce the conceptual space between inexhaustible nature and encroaching chaos. Moreover, for a man of "about twenty" to achieve that resignation is one thing whereas for a man beyond fifty it is quite another, since long before fifty it becomes a habit of thought to understand the life-stream and the death-stream as a single flow. So the will reaches toward freedom and the mind reins it back—"*Optimism of the will, pessimism of intelligence*" (p. 182)[34]—a relentless, reciprocal action that chews experience into fragments and shreds. Within the borders of a single poem the poet perceives himself as shivering "up vertical like a baby pigeon, / palate-sprung for the worm, senility"; and in the next moment as strapping "the gross artillery to my back, / ...destroying what I lurch against, / not with anger but with unwieldy feet"; and in the next as "croaking" with King Solomon "'This too is vanity; / her lips are a scarlet thread, her breasts are towers'"—"hymns of the terrible organ in decay" (pp. 97–98). Williams's "nameless religious experience" can be described, as Miller has shown, in the language of Heidegger as a rejection of the secure, fallen state of the One for the fearful venture into self, being, and potentiality. With Lowell, the venture is repeatedly undertaken but blocked at the point of opening to potentiality:

A large pileated bird flies up,
dropping excretions like a frightened snake,
its Easter feathers; its earwax-yellow spoonbill
angrily hitting from side to side to blaze
a broad passage through the Great Northern Jungle—
the lizard tyrants were killed to a man by this bird,
man's forerunner. I pick up stones, and hope
to snatch its crest, its crown, at last, and cross
the perilous passage, sound in mind and body...
often reaching the passage, seeing my thoughts
stream on the water, as if I were cleaning fish.

(*Notebook*, p. 99)

A year's black pages. Its hero *hero demens*
forcing his ship past soundings to the passage—

(p. 172)

In my dream my belly was yellow, panels
of mellowing ivory, splendid and still young,
mellowing toward life-end like myself;
my green and brown backscales are cool to touch.
For one who has always loved snakes, it's no loss
to change to nature. My fall was elsewhere—
how often I made the woman bathe in her waters.
With daylight I turn small, a small snake
on the towpath writhing up the jags....

(p. 99)

The doubtful ambivalence is that of an intellectual being considering his creatureliness, led out by Heidegger, as it were, and drawn back by Kierkegaard.

there's a new poetry in the air, it's youth's
patent, lust coolly led on by innocence.
Gardens, how far from Eden fallen, though
still fair! *Hoc opus, hic labor est*—the lust
of Ulysses landhugging from port to port for girls....

(p. 71)

Optimism of the will, pessimism of intelligence. "Truth, alas, is the father of knowing something" (p. 32), and "the mind. . . is also flesh" (p. 106).

The consciousness of death is registered everywhere in these pages with a persistence and prominence that cause it to become in the mind the matrix (that which gives origin or form to a thing, or serves to enclose it) of the volume's full range of perception, thought, and feeling. It is implicitly present in the seasonal pattern itself and in the specific character with which that pattern is rendered. Although the journal encompasses a period of roughly three years (1967–1970), the book made from it comprehends only a single seasonal spectrum: from the end of one summer to the end of the next. "My plot rolls with the seasons," Lowell says in the "Afterthought"; and his wording, as well as the fact itself, implies the subordination of art to nature—"A little further on, and I am nature" (p. 139).

> To summer on skidding summer, the rude spring rain
> hurries the ambitious, flowers and youth;
> the crackling flash-tone's held an hour, then we
> too follow nature, imperceptibly
> change from mouse-brown to the white lion's mane,
> to thin white, to the freckled, knuckled skull,
> bronzed by decay, by many, many suns. . . .
>
> (*Notebook*, p. 22)

In the first summer phase, the emphasis falls upon transition rather than fruition: "greedily bending forward / for the first handgrasp of vermilion leaves, / clinging like bloodclots to the smitten branch— / men, like ears of corn, / fibrous growths. . . green, sweet, golden, black" (pp. 30–31); "we asked to linger on past fall in Eden" (p. 30); "The thick-skinned leaf flickers along its veins / . . . dancing its weekend jig in blood" (p. 44); "The green paint's always peeling from the prospect" (p. 47); "Randall, the same fall lunges on the windshield, / the same apples ripen on the whiplash bough" (p. 50); "the leaves light up, still green, this afternoon, / and burn to frittered reds" (p. 53); "the girls age not, are always young as last week, / wish all rains one rain—this, that will not wash / the fallen leaf, turned scarlet, back to green" (p. 65); "The sycamores throw shadows on the Charles, / while the fagged insect splinters to rejoin / the infinite, now casting its loose leaf / on the short-skirted girl and long-haired escort" (p. 66); "Youth's mobile, but no friend of the waste leaf" (p. 71).

Winter is an urban nightmare—blockage, congestion, cold inertia: a "defoliated playground" mocked by a "green copper cupola" (p. 79); "night-black days— / blanch flesh" (p. 92); rich, snow-struck New Yorkers "stranded" and "staring with the wild, mild eyes / of steers at the foreign subway" (p. 93); "snow mucking to pepper and salt, to brain-cell dull, / to ink" (p. 110); "the blind snow, blind light everywhere, / the sad, metallic sunlight of New York / throwing a light on something about to die" (p. 112); the purifying snow soiling "with poison when it hits / the Hudson's prone and essence-streaming back" (p. 126); the "minor sun, / our winter moon bled for the solar rose" (p. 126); the swan's "great glacier of flights that never fly" "hoarding under ice," "the great boredoms" that "blaze in the sterile winter" (p. 133); and, from Frank Parker's title-page illustration, Death astride a horse above Boston, "the eternal, provincial / city Dante saw as Florence and hell": "In daylight, the relaxed red scaffolding is almost / breathing: *no man is ever too good to die*" (p. 141–142).

O when will we sleep out the storm, dear love,
. . . . .
see at the end of our walk some girl's burnt-yellow legs
glow, as if she had absorbed the sun?
(Notebook, pp. 126–127)

Even the summery, erotic interlude, midwinter in tropical Mexico, is caustic with the savor of corruption and loss: an Aztec woman singing "adultery ballads"; "dry twigs and salt grasses. . . dust and bits of adobe, / lizards, rats and worms" (p. 104); "Toltec temples changing to dust in the dusk" (p. 102).

The soul groans and laughs at its lack of stature—
if you want to make the frozen serpent dance,
you must sing it the music of its mouth.
(p. 105)

Spring is scarcely perceived along this continuum, and then it is no renewing advent but an ironic counterpoint: water hyacinths sucking life from Lake Nasser, snails "with wormlike bloodflukes" poisoning the new canals below the Aswan Dam—"Pharaoh's death-ship come back against the tide" (p. 158); a "fountain's Dionysiac gushes, / water smote from marble. . . / going underground to the stone museum" (p. 151); sleep for the poet—"if such sleep lasts, I touch eternity" (p. 144); violence, atrocity, and chaos without—the Six Days' War, Martin Luther King's murder, Robert Kennedy's murder, the Columbia riots. Michael Tate is dead in July. "Hope is the must-be, the tomb of a small child" (p. 177).

In the returning summer, only "corruption serenades the wilting tissue" (p. 249). Rot proceeds without renewal.

> The wooden rooms of our house
> dry, redoubling their wooden farmhouse smell,
> honest wooden ovens shaking with desire.
> We feared the pressure might be too curative.
> Outside, a young seal festered on the beach,
> head snapped off, the color of a pig. . . .
>
> (Notebook, pp. 224–225)

The Democratic Convention "throws out its Americana like dead flowers"—"what can be" becomes "only what will be." The premonitory, predatory swallows return. Consciousness and awareness dim as if controlled by a faulty rheostat. The blood, "nine-tenths of me" yet "lousy stuff," is "lukewarm": "All else—the brains, the bones, the stones, the soul— / is peripheral flotsam in this live flow" (p. 223). Both will and intelligence here seem to evacuate or disperse into the setting of the seasonal torpor: "Some mornings now my studies wane by eleven, / afternoons by three. The print, its brain, / clouds in mid-chapter, just as I will go" (p. 216).

> Man turns dimwit quicker than the mayfly,
> asks sleepless drowsiness, not lucid moments;
> the tissue sings to sinew, "Passerby. . ."
> Dying beside you, I feel the live blood simmer
> in my palms and my feet, and know I am alive.
>
> (Notebook, p. 218)

Palms, feet, and blood are extremities of the self, and this minimal human contact is the deprived extremity of romance. The summer delivers what its spring has promised—the *nostalgie de la boue* that shelters ape / and protozoa from the rights of man" (p. 178). Lowell's "plot rolls with the seasons," but the seasons themselves are moved by a common undertow; each is a different dying. At the end of the volume's first summer season, the summer dwellers in Castine are departing, heading, in their own metaphor, back into time: "We asked to linger on past fall in Eden" (p. 30). At the end of the last summer, the fateful sign on the highway shining to Bangor is "the usual autumn / flight of Canada geese" V-ing above it "moonborne, / the path too certain; Dante found this path / even before the first young leaves turned green, / stark seniority that spined his youth" (p. 245). Here Lowell's is not the moonborne path; nor for him is the spine or the sinew of vision that might in "lucid moments" sing back to "the wilting tissue." This loss is the price of containment within the seasons of life and dying; and the only recourse clearly affirmed is that of his "Revenants" (p. 179): to savor "the healthy bite in the south wind," the "Spring. . . echo of heaven's single day," and "sun naked like earthworms on the puddly mall"—without their enviable option ("as little wanting our dust as we want theirs") of moving on.

With a somewhat different emphasis in mind, R. P. Blackmur once wrote of Williams that his poetry was almost wholly "unexpanded notation" that "isolates and calls attention to what we are already presently in possession of"; he added that "the advantage is the strength of isolation as an attention-caller to the terrible persistence of the obvious, the unrelenting significance of the banal."

> Dr. Williams perhaps tries to write as the average man—that man who even less than the normal man hardly exists but is immanent. The conviction which attaches to such fine poems as "The Widow's Lament in Springtime," "Youth and Beauty," or the first section of "Spring and All," perhaps has its source, its rationale, in our instinctive willingness to find ourselves immanently average; just as perhaps, the conviction attaching to tragic poetry is connected with our fascinated dread of seeing ourselves as normal. Dr. Williams has no perception of the normal; no perspective, no finality—for these involve, for imaginative expression, both the intellect which he distrusts and the imposed form which he cannot understand.[35]

I cite Blackmur's critique here for two reasons. It illustrates, for one thing, how close Lowell is running at this point to Williams's example. On the other hand, it also illustrates a vivid difference between the two poets: however Lowell may distrust intellect, and with it the "imposed form" that Blackmur implies is a natural corollary, he is nevertheless stuck with it and with the "fascinated dread of seeing ourselves as normal"; no matter how vigorously he labors to achieve Williams's "contact," to yield openly to the world, the intellect with its store of erudition and ingrained formal imperatives will invariably intervene.

So for Lowell even more than for Williams, the obvious and the banal which persist so terribly are within as well as without, built into nature and the self, and this dispiriting realization is nowhere more apparent than in his consideration of his own death. That unremitting necessity averages everything out, *is* the "immanently average" in demythologized nature—Edward King, instead of Lycidas, weltering "to the parching wind," without a prospect of the loving ministrations of choiring angels and the dignifying redemption through Him "who walked the waves." The weight of this thought exerts a demoralizing influence upon the creative will, upon the resisting gestures of language; and when Lowell turns sententious on the subject, it is addressed with a stark, awful banality that compromises humanness itself—another triumph of the objective over the self, as it infiltrates and then reemerges to corrupt the only redeeming grace, transcendence in language, that the poet can lay claim to: "A little further on, and I am nature: / my pinch of dust lies on the eternal dust tray" (pp. 139–140); "we [are] aging downstream faster than a scepter can check" (p. 30); "from the first God heeded His socialistic conscience, / gave universal capital punishment" (p. 142); "we are ice returning to water" (p. 246); "*no man is ever too good to die*" (p. 142); "man in the world like the whirlpool in a river" (p. 143). There is something coarse and inhibited in this material—a sullen refusal of the consolations of form, as though from a compulsion to trivialize and demean the self in order to lessen the significance of the event—either way, to average it out. In this context, Lowell's elsewhere representing "Fame" reductively as "a bouquet in the niche of forgetfulness" (p. 139) or writing in "Marlowe" (p. 167) that "Tragedy means to die . . . / for that vacant parsonage, Posterity, / tabloid stamped in bronze, our deeds in dust," calls to mind the supreme expression in our language of precisely this subject, "When I Have Fears that I May Cease to Be," and with it, two associated thoughts: that the assured command of language, syntax, and structure in Keats's sonnet was made possible for him by the small visionary margin implied in the slightly hedging "fears" and "*may* cease to be"; and that all things being equal, that small margin can make the remarkable difference between inspiration and total demoralization.

On the other hand, in *Notebook* the rest of the whole story is always somewhere else; form and idea change shape kaleidoscopically before any one shape can be fully assimilated. Reflections upon death and dying at other points, under covert pressure from the intellect, shape into a strangely figured and cerebral density. The notational style prevails over the syntactic organization, and so nothing like Keats's paradoxically authoritative formality can be achieved; but where the poems rise to the occasion, the effect seems close to the opposite of the willful subsidence that is evident elsewhere in such passages as those I have just cited. The authority that is lost with the rejection of firm rhetorical organization is to some extent recovered by reliance upon an alternative source of power—the displacements, rearrangements, and occult associations of dream logic.

> Both my legs hinged on the foreshortened bathtub,
> small enough to have been a traveler's. . .
> sun baking a bright swath of balsam needles,
> soft yellow hurts; and yet the scene confines;
> sun falls on so many, many other things:
> someone, Custer, leaping with his wind-gold scalplock,
> a furlong or less from the old-style battle,
> Sitting Bull's, who sent our hundreds under
> in the Indian Summer—Oh that wizened balsam,
> the sunlit window, the sea-haze of gauze blue
> distance plighting the tree-lip of land to islands—
> wives split between a playboy and a drudge.
> Who can help us from our nothing to the all,
> we aging downstream faster than a scepter can check?
>
> (Notebook, pp. 29–30)

The image of the poet awkwardly wedged into a miniature bathtub—a visual epitome of the pedestrian self-deprecation present in the idiom elsewhere—reaches across the body of this poem to associate with the fading balsam, the thinning haze, and then unmistakably with the poet himself as alternately playboy and drudge. The expanding reach of the lines between is the ironic conductor for that contact: "confined" by the scene, the poet's mind ranges with the sun back into the open space of history and there circles the time-frozen and mythicized epitome of a naive majesty in death—both Custer's and, from that heroic meridian point, the Indian nation's. The effect upon reentry is one of reductive contrast. In the flood of light from the past, the self—the moral and creative being—is seen sharply as both diminished or ineffectual and dying, without ceremony, and the two conditions adhere immediately on contact. "Aging downstream"—the drawing out of "our nothing"— is death as a wizening of both the flesh and the moral nature. The poet in his own poem has come to this realization not by searching it out, but by yielding passively to the random epiphanies of associations.

The poem called, with simple irony, "Nature" is a more firmly directed meditation on the same theme, and because it exploits a similar image system it can be read as a gloss for the poem just cited (Poem 12 from "Long Summer")."Nature" uses its own potential structure—a conventional Petrarchan structure—in a way that most of the Notebook poems do not, and thus it stands as one of the most cogent formal statements in the volume, moves Lowell as a poet slightly back toward the formal authority exemplified previously by Keats.

> The circular moon saw-wheels up the oak-grove;
> below it, clouds—a permanent of clouds,
> many as the waves of the Atlantic, and shingled.
> It makes men larger to sleep with the sublime,
> the Magna Mater *had*, shivers under oak, moon, cloud.
> Such cures the bygone Reichian prophets swore to,
> such did as gospel for those virgin times—
> two elements were wanting: man and nature.
> By sunrise, the show has shifted. Strings of fog,
> such as we haven't seen in fifteen months,
> catch shyly over lobsterboats and island:
> smoke-dust the Chinese draftsman made eternal.
> His drawing wears; the hand decayed. A hand does—
> we can have faith, at least, the hand decayed.
>
> (Notebook, pp. 246–247)

In the first two lines, the sublime is represented majestically as both action and stasis—a Van Gogh image in language, and a persuasive appeal to the exertions of the spirit. But by the point of the fourth line, reflecting on that illusion, it is clear from the sardonic inflection of "sleep with" that the enchanting fabric of this vision is about to be undone. Thus, Reich and the mystique of orgone therapy and its entire romantic origin are seen as the appealing delusions of a compulsive innocence. The point is then illustrated by another image and a corrective meditation. The exalting and measuring spectacle becomes simply a "show" and slips away, the spirit with it, into "strings of fog." This image gives way inevitably to a corollary in art. Even the stylized, de-natured image of the Chinese draftsman wears in time, and the hand that makes it ages in the moment it is drawn back. Death again is a wizening—eventual in different forms, but assured. The spirit wizens as the mind learns of the hand's decay. Death always has this chastening role in Lowell's meditations, an agent less of punishment—for moral foolishness in the first of these two examples and for pride in the second—than of poetic justice.

Seen from a slightly different angle, these two poems may be read as being concerned not simply with the subject of death but also, perhaps primarily, with the forms that death takes in the mind, with the way in which the thought of impending death surfaces unpredictably in response to any setting or memory, once the awareness or the obsession has set in. A third example, "Nantucket: 1935 (To Frank Parker)" makes this tendency clear.

> She never married, because she loved to talk,
> "You watch the waves *woll* and *woll* and *woll* and *woll*,"
> she lisped, and that was how we picked Nantucket.
> I watched but little, though I tried the surf,
> hung dead on its moment of infinity,
> corked between water, sky and gravel, smothered,
> smitten loose from volition. When I breathe now,
> I hear that distant pant of gulls in my chest,
> but death then was our classmate killed skidding on
> a Vineyard sand-swerve—a first death, and its image:
> your seascape of Moses breaking the Ten Commandments
> against a mount of saltgrass, dune and surf,
> repainted, then repainted, till the colors browned
> to a whirl of mud in the hand of Michelangelo.
>
> (*Notebook*, p. 48)

Without access to Frank Parker's painting in its different stages, the import of the "image" introduced in line ten is obscure. (Privacy of allusion thwarts explication more than once in the *Notebook*.) On the evidence of his drawings for Lowell's volumes, it is easy enough to believe that Parker's literal response to the classmate's death would be as overt as a painting of Moses breaking the Ten Commandments. What redeems that "image" from banality here is the poet's transvaluation of it in the reconstructing activity of memory. The apparent implication is that there are four stages of cultural transition: from Moses to the breaking of faith and authority to Michelangelo to now (the whirl of mud). How this conceit coheres with, let alone issues from, the material of the "octave" is difficult to make out, but the integration of associations achieved there is a model of Lowell's uniquely laconic eloquence—an eloquence that despite the casual appearance is, underneath, an eloquence of form. The maiden lady of the first lines (who, we learn in *History*, was Parker's sister) by a devious indirection sets an innocent perspective for the action that follows. She never married, she *watches* the sea, and from her literal and metaphysical distance the sea is merely a tranquil, tranquilizing, and stylized rhythm. For the poet who tries the surf, a shadow death is experienced in two forms: the exhilaration of the suspension above nature and time and the sudden terror of "being smitten loose from volition," a proleptic identification with the classmate killed in the automobile wreck. But the true focus of this poem, as of the other two, is the perception that death in the mind matures and ages—seasons—with the mind itself, loses its aura of both beauty and terror, subsides into a demoralizing and chronic pain that must be endured: "When I breathe now, / I hear that distant pant of gulls in my chest." Conceivably, this is the point of connection with the forms of Frank Parker's painting. Each metaphysical crisis is to a certain extent a crisis of identity as well, and the curve traced in the painting, from Moses to mud (recalling the "mud-flat detritus of death" from "Colloquy in Black Rock") may be understood as a reorganization of the curve implied in the sequence of associations of the first section. Dying is evil enough, but the attrition, the de-gradation, that the thought of death works upon the spirit is worse. The imagination may touch thought and vision into life in an image or in the arrangement of images for a transcending form, but real dying and real death is a gravitational influence that seeks the level of banality. Nothing but that is clear or trusted in the complex experience of *Notebook*; no life in *Notebook* is directed truly by will or hope or sustained by the model of art.

In *Notebook*, it is alone the ground of being that gives and the ground of being that takes away. Lowell's "Returning Turtle" is surely no deliberate and irreverent parody of Williams's plunge into "the filthy Passaic"; but to perceive at least an echo does not seem quite so ludicrous at the end of the poem, where the turtle is said to look back at "us" and blink. At that time the turtle is rushing with joy into the sleazy, fly-infested Orland River, freed from the prison of the enameled bathtub, and it is the human beings watching who are suddenly homeless. In the third poem of "In the Forties," the poet recreates an autumn day on Prospect Pond: "Our day was cold and short, love." The poet rows for the reflection of the sun,

                                          but it slid
between my fingers aground.... There the squirrels,
conservatives and vegetarians,
hold their roots and freehold, love, unsliding.
                                  (*Notebook*, p. 85)[36]

All of Lowell's creatures are conservative in this special sense: they
accept their state, in a contaminated river can swim an "uncontaminated
joy." In "Sounds in the Night" the animals are cats in heat and mating,
and the poet is again conscious of his preternatural isolation:

Sleepless I drink their love, if it is love.
Miles below heaven, luminous in some courtyard,
dungeoned by primitive wall-brick windowless,
the grass conservative cry of the cat in heat—
"Who cares if the running stream is sometimes stopped?
Inexhaustible the springs from which I flow."
Cats will be here when man is prehistory,
man doomed to outlast his eternal work.
                                  (*Notebook*, pp. 191–192)

The phrase "miles below heaven" recalls from an earlier poem, Poem 8 of
"Long Summer," the image of cattle "kneedeep in the cowpond...lap-
ping soiled water indistinguishable from heaven." The cattle, too, stop and
watch "us." The cats through a form of synaesthesia (the poet's contribution to their being) are "luminous" in man's unnatural habitat, the
"windowless" dungeon of the metropolis. To say that man is doomed to
outlast his "eternal" work is to say that he will outlast its import, its
measure. This poem seems deliberately placed against the one that follows
it, "Civilization":

Your skirt stopped half a foot above my knee,
personal birthmarks varied your black mesh,
and yet I praise your legs as generic legs—
and who would want to finger or approach
what ruminated through your printed sweater?
Civilization will always outdo life,
its toleration means to bear and ache,
hate, hurt oneself, as no one wants to twice.

> That's Locke, that's Mill; the Liberal lies with that,
> bites his own lip to show his icy tooth.

The liberal here is the minotaur stranded in the maze of his own eloquence, dissociated. He is the hopelessly bemused quester of the volume's first poem, slicing through fog—

> round
> the village with my headlights on the ground,
> as if I were the first philosopher,
> as if I were trying to pick up a car
> key. . . It can't be here, and so it must be there
> behind the next crook in the road or growth
> of fog—there blinded by our feeble beams
> a face, clock-white, still friendly to the earth.

He is the poetic self who might very well write the perfect English sentence and go to bed Lord Byron, but overnight change to an empirical self once more and wake up bald. Civilization—restraint, sublimation—is his chosen milieu; when sleepless he drinks the love of the cats in heat, he bends toward the earth, toward the "inexhaustible. . . springs"—toward the ground of being, which is nature in time. What is sought there is not salvation (since in *Notebook* salvation is beyond reach) but a recovery of the lost self, the life that this sphere of being yields in exchange for death. To arrive there, the rich man must pass through the eye of the needle.

> In backward Maine,
> ice goes in season to the tropical,
> then the mash freezes back to ice, and then
> the ice is broken by another wave.
>
> (*Notebook*, p. 216)

Bending the poetic self makes for an awkward posture when it involves maneuvering the armor of a lifetime's definition, cultural conditioning, and ethical idealism. When the poet says of a painting of Rembrandt's, "his faces crack. . . if mine could crack and breathe!" (p. 143), it is identity that he seems to be speaking of, so taut and constraining that it is felt and registered as a physical sensation. At another point, writing of the ambition of Marshal Ney (or, taking liberty with the facts, a symbolic figure resembling Ney), "He went on to be Lord Mayor or guillotined, / passed many varieties of untried being."[37] The personal relevance of this allusion is focused in the same poem by two images before and after it that contrast the past and present:

> In the village, the lovers
> stop for its unreliable clock and bells,
> kept straight by intuitive tact and considered malice.
> . . . . .
> The New York streets drink changes like a landscape.
>
> (*Notebook*, p. 34)

Change, the trying of stages of being, is the ruling concept of this poem, and it provides the common field for the otherwise gratuitous association between the New York streets and nature. In "The Nihilist as Hero," it is said that "Life by definition breeds on change." In a poem from the group called "Charles River," the point is put differently but comes to the same thing:

> If we leaned forward, and should dip a finger
> into this river's momentary black flow,
> the infinite small stars would break like fish.
>
> (p. 66)

In itself, change as a value is neutral, but in the familiar modern paradox it is also an order of continuum. In any case, it is a reality that cannot be evaded once its end, for the self, is firmly wedged into the mind. It is the *ideas* of order and stability that break under pressure—the infinite small stars. The river's "momentary" flow remains. Bending toward that flow is a labor of deference to the empirical identity and to the zone of reality that gives it being. The poems that address this subject are not cheering or naive celebrations of the life-force, but expressions of labor and conflict; and in their awkward honesty is the beauty, as in Hopkins's poem, of breaking and plowed-up things.

The above excerpt from the sequence called "Charles River" is from a love poem. It appears with the sonnet that, in a different connection, associates "first love" and "the hideous concrete dome of M.I.T." and with the sonnet that concludes, unpromisingly, with the lovers lying awake and unmoving "parallel" to each other and to the river and to the six roads without cars that also parallel the river. The group of poems relates a brief recovery (in memory, and apparently in fact as well) of an affair from deep in the poet's past—an affair that had promised fulfillment and had ended in manic rebellion. The rending violence in the poet's family has survived in his continuing, irredeemable remorse: "not until death parts us, / will I stop sucking my blood from their hurt. / They say, 'I had my life when I was young'" (p. 68). The course of this sequence is perceptibly downward, but before the pain of the past forces its way into memory, the flow of feeling follows the voluptuous curve of the river: "And now, the big town river, once hard and dead as its highways, / rolls blackly into country river, root-banks, live ice, / a live muskrat muddying the moonlight" (pp. 66–67). The deliberately antipastoral texture of this image is Lowell's way of objectifying subjective extremes, a way of pressing the register of feeling past the level of stylization that poetry ordinarily heads for as if for home. The river of the country is the river the turtle returns to, infested with life. Sexual love is like this in *Notebook*: both an end in itself and an access, the eye of the needle through which the poet must pass, or (to alter another of Plato's parables, and with that to invert the entire mission of courtly love) the ladder he must descend. At one point in a dialogue poem, someone, perhaps the poet himself, remarks that love is "all that keeps off death at any time." The line echoes Auden's assertion in "September 1, 1939" that "We must love one another or die," and both simple observations come to the same point: love does not in reality keep off death; it may not keep the thought of death at bay in the mind; but it prevents one from dying inside before one's time, opens the big town river, hard and dead as highways, to the flow and teeming profusion where the muskrat muddies the moonlight—as the stars touched on the water break like fish.

Sexual love in *Notebook*, both domestic and adulterous, wavers in character between poles that are suggested in broad outline by frequent allusions to Dante and Beatrice on the one hand and to Orpheus and Eurydice on the other. The poet of *Notebook* has always met his Beatrice too early or too late; and so it seems that the figure who might have been Beatrice in another time is in this one Eurydice, whom, in her opposed mythic sphere, the poet must face death to claim. The ancient myth and its recurrence in this new form do not coincide at every point; but at the point, for instance, where a covert meeting of lovers is described in these terms:

> your tongue as smooth as truth, your record player
> singing Gluck's *Orfeo*, the contralto's

"Where shall I go without Euridice?"
dying in our undergrowth, dense beyond reward...

(Notebook, p. 45)

the association is unmistakable. A parallel implicit in the contact in the mind between under*growth* and under*world*, a parallel that suggests a proximity of the two realms of being, again locates the ground of being for us as life embraced on the edge of death. An implied *contrast* both reinforces and complicates that implication, the contrast between art and experience, between the mouth and tongue as the implements of voice and music, and the mouth and tongue as implements of a sexual contact that is as smooth as truth, *is* an irreducible truth in this context, and in that sense "dense beyond reward." The relationship between the operatic and mythic expression of love and the carnal experience of it is in essence a recapitulation of *Notebook*'s generative theme, last alluded to here in the image of the muskrat muddying the moonlight. It is made more explicit at the end of this same sequence, "Through the Night."

We are firemen smashing holes in our own house.
We will each breath, and make our peace with war,
yearning to swoop with the swallow's brute joy,
indestructible as mercy—the round green weed
slipping free from the disappointment of the flower.

(Notebook, p. 47)

The proximity of the undergrowth of experience to Orpheus's underworld is at best a cautionary apposition. It serves to remind us that being and becoming in *Notebook* are not to be identified with joy or romantic transport and cannot be transmuted into spiritual revelation. The contrast between weed and flower implies a choice—of reality over possibility, of the suddenly experienced full intensity of being of the swallow, of life experienced as texture as opposed to form and idea, a density that is not so much beyond good and evil, reward or punishment, as prior to these and primordial.

Since there is no point in *Notebook* where the challenge of being is more than episodically realized, when *mutatis mutandis* "you are the music while the music lasts," as Eliot expressed it, guilt, doubt, and ironic self-recrimination are pervasive aspects of the chosen texture, contaminants in the river of experience. The liaison depicted in "Through the Night" moves from outside the experience, when the poet-lover hesitates in sardonic self-deprecation—"it's the same for me / at fifty as at thirteen, my childish thirst / to be the grown-up in his open car and girl" (p. 44)— to the center of the undergrowth and in the moments afterward "trying to extend the dark unspent minute, / . . . as my backbone swims in the sperm of gladness" (p. 45), to the point on the edge of reentry where the two lovers, still mentally invertebrate, are each other's exploiters, "two species even from the inside— / a net trapped in the arms of another net" (p. 45). Then, with day, surface the inevitable, ironic measuring images: an eighteenth-century oil painting, expressive of a vanished noblesse and naive order, "unfamiliar here" in the room, in the situation; on the walk home, "wrecked gingerbread Gothic" neighborhoods meeting a "pop-art playground of psychedelic reds"; images from the past of ancestors, "stern executors of justice"; Saint-Just, *Notebook*'s anti-Giovanni; the Duc de Guise, companion in fate of the poet; then, apparently, the vision of a formerly and naively imagined futurity, "a man of eighty with the health of sixty, / strolling his lawn shaved smooth as a putting green— / this scene I could touch as I touch your hand" (p. 47)—an image prefaced by an observation on the morphology of all imagined futures, "the green paint's always peeling from the prospect." The passage through this cluttered, distracting landscape earns authority for the contrast between weed and flower.

In the erotic episode recounted in "Mexico," the weed of selfhood thrives upon anonymity, escapes the confining decor of personal history, and finds physical nourishment in decay. "South of New England, south of Washington, south of the South" (south of time, in effect), the lovers find themselves to be bull and cow "obliviously pairing," "drawn on" only by "unlimited desire"; the poet's "grizzled laurels" become "spines of hay." On an aimless walk, they are "shown up" briefly by the headlights of a passing car, then once again they are "gone," back into the darkness, living in history (p. 103). A lizard is regarded enviously:

> [He] does nothing for days but puff his throat
> for oxygen, and tongue up passing flies,
> sees only similar rusty lizards pant:
> harems worthy this lord of the universe—
> each thing he does generic, and not the best.
> How fragrantly our cold hands warm to the live coal!
>
> (*Notebook*, p. 102)

Generic here is normative, the ground of prehistory. The season is inverted: "Midwinter in Mexico, yet the tall red flowers / stand up on many trees, and all's in leaf; / twilight bakes the wall-brick large as a loaf of bread" (p. 103). The lovers seek the unity and calm of a generic oblivion at the bottom of time: "we two are clocks, and only count in time" (this means both things: only count time in time and only matter in time), "the hand's knife-edge is pressed against the future" (p. 101); "we sit on the cliff like curs / . . . / two clocks set back to the Toltec Eden" (pp. 102–103). When the two are together, time and space are a continuous flow—"the bricks glide; the commonest / minute is not divided." When they are separated, time recovers definition—"each hour of the day, / each minute of the hour, each second of the minute" (pp. 103–104). They walk willfully *downhill* into corruption—"devotion hikes uphill in iron shoes" (p. 105)—and in this sustaining oblivion their roles and motivation become briefly typological, their identities ancient. They may be Aztec in the age of the Fifth Sun—"We sun people know the sun, the source of life, / will die unless we feed it human blood" (p. 101); or Toltec earlier, "as if we still wished to pull teeth with firetongs— / when they took a city, they too murdered everything: / man, woman and child, down to the pigs and dogs" (p. 103); in either role cruelly obedient to a primitive God. But anywhere in a Lowell poem is above the epicenter of modern time. In Mexico it breaks through the ambience in the form of the heretical order of Emmaus of Cuernavaca with its avant-garde crucifixes, gay prior, "lay-neurotics," and whitewashed cabins, "named / *Sigmund* and *Karl*" (p. 102) or mnemonically as the tea, bouillon cubes, and cookies "bought and brought from Boston" (p. 105). The grip upon the dream is loosened and "those *other yous*" surface on the other side of the inversion.

We're burnt, black chips knocked from the blackest stock:
Potato-famine Irish-Puritan, and Puritan—
gold made them smile like pigs once, then fear of falling—
hipbones finer than a breast of squab,
eyes hard as stars, hearts small as elves, they turned
the wilderness to wood, then looked for trees.
They are still looking. Now our hesitant
conversation moves from lust to love;
friendship, without dissension, multiplying
days, days, days, days—how can I love you more,
short of turning into a criminal?

(*Notebook*, pp. 106–107)

Implied here is an analogy between the mutual Puritan forebears' turning
the wilderness to wood and then looking for trees, and "our" conversation's
moving from lust to love. That recognition alone is a reminder of how
obedient any poem or experience of Lowell's is, even in resistance, to the
rule of intellect, and of how that obedience is not so much willed as it is
locked in. When this episode is recalled in the brief sequence "Eight
Months Later," its deciduous character is the focus and, grimly, its full
symbolic meaning—especially as it foreshadows (unwittingly, of course, at
this stage) the contentions and doomed third marriage of The Dolphin and
Day by Day.

> Where is Mexico?
> Who will live this year back, cat on the ladder?
> (Notebook, p. 209)

> The mule-man lost his footing in the clouds,
> seed of the dragon coupled in the caves. . .
> The cliff drops; over it, the water drops,
> and steams away the marks that led us on.
> (Notebook, pp. 209–210)

Notebook, taken as a poem, is a traditional work in that it wrestles in
an ancient conflict—another monument to the fate of human beings (in a
world with or without God) which requires them to find a place in the
incompatible environments of mind and nature. Its specifically modern
realization is expressed in its form: the equation is not resolved in whole
numbers (as it is, for example, in Pope), but in a series of infinitely
reorganizing and receding fractions. The ironies are immense, foreseen,
and willingly undertaken. Like Eliot's Gerontion, the poet of Notebook
finds that in imposing the action of thought ("think. . . think now. . . think
at last") upon the content of thought, he produces instead of the desired
effect of coherence, form, and energy the very opposite effect of dispersal,
confusion, and inertia. Each either savors or seeks an optional mode of
being in fantasy or fact: being in action knee-deep in a salt marsh in the
warm rain bitten by flies heaving a cutlass—or being in sexual love:

> I'm through with looking steadily at the worst—
> Chaucer's old January made hay with May.
> In this ever more enlightened room,

I wake beside the early rising sun,
sex indelible on the flowering air—
shouldn't I pray for us to hold forever,
body of dolphin, breast of cloud?

(*Notebook*, p. 92)

In both contexts, the subtle distinction between *holding* and *being* is
the field of action of the poem and finally its *raison d'être*. Resolution,
except in death, is a culturally conditioned mythology, receding in this
book and its time to join other fatalities of the imagined life. The only
remotely available transcendence is the cold comfort of understanding; and
yet understanding in *Notebook* is its most excruciating irony. Two of the
many poems about creatures of nature—"Trout" and "Seals"—seem to
epitomize this aspect of the volume's subject, as well as the strangely
demoralized honesty and fortitude with which it is faced. The first, a fairly
faithful rendering of Schubert's "Die Forelle" (poem by Christian
Schubart) becomes in Lowell's context a parable or allegory, and
describing it as such makes interpretative commentary virtually redundant.

I lean by a bridgehead watching the clear calm,
a homeless sound of joy is in the sky:
a fisherman making falsecasts over a brook,
a two pound browntrout darting with scornful quickness,
drawing straight lines like arrows through the pool.
The man might as well break his rod in his fist,
his trembling boot or finger scares the fish;
trout will never hit flies in this brightness.
The man with the rod keeps watching on his bank,
he wades, he stamps his feet, he muddies the water;
before I know it, his rod begins to dip.
He wades, he stamps, he shouts to turn the run
of the trout with his wetfly breathed into its belly—
broken whiplash in the gulp of joy.

(*Notebook*, p. 98)

The "trout" making straight lines in the clear pool is charismatically
beautiful and affecting, as though an echo from a prelapsarian past; and the
trout is the poem's protagonist, striking the fly—taking the main chance—
only when his vision is clouded. In the second poem, "Seals," the theme
of "Trout" is reconsidered and the irony, as a consequence, is overt, a

visible part of the poem's action. "Seals" is a New Jerusalem poem, a "Sailing to Byzantium" in reverse, beginning where the imagined journey of Yeats's poem is ambiguously resolved.

> If we must live again, not us; we might
> go into seals, we'd handle ourselves better:
> able to dawdle, able to torpedo,
> all too at home in our double elements,
> our third of rocks and ledges—if man were dormant. . .
> We flipper the harbor, blots and patches and oilslick
> so much bluer than water, we think it sky.
> Creature could face creator in this suit,
> fishers of fish not men. Some other August,
> the easy seal might say, "I could not sleep
> last night; suddenly I could write my name."
> Then all seals, preternatural like us,
> take direction, head north—their haven
> green ice in a greenland never grass.
>
> (*Notebook*, pp. 249–250)

The obvious difference is that whereas Yeats conceives the journey away from nature and out of time as an effort of the creative will, for Lowell it is predetermined, the curse of a genesis under the wrong sign. On the other hand, given the resemblance between Lowell's "greenland never grass" and the eerie inertia of Yeats's Byzantium and the implied yearning, therefore, of his golden bird back toward the realm of "what is past or passing or to come," the two poets are perhaps not so far apart as at first they seem. It might be said that all poets who attend the opposed voices of the self and the soul move eventually in the same circles.

   Notebook became *History* as an afterthought. Lowell's friend Frank Bidart, who participated in *History*'s revisions, confirms what Stephen Yenser had guessed at: that *For Lizzie and Harriet* was the first book to be made from relevant materials excised from *Notebook* and that the plan of *History* came about as a device for reorganizing the materials that were left (along with the new poems to be added).[38] Without the personal poems that had formed the basis for *Notebook*'s seasonal structure, the remainder of *Notebook* was left with no structure at all. The solution that presented itself was to arrange the surviving and new poems in a rough chronological sequence, beginning with the very beginning of time. This was a resourceful but also somewhat arbitrary strategy, a virtue made of necessity; and since the results, in any case, are now fixed in place, *History* will eventually have to be dealt with on its own terms. Those terms, however, are markedly different from *Notebook*'s and not always to the later volume's advantage.

One damaging effect of the transformation of *Notebook* into *History* is that the eccentric style of the new volume is left without formal authorization. It is a notebook style, brilliantly effective at its best at registering what experience is like at the fluid border between subject and object, in the continuing present that is the consciousness-time of the original poem. *Notebook* is not a memoir or an autobiography or history but what it declares itself to be, which is its reason for being. The style of *Notebook*, in other words, is essentially appropriate for interior monologue in a moving present and justifiable only to the extent that it is harnessed securely and comprehensibly to that purpose. *History*, however, has no firmly identified protagonist whose consciousness we are attending; it is not invigorated by the quirky, palpable atmosphere of specific settings (Cambridge, New York, Castine, Mexico), and it presents no characterization of time whatever. Time in *History* is merely an idea, an abstraction, not a medium within which we live: the day-to-day, the seasonal, the real rhythm of experience, in other words, from which the written word of *Notebook* seems inseparable. The sense of intimacy that gave *Notebook* its mysterious life does not survive the transformation. *History* is not altogether successful, therefore, as a formal enterprise because it has merely adapted a style conceived for one design to a new design for which it is not suited. In this respect it is *History* rather than *Notebook* that is random, and careful readers of both volumes may perceive readily how the poems transposed from *Notebook* are stunned by *History*'s mechanical, symmetrical organization into the poetical equivalent of an inorganic state. This odd discontinuity—in effect, between style and point of view—is marginally less conspicuous after the chronology enters the time of Lowell's own life span, roughly at the point of "Wolverine, 1927"; but of course at that point the history paradigm itself has ceased to be relevant. The poet's consciousness is born, as it were, halfway through, and the experience in that subsequent time period is more personal and at least contemporaneous; but the first half of the book is then left seeming vaguely stranded.

Another important effect is that, epistemologically speaking, *History* turns *Notebook* inside out. It changes what was overtly subjective into an ostensibly objective structure, with the effect of hardening the attitudes.

Whereas in *Notebook* the focus was first of all on the activity of consciousness and second on the contents of that consciousness, in *History* the content has achieved an autonomous status, and the mind's influence upon that material, though still evident, of course, in the idiosyncratic style, is downplayed. What was dominant in one volume is recessive in the other and vice versa. In *Notebook* the cynicism shown toward historical figures could be taken at least partially as a projection of the poet's own identity, an aspect of an ongoing process of self-discovery; but in *History* Lowell takes the long aerial view, and the verdicts have edged toward the absolute authority of fact. *History* is therefore by a wide margin the more pessimistic of the two volumes. It is all the more so since the poignantly few domestic and extradomestic romantic interludes that gave *Notebook* a faltering sense of human purpose, an affirmative orientation, in *History* have been cut away. The feeling man in the poems in *History* is claimed almost wholly by his own cynicism. Moreover, by linearizing for *History* the basic material of *Notebook*, Lowell has made the former volume's implicit antimeliorism retroactive and therefore more emphatic. *History* fiercely spatializes time and human experience, and our moral nature in that stasis becomes inert. The obvious effect is that the familiar modernist recourse of nostalgic time-travel is disallowed. As there is no refuge before us (except death), there is now none behind us either, for whatever comfort the past may have been in any case. The powerful men and women of history in the new arrangement are more obviously simply replications of each other, demotic versions of Ozymandias; and their story, so exposed, becomes numbingly redundant, and poetically less interesting. It is not only no longer possible to be placated by illusions; it is also no longer possible to revere—or simply not be bored by—the truth.

When we move from *Notebook* to *History*, nothing ontologically has truly changed—human life is unfulfilling in either setting; but the emphasis is noticeably different. Yenser points out that *History* can also be read as his-story. The pun shows the margin of difference between the second version and the first, and the life of the one within the other. All of experience for Lowell tends to be "his story," no matter how it is laid out. It is all appropriated and internalized in radically personal ways. *History* as a concept seems grandiose, especially compared with the modesty of its predecessor, but it may in fact be quite the reverse—that is, a concession on Lowell's part of his failure to free himself from the confining patterns of his own thought.

The volume's first poem, itself called "History," foretells the themes of the volume by modifying the most familiar symbol of a more credulous romantic era.

> As in our Bibles, white-faced, predatory,
> The beautiful, mist-drunken hunter's moon ascends—
> a child could give it a face: two holes, two holes,
> my eyes, my mouth, between them a skull's no-nose—
> O there's a terrifying innocence in my face
> drenched with the silver salvage of the mornfrost.

It is important to recognize in passages such as this one the ambivalence that is indicated, almost unwillingly, in the diction—a conflict between a residual lyricism and the poem's grinding fatalism, which in the end prevails. In the preceding lines of the poem, it is made clear that the poet is unable to envision our mythic beginnings in innocence without subordinating the Edenic aspect to the post-Edenic; what is stressed is the admonitory episode of Cain and Abel. The "terrifying innocence in my face" associates the poet with the moon's skull face and with the innocence of Abel and its fateful consequence. If there is, as Yenser suggests, a bizarre pun on "no-nose," it might be understood to refer not only to a cosmic tyranny but also to a denial of possibility—a denial that the death's head in the moon's face only reinforces. But the moon's face is also Lowell's and therefore no portal but a mirror, another dead end. Perhaps that is an innocence—an inviolability of the ego—that is justly terrifying in its own right.

In "Flaw," later, that projecting solipsism is associated with the physically harmless but psychically pathogenic defect of his "old eye-flaw,"

>   sprouting bits and strings
> gliding like dragon-kites in the Midwestern sky—
> I am afraid to look closely and count them;
> today I am exhausted and afraid.
> I look through the window at unbroken white cloud,
> and see in it my many flaws are one
> a flaw with a tail the color of shed skin,
> inaudible rattle of the rattler's disks.

Both curious and typical in this episode is the way in which this common spectacle of air travel, exhilarating to some observers (as is the moon), becomes for Lowell in a mood of anxiety and exhaustion simply one more sinister portent, a not merely hopeless but even threatening prospect. The shed skin becomes a rattler's disks—eerily inaudible—and the disks "the first scrape of the Thunderer's fingernail." The large meaning is hidden in the small, as the minute flaw is magnified in perspective upon the clouds. This is a gloss upon Lowell's many juxtapositions in both *Notebook* and *History* of the momentous and the trivial; but as both "History" and "Flaw" imply, he has somehow lost control over his own powers of signification. This theme stays in the foreground in *History*, especially in poems that have to do with the subject of his failing eyesight. Thus, in "Fears of Going Blind (For Wyndham Lewis)" two levels of meaning are quite clearly intended:

> I see non sequitur:
> *Watch the stoplights, they are leopard's eyes;*
> *what's the word for God if he has four legs?* . . .
> Even the artist's vision picks up dirt,
> the jelly behind the eyeball will leak out,
> you will live with a constellation of flusters,
> comet-flashes from the outer corners . . .
>
> *(History,* p. 141)

Lowell is as ready to deglamorize the artist's vision as he is history, that vision's subject matter, and to concede that the vision is necessarily flawed and doomed. The non sequitur he speaks of is evidently the paranoid transition from simple stoplights to sinister leopard's eyes, and from the leopard to a four-legged predatory God. This nameless God is to the Christian vision what leaking eyeball jelly is to the artist's. His own vision is not something that he chooses, or by which he is redeemed or even gratified; it is something that he cannot escape. The "failed surgeon" who in this poem cannot save the eye and exits "with a smile" suggests with irony "the wounded surgeon" of Eliot's "East Coker" whose "sharp compassion of the healer's art" resolves "the enigma of the fever chart" and saves the patient whose suffering in the world ensures his spiritual health.

Alan Williamson points out that the "concept 'God' has been making a surreptitious comeback in Lowell's [recent] poetry."[39] *History* contains as many as forty poems that make direct reference to God, but the God of this vision is no being with whom one would cheerfully consort. He is at best as featureless as the God of Christian existentialism; at worst he is sinister and unpredictable, an adversary of humanity rather than an ally:

> But was there some shining, grasping hand to guide
> me when I breathed through gills, and walked on fins
> through Eden, plucking the law of retribution from the tree?
> Was the snake in the garden, an agent provocateur?
> Is the Lord increased by desolation?
>
> ("Our Fathers," *History*, p. 26)

Strictly speaking, this question is not necessarily facetious. Since in the Hebrew tradition, and in the Old Testament generally, there is no autonomous evil force such as the Christian Satan opposing God, there is logically no being for the serpent to represent in the unfallen garden but God himself. God and man in Lowell's revisions of history are therefore off to a considerably worse start than is generally supposed, each guilty of having betrayed the other. We are familiar with this contest from *Lord Weary's Castle*, where it is prosecuted less explicitly but with greater intensity. That it should now reassert itself at this later point in Lowell's career shows how deeply entrenched his religious nihilism has been all along. There is this difference now, though: the God of *Notebook* and *History* is so remote as to have become a kind of overbearing abstraction to whose existence may be attributed any number of recurring human tribulations. Cumulatively, the references to God in *History* insinuate that there must be some scheme at work in the universe that is vastly beyond our capacity for knowing—some principle that may as likely be irrational as rational or destructive as creative, having nothing remotely in common with the Gods of traditional religions, but somehow *there*. The idea of God in the poems of *History* signifies Lowell's unwillingness to envision a universe without a cause, or without an ultimate metaphysical boundary or limit. This may be the mystery that the nude and faceless figure in Frank Parker's frontispiece drawing broods upon as he sits amid ruins of war and glory glared down upon by evil faces in the sun *and* moon, with his own death waiting at his shoulder, half in shadow. So God in *History* at first is He "with whom nothing is design or intention" ("In Genesis," p. 26). Or later, "God is design, even our ugliness / is the goodness of his will" ("Flaw," p. 177). And at the last, "'God's ways are dark and very seldom pleasant'" ("Death and the Bridge," p. 205). History and God have this in common: each is, as Yeats said of Plato's nature, a "ghostly paradigm that plays upon the spume of things." The paradigms are indecipherable, but without them the things—the events and intuitions of human life—cannot be assigned certain value, except, seemingly, the negative value that owes to their contrast with the grand, failing paradigms themselves. With *History*, these grand paradigms have therefore been put away for good. From this point on, the poet's life will be conducted willingly—however unappeased—in the more intimate spaces of the world.

7. "My Eyes Have Seen What My Hand Did"

The Dolphin should properly be considered a sequel for Notebook, and it seems at first to be a coda as well but turns out to be a false one. In The Dolphin, the major themes of Notebook converge in Lowell's account of his separation from Elizabeth Hardwick, the birth of his new son, conceived out of wedlock with Caroline Blackwood, his divorce, and, we assume, his marriage to Caroline—hence a potential emphasis in the plot upon resolution and new beginnings. But the booklike linearity of such a progression cannot be accommodated by the form of real life, and so once again the reverse torque of the poet's awareness subjects him to the incoherence of irresolution and ongoingness. "Even the licence of my mind rebels," he says, homing in precisely upon one of the odder paradoxes of his own nature: "[I] can find no lodging for my two lives. / Some things like death are meant to have no outcome." This thought occurs only four pages before the volume's end. It cannot be argued that the intention of The Dolphin is to show anything romantically resolved. The Dolphin wants to be a volume that it cannot be; and it cannot be the book it wants to be, that it dreams of being, because of its author's inability to be self-deceived. Nihilism is held at bay but not transcended. We may think we see in it the happy erotic ending that we hope all such stories will achieve, but Lowell is scrupulous to present this outcome unsentimentally, as only one dimension of an existential palimpsest. We expect a Lawrentian breakthrough that never comes. "Beatrice / always met me too early or too late," he had said in *Notebook*, and by the end of *The Dolphin* we understand this to mean that *any* time would have been one or the other.

The Dolphin, moreover, is in many apparent ways—which are directly related to its subject and theme—the most enervated of Lowell's works. As a matter of course, it indulges his worst tendencies. "The visceral stream of consciousness that Lowell has been developing ever since *Near the Ocean*," Stephen Yenser says rightly, "takes its most extreme form in this volume: ellipsis after ellipsis, non sequiturs and metastases, fragmented sentences, and all manner of mannerisms that contribute to a quirky opacity."[1] Yenser's oxymoronic phrase, "visceral stream of consciousness," points to the nature and depth of the problem. The diarylike style of *Notebook* has become so introverted and narcissistic as to threaten to waive relationship with the intelligible world altogether, the world represented by us, as readers, and the world that otherwise constitutes the setting of his own story. Parts of speech lose definition: "Clouds go from dull to dazzle all the morning" (*The Dolphin*, p. 61); verb forms lose conventional transitive or intransitive status: "I roam from bookstore to bookstore browsing books" (p. 49); syntax loses its logic: "your eyelashes are always blacked, / each hair colored and quickened like tying a fly" (p. 55).

There are virtually no other characters in the book besides the three main ones and their children; no human world intrudes that does not have immediate bearing upon the personal circumstance of the story. Lowell makes a point of this: at home, he says, in America, "the colleges are closed for summer, / the students march, Brassman lances Cambodia— / ... / Is truth here with us if I sleep well?— ... / we have climbed above the wind to breathe" (p. 17). Metaphorically, sleeping well has a very high priority in *The Dolphin*, even though it means excluding the harsh truth of the ongoing historical world. The inwardness of the book, reflected in its style and content, is a chosen state, and though Lowell's reticence and obliquity often keep us from seeing the point, they are also themselves aspects of the point. "Our dream has been more than life is solid," he says to Caroline (p. 53), meaning to praise her for what she has enabled him to achieve.

Rather than being saved by Caroline, Lowell in *The Dolphin* is sealed off with her in a glassy unreality, submarine in feeling in a way that gives the book's preoccupation with sea-creatures as metaphors an ironic twist. This condition is as close to a wordless state as Lowell ever comes. It is even implied that he would not be writing at all if he were not, in the simplest sense, making a living from it. "There are ways to live on words in England" (p. 28); "God; / but it's moonshine trying to gold-cap my life, / asking fees from the things I lived and loved" (p. 29); "but you and I actually lived what I have written, / the drunk-luck venture of our lives sufficed / to keep our profession solvent, was peanuts to live" (p. 52). Though Caroline herself is a writer, that fact is not made much of in the text because the beauty of their association—insofar as wishful thinking can sustain it—is preverbal. "When I was troubled in mind," he says to her in "Dolphin," the book's last poem, "you made for my body / caught in its hangman's knot of sinking lines" (p. 78). In the volume's first poem he speaks of poetry as if poems themselves, on the page or read aloud, were merely the embalming of the living poet, whereas in their making, their sole important phase for the poet himself, they have been only a means toward the end of capturing and heightening experience.

> I know I've gladdened a lifetime
> knotting, undoing a fishnet of tarred rope;
> the net will hang on the wall when the fish are eaten,
> nailed like illegible bronze on the futureless future.

This theme is familiar to us from *Notebook*. In *The Dolphin*, its implications are acted out: thus the variations throughout on the corollary theme that words invariably falsify:

> Surely good writers write all possible wrong...
> *(The Dolphin*, p. 28)

> I waste hours writing in and writing out a line,
> as if listening to conscience were telling the truth.
> (p. 28)

> Some meaning never has a use for words,
> truth one couldn't tell oneself on the toilet...
> (p. 40)

which is truer—
the uncomfortable full dress of words for print,
or wordless conscious not even no one ever sees?
The best things I can tell you face to face
coarsen my love for you in solitary

(p. 67)

Everything is real until it's published.

(p. 72)

Everything is real until it is published because once put into a fiction in words ("life never tells us which part is life") the lived experience becomes false and mythicized, the poet as himself embalmed; the net itself as rope and tar becomes bronze.

In *The Dolphin*, what matters the most is the *ur*-dream and learning to become relinquished to it, an erotic and psychic kingdom beneath the sea, ruled by the Dolphin, Caroline. Caroline's objective is simple, but her role is complex. She is not only a dolphin, the bearer of men to enchanted isles; she is also a "baby killer whale, / free to walk the seven seas for game, / warmhearted with an undercoat of ice" (p. 36); or she is a mermaid who "serves her winded lover's bones in brine, / nibbled at recess in the marathon" (p. 35). These images suggest that the new life she offers—for those who "grapple for the danger of [her] hand"—entails both sexual risk and the threat of death to the ego. "No one swims with her and breathes the air"; "you are packaged to the grave with me, / where nothing's opened by the addressee" (p. 35). In one aspect she is the poet's antithesis, lithe, buoyant, athletic, reckless, sensual, decisive, where he is burdened, guilty, doubting, clumsy, ambivalent, cerebral. "Do this, do that, do nothing," she says to him; "you're not chained.... / I spout the smarting waters of joy in your face— / rough weather fish, who cuts your nets and chains" (p. 54). But whereas in one regard she is a rescuer, because other, an antiself, in another regard she is a danger because they are alike, because she becomes dissolved into the poet's narcissistic dream. This creates problems for Lowell's narrative, for Caroline finally does not stand sufficiently apart as herself to pull her weight against the counterforce here, represented by Elizabeth Hardwick, "Lizzie" in the text. She is a symbol, largely, and therefore a projection of the poet's dream and finally, therefore, not only an object in the dream but continuous with the dreaming state itself.

Given Caroline's nature as it is presented through metaphor, we expect animation from their relationship, some discord, sexual ardor, engagement, charisma. But they are joined instead in a voluptuous leisure, seemingly always at the edge of morning or evening, or sleeping and then waking together, as if living from day to day were a prolonged aubade. At best in these states consciousness is fluid, without edge, unattuned to the world.

> The sky should be clearing, but it cannot lighten,
> the unstable muck flies through the garden trees,
> there's morning in my heart but not in things.
>
> (*The Dolphin*, p. 56)

London's closed, clouded sky is "welcome to us as insulation" (p. 44). Hence, even feeling strength, having walked five miles, the poet still desires, he says, "to throw / my feet off, be asleep with you. . . asleep and young" (p. 56). "My hand / sleeps in the bosom of your sleeping hands, / firm in the power of your impartial heat" (p. 57). Without feet and with only sleeping, unfunctioning hands, this imagined insulation seems complete, like a "final calm." "[It's] enough to wake without old fears, / and watch the needle-fire of the first light / bombarding off your eyelids harmlessly" (p. 61). Perhaps deliberately recalling "Fern Hill," this "first light" suggests Eden, as does the observation a line earlier that the two have not "met Satan like Milton going blind in London." And although that Eden seems to survive only in the margin of morning (each day in the "first light"), even the transitory release from fear is made to seem worth the cost. "[New] wine floods our prehistoric veins— / the day breaks, impossible, in our bed" (p. 51). One miracle is waking itself— having deferred dying; another is "Sleeping, [then] always finding you there by day" (p. 63). The unnaturally endless daylight of the English summer is overbearing, and evening, therefore, brings release as well: "So country-alone, and O so very friendly, / our heaviness [is] lifted from us by the night" (p. 62). A sense of weightlessness pervades these interludes, suggesting a transcendence of gravities. "When I sit in my bath, I wonder why I haven't melted like a cube of sugar" (p. 52).

The mood of suspended animation, inward and enchanted, prevails mainly in the last third of the volume and is deepest in the section called "Marriage," which also includes the account of the birth of their son. Sheridan's birth, characteristically, is as much a symbolic as a natural event; it marks an end to vacillation and requires the real, or at least putative, new birth of the poet. "'Darling, / we have escaped our death-struggle with our lives'" (p. 61). His old life "settles down into the archives" (p. 61). Sheridan is sealed off with them, "bracketed" within a larger text. Within the brackets, "Living with you is living a long book / *War and Peace*, from day to day, / unable to look off or answer my name" (p. 51).

This is the dreamed life as one part of the self would have it. We are jolted out of it repeatedly, however, by a shocking and inspired device: Lizzie and her voice in the form of her own letters. Lizzie is not within the brackets but of the main text, the world. She is unsubmissive, complex, passionate, clearheaded, and articulate. Because she is not written by Lowell but instead writes herself, and because her "poems" are powerfully coherent—models, by contrast with Lowell's own, of "articulate energy"—she is decisively other. Caroline is allowed to emerge from the shadows only occasionally and then usually only into metaphor, and she is therefore no match for Lizzie forensically. This is true not only because Lizzie is both real and sensible but because she introduces into the story another form of human love, which is mature, complicated, and worldly.

> "Your student wrote me, if he took a plane
> past Harvard, at any angle, at any height,
> he'd see a person missing, *Mr. Robert Lowell.*
> You insist on treating Harriet as if she
> were thirty or a wrestler—she is only thirteen.
> She is normal and good because she had normal and good
> parents. She is threatened of necessity. . . .
> I love you, Darling, there's a black black void,
> as black as night without you. I long to see
> your face and hear your voice, and take your hand. . . ."
>
> *(The Dolphin,* p. 41)

We can see from this alone why it was necessary for Lowell to offend decorum by including privileged material: her voice by this means remains distinct and incontrovertible. The fact that Lowell edits and modifies these letters (and, indeed, includes in them portions of letters from other correspondents) does not alter this case at all. The important factor is that Lizzie is not and must not seem assimilated. She is a last, saving contact with the world; and after the dreaminess of the foregoing twenty pages or so, even the simple names and dates of things she brings to the text are bracing and beautiful:

> Will you go with us to *The Messiah,*
> on December 17th, a Thursday,
> and eat at the *Russian Tearoom* afterward?
>
> (*The Dolphin,* p. 69)

It is Lizzie who perceives that Lowell and Caroline are dangerously more alike than different. You are "doomed," she writes, "to know what I have known with you, / lying with someone fighting unreality" (p. 31). Her shrewd humor prevents her wisdom from becoming tendentious and grandiose, gives it the appeal of sane detachment: "Why don't you lose yourself / and write a play about the fall of Japan?" (p. 77). Lowell is perhaps shrewder, generously, for by allowing Lizzie to pass all of the precisely right judgments—both of the ones just quoted go directly to the heart of the volume's crisis and theme—he avoids making those judgments himself and thus resists the temptation of evading censure by taking credit for them. This appears to be the point of his tampering with the chronology of the true story and putting himself, at the end, on Lizzie's turf: America, and, specifically, New York. New York's "romance" is not voluptuous and enclosed but "austere" and "geometrical"; its skyscrapers suggest an un-Keatsian "irritable reaching after fact and reason"; the runway of its airport is "wintry and distinct." Lizzie's insistent presence in the book keeps alive the poet who finally puts the book together, and he concedes this readily:

> All too often now your voice is too bright;
> I always hear you...commonsense, though verbal...
> waking me to myself: truth, the truth, until
> things are just as if they had never been.
> . . . . .
>
>   —I too,
> because I waver, am counted with the living.
>
> (*The Dolphin,* p. 77)

In this last section it becomes clearer that his affair with Caroline all along has seemed vaguely unnatural, disturbingly unsynchronized with the normal pattern of his time in life. He is required by his choice to abandon his first child. The poems touching on his pain and Harriet's are among the strongest in the text: "Summer Between Terms: I"; "The Mermaid Children"; "Harriet's Donkey"; "During a Transatlantic Call." In England the strangely drawn-out seasons, the sprawling summer days, the whole of nature, seem unreal, of another life rhythm.

> The soaking leaves, green yellow, hold like rubber,
> longer than our eyes glued to the window can take;
> none tumble in the inundating air. . . .
> A weak eye sees miracles of birth in fall,
> I'm counterclockwise. . . .
>
> (*The Dolphin*, p. 29)

"Change I earth or sky," he concedes, "I am the same; / aging retreats to habit, puzzles repeated / and remembered, games repeated and remembered" (p. 66). Lowell implies here that upon reaching this certain age, habit itself becomes therapeutic whether the habits seem appropriately sedative or not: better the habit of doubt than the unfamiliar novelty of peace. He perceives (underscoring this point, which separates him from the Dolphin realm) that he is "overtrained for England" (p. 66). Albeit unwillingly, he is lashed to a mast. On the plane headed toward New York he is moved by the thought of the new joy he has found with Caroline—a joy, however, that he cannot precisely focus:

> I hardly want to hide my nakedness—
> the shine and stiffness of a new suit, a feeling,
> not wholly happy, of having been reborn.
>
> (*The Dolphin*, p. 72)

This perverse discontinuity will remain the raw nerve in his new life: "What is worse than hearing the late-born child crying— / and each morning waking up glad we wake?" (p. 62).

Putting the matter too simply, there is a Lizzie-self in *The Dolphin* that belongs in America on the edge of being, and a Caroline-self that belongs in the quiescence of England; and both selves survive the story.

The last section, "Flight to America," makes this clear, as does the final, curiously disjunctive, title poem, a tribute to Caroline. This is too simple, however, because there is a third mysterious being involved—one who transcends the man, who puts together the book composed of fragments of his self-absorbed journal, achieves a paradoxically objective understanding of his own self-inversion. In this respect, the Lowell who writes poems has, because of the way they are written, the same fictional status as his two other fictional characters. It is forgivable that we do not always see this distinction between writer and maker, but not to see it is to miss the point. It is even not very forgivable in the case of *The Dolphin*, since its last line states the matter plainly (if not simply, since "hand" refers both to writing and doing): "my eyes have seen what my hand did." It is characteristic of Lowell's unique contribution to our literature that he can transcend the failure of his own life and of human life generally only by not transcending it. He seems to have made a parable of this point near the end of *The Dolphin* in a poem called "Purgatory," which is based, apparently, upon an imperfect reconstruction from memory of Domenico di Michelino's fresco portrait of Dante in the Duomo of Florence.[2]

> In his portrait, mostly known from frontispiece,
> Dante's too identifiable—
> behind him, more or less his height, though less,
> a tower tapering to a fingerend,
> a snakewalk of receding galleries:
> Purgatory and a slice of Europe,
> less like the fact, more like the builder's hope
> It leans and begs the architect for support,
> insurance never offered this side of heaven.
> The last fifty years stand up like that;
> people crowd the galleries to flee
> the second death, they cry out manfully,
> for many are women and children, but the maker
> can't lift his painted hand to stop the crash.

The old ambiguities of freedom and determinism thrive in *The Dolphin* because of the recurring sensation throughout its pages that life and human actions—our own as well as those of others—will not respond to the instruction of reason, seem orchestrated by some force outside the compass of human will. The act of writing down the life seems to allow a degree of purchase, a share in the control; but that also is an illusion—cherished by laymen and endured, at best, by the truthful artist. The maker cannot lift his hand to avert the crash of the tower because he and the hand are painted, too.

8. THE AUTHORITY OF THE ORDINARY

The difficult emotional and intellectual richness of *Day by Day*—complicated by its ramifying themes from *The Dolphin*—may be approached through the simple access of one of Lowell's characteristically inverted epigrams (from "Jean Stafford, A Letter"): "we learn the spirit is very willing to give up, / but the body is not weak and will not die." This demoralized experience of living on redundantly from one day to the next, without willing or meaning to, is one attitude signified by the volume's title. It is typical of Lowell's frame of reference that he would take one platitude and turn it unceremoniously into another, as if to point out that the common wisdom of the race never prepares us for what turns out to be the common truth of human life. In a previous poem he has adapted a line of his dead friend John Berryman (who is said to have "got there first"): "something so heavy lies on my heart." Berryman did not know what the something was—the thing that sat heavy on Henry's heart ("often he reckons, in the dawn, them up. / Nobody is ever missing"). Nor did Lowell. And yet it was such a grief—nameless; *something*—that both men struggled in their poems and in their lives to understand and fend off. "It's not death I fear," Lowell says (as Berryman, in turn, might have), "but unspecified, unlimited pain": unspecified *and* unlimited. *Day by Day*, first of all, commemorates a chastened obedience to necessity, an abdication of pride and will before the authority of the ordinary.

Accordingly, the book refuses us again the catharsis of lyrical idiom and form, since otherwise its poet would be implicitly representing himself as having transcended the human process; instead, he makes a point of acknowledging his continuity with it. In *Notebook*, Lowell had written in another poem for Berryman, "John, we used the language as if we had made it"; and it should have been clear there, for it certainly is here, that Lowell meant such statements as acknowledgments of his own hubris, as admissions that making the language in no sense makes or even changes the life. However exotic and autonomous the world of one's creation may be, one's destiny in real life is common: "Can one bear it; in nature / from seed to chaff no tragedy?" This complaint is in a poem for Caroline Blackwood called "We Took Our Paradise," the point of which is that we take our paradise here, in a particular time and place (there being no other paradise), and then it is gone, and time and the world simply proceed, promising and luring us but remaining unwilling to make special dispensations for human beings generally or to invest individual fates with tragic dignity. On this issue of the ironic disjunction between art and life, Lowell's glum knowingness is unrelieved and its ironies apparent to him everywhere.

> We asked to be obsessed with writing,
> and we were.
>
> Do you wake dazed like me,
> and find your lost glasses in a shoe?
> ("For John Berrryman")

The joke in the image, showing the visionary subdued to the pedestrian, is a dispirited one and the stage in human life that it depicts is not enhanced even by being remarkable. On the contrary: "Yet really we had the same life, / the generic one / our generation offered." The fact of life for the poet is that one cannot write one's way out of the commonplace after all, and that one's writing and one's vision therefore mock one's life. In a poem for Frank Parker, Lowell has Parker say (during a visit by Lowell to Parker's house), "'Let us go into the garden, / or shall I say the yard,'" and then asks, "Why have you said this twice, Frank?" What may in fact have been mere absent-mindedness on Parker's part happens also to call attention nicely to the poem's subject, the transition from youthful dreams to real outcomes:

The garden has no flowers,
or choice of color,
the thick wet clump of grass
thins to red clay,
like an Indian's shaved and tufted head,
or yours—

Earlier in the poem, Lowell has recalled that "we looked in the face of the other / for what we were," expressing in only one of several ways his preoccupation in *Day by Day* with the notion that whole selves in one lifespan simply disappear into the recesses of time.

That same reflex by which past and present are made to coincide in his mind's eye responds to a more contemporary circumstance in "Last Walk?"—the poem that marks the end of the seven years with Caroline Blackwood. It is the death of that union, of course, which has actuated the theme of failure in *Day by Day* and which, when combined with the meditations on aging and time, accounts for its hopeless outlook. "Last Walk?" covers familiar autobiographical territory—from seven years back—through the paradigmatic story of some Irish swans, particularly of a male who escaped his "safe, stagnant, matriarchal pond" to gallant "down the stout-enriched rapids to Dublin, / smirking drunkenly, racing bumping, / as if to show a king had a right to be too happy." All of that now seems mostly comical to the couple—now that even "nostalgia [is] pulverized by thought." The "misleading promise / to last with joy as long as our bodies" has come down to having "nothing to do but gaze," "nothing but a diverting smile, / dalliance by a river" and finally, unbearably, "all whiteness splotched." Lowell alludes here to the Irish legend Yeats used in "Coole Park and Ballylee, 1931"—that the swan's whiteness is of such a purity that "It can be murdered with a spot of ink"; and the reference seems to indicate that the failure of this individual human chance shows on a small scale the failure of all. The line about lasting "with joy as long as our bodies" will be conceptually rhymed seven poems later in the poem for Jean Stafford, with its scrambled platitude: "the spirit is very willing to give up / but the body is not weak and will not die." Both affirm a kind of minimal desire to survive thwarted expectations—to be; but both waive, it seems, vain designs upon the quality of the life that remains. "Jean Stafford, A Letter" is interesting in relation to both "Last Walk?" and "To Frank Parker" because it both clearheadedly and self-defeatingly points out an inherent limitation in nostalgia: that it can become a means by which one ignores necessary truths about other human beings. "I can go on imagining you," Lowell says of the period of his and Jean Stafford's courtship and early marriage, "in your Heidelberry braids and Bavarian / peasant aprons you wore three or four years / after your master's at twenty-one." This image is among his diminishing "little set / of favored pictures." But the image is false insofar as it is a projection of his own need—and perhaps was false at the time—and it has the effect of enabling him to evade the difficult fact of his first wife as a mature woman, as herself.

> You have spoken so many words and well,
> being a woman and you ... someone must still hear
> whatever I have forgotten
> or never heard, being a man.

Lowell's capacity for being simultaneously self-deceived and unself-deceived no doubt contributes in large measure to his demoralized sense of being existentially stranded and will-less. He says later: "It's impotence and impertinence to ask directions, / while staring right and left in two-way traffic" ("The Downlook").

But even in these lowest and defeated points in *Day by Day* we notice—eventually, if we see what we are looking at—that in some sense the "spirit" has not given up, even though it be willing to; that whatever the prognosis for the poet's own personal life might be, or for other human lives like his, his residual idealism remains intact, diminished but viable; and that idealism seems to be precipitated finally from human enterprises as if thereby to save it from adulteration or dilution. One must be very careful, in thinking of this subject, to distinguish what is from what is not the case. There is no more craving after personal happiness in *Day by Day*; there is no sense that what Lowell has failed to achieve in life others might—on the contrary, the "others" in *Day by Day* are more often than not extensions of Lowell himself and he of them. There is no turning to God or away from the world. There is simply the fact that one still believes that, as Lowell says of Israel Citkovitz, "somewhere" the "spirit" has "led the highest life" and that "all places matched / with that place / come to nothing"; and that some quality in the world urges us still to "pray for the grace of accuracy" and to retain the capacity to revere. Meanwhile, the poet himself has failed in his own eyes as a human being, failed to make his life right. He has few cherishable childhood memories that he can trust, and therefore, no alluring past to retreat into. He has more reason than most to be skeptical of the Sartrean thrust into the future ("Man first of all is a plan which is aware of itself," Sartre said, and "will be what he has planned to be").[1] So he stays in place in the moment, choosing being rather than becoming, as Nietzsche enjoins through Marcuse in the passage Lowell modified for "Obit." Warner Berthoff has suggested that the source for the title of Lowell's volume could have been Henry Miller's *Tropic of Cancer*, where the phrase recurs in affirmative forms: "The present is enough for me," says Miller. "Day by day"; and then again: "Day by day. No yesterdays and no tomorrows."[2] Lowell's version of Miller's allegiance to pure being—whether the parallel is coincidence or not—is less exuberant and tonally more ambiguous than Miller's, but the fact that the phrase can be read in Lowell's title to signify contradictory attitudes, both resignation and acquiescence, suggests that the poems will express intricately ambivalent states of mind.

The autobiographical poems in *Day by Day* that recount, not always clearly, the period of Lowell's life after *The Dolphin* are concentrated upon the erratic course and eventual end of his marriage to Caroline Blackwood. This puts at the center of the volume the subject of a last, failed, erotic dream. The chronology of this story is manipulated, however, so that its end is described after the volume's brief first section. That first section, in other words, carries us farther in chronological time than the last section, which has as its frame the last period of Lowell and Caroline's life together in England, at Milgate and in London, before their final separation. (One indication that this time scheme has been inverted is the fact that in the poem "Notice," in part three, the last section, Lowell pointedly mentions jotting down an image that appears as an integrated, finished line in the fourth poem, "Suicide," of part one.) In the first poem of the volume, this entire period of Lowell's life is foreshortened and enclosed in a caustic version of the *Odyssey*—a version in which he himself as a "bleak-boned" Ulysses, escaping Circe, returns, relentless and dangerous, to his Penelope (who would be Elizabeth Hardwick) "ten years fro and ten years to." The effect of this chronological arrangement is to get the worst of the *life* story over at once and to allow the volume to end on a note that, though not exactly buoyant, is at least open to possibility. By this means, in other words, Lowell is able to separate the essence or value of personal history from the outcomes of personal history, and therefore to shift the focus of relevance in the volume away from personal history altogether. The structure also allows the themes of human love and art, twin offspring of

Eros, to come together naturally and augment each other indirectly without the one's prospects overpowering the other's. In effect, then, this method causes Lowell's career to end where the last, distinctive phase of it began, at the indefinite point of contact between unmediated existence and the mediating power of imagination. What faith in the latter survives, however, does so only after folly, guilt, sickness, humiliation, failure, and age have chipped and whittled away the ego. To "pray for the grace of accuracy," as Lowell puts it in the last poem of *Day by Day*, means grace in an almost but pointedly not quite theological sense: he means by it whatever it is in art that seems continuous with the elusive quality of life— mysterious, but not, sadly, delivering—that appears to come from beyond the self and momentarily, episodically, to redeem the world. The whole of *Day by Day* to that point carries on a struggle to earn the right to even minimal affirmation, and this necessitates a torturous process of self-renunciation. With the self discounted, what there is of worth in individual experience stands clear, to be redeemed.

A large group of poems of *Day by Day*, then, record the winnowing of the self from what the self dreams and achieves. Personal memory in this text serves only to injure and to chasten pride. The language at the poet's command is not allowed to ritualize and therefore transcend the banal truth of its subject matter. Generic human experience repeatedly displaces and absorbs whatever is individual and unique. Intelligence, which one would otherwise think of as a gift, instead foreknows and foretells all, shadowing joy and hope, and becomes a flaw of vision. Each of these constraints affects and is an effect of the other, and collaborating in this way they close off all access to better prospects. Helen Vendler points out that *Day by Day* records "the very worst memories suppressed from *Life Studies*,"[3] and putting the matter in that way indicates how little recourse Lowell had in the end to the commonest, sanity-saving, psychological mechanisms and how deeply immersed he was (as was the aesthetic he worked from) in a self-destructive reality principle more darkly and fatalistically Freudian even than Freud's.

What is happening generally in *Day by Day*, to the ego and the spirit, is expressed symbolically in the poem "Turtle," which is positioned as the first of the volume's last subgroup of poems. In it the turtles of "Neo-Classical Urn" return to exact revenge. This happens in the poet's mind's eye, in the hallucinogenic margin between sleep and waking, where, dreamed, the turtles are sinister and purposeful: "You've wondered where we were these years? / Here are we." They are like grotesque, patient gods whom the hero has defied and must now propitiate. Memory throws up a specific occasion, turtle hunting, when the boy Lowell had drawn a snapping turtle out of the muck by what he thought was its tail but was in fact a foreleg: "I could have lost a finger." Now that memory is rerun, and what did not happen in that moment becomes transformed into a metaphor of what did happen in time:

> the snapper holds on till sunset—
> in the awful instantness of retrospect,
> its beak
> works me underwater drowning by my neck,
> as it claws away pieces of my flesh
> to make me small enough to swallow.

The poet has said in the beginning, "I pray for memory"; and this is ironically what memory achieves. The turtles in memory destroy the ego, show it destroyed. They are a murderously innocent reality, with their attributes of corruption and impersonal cruelty, and now there is no neo-classical urn, ironic or otherwise, to offset them.

> what is dead in me awakens their appetite.
> When they breathe, they seem to crack apart,
> crouched motionless on tiptoe
> with crooked smiles
> and high-school nicknames on their tongues,
> as if they wished to relive
> the rawness that let us meet as animals.
> Nothing has passed between us but time.

By the "rawness" and "what is dead in me" the poet and the turtles become identified: he is already small enough to swallow. Time has disclosed this truth. As a child, he had been at home in the turtles' primal element, bizarrely intrigued by, wedded to, grotesqueness and danger. Now he is also a turtle—*the* turtle of the title:

> absentminded, inelastic,
> kept afloat by losing touch ...
> no longer able to hiss or lift
> a useless shield against the killer.

His vanity destroyed, he has come full circle. The only exemplary ego left is dissolved in the eerie power and authority of the poem itself.

"Turtle" presents eidetically an experience of the poet's relation to memory and time that other poems present in a more conventional, representational way. One such is "St. Mark's, 1933," where we learn not only of the psychological torture Lowell seems to have invited from his classmates in boarding school, but of the reductive and dehumanizing—if also familiar and conventional—form that it took. It is significant that this particular memory has waited, like the turtle, to surface here.

> "Why is he always grubbing in his nose?"
> "Because his nose is always snotty."
> "He likes to wipe his thumb in it."
> "Cal's a creep of the first water."
> "He had a hard-on for his first shower."
> . . . . .
> "Cal is a slurp."
> "A slurp farts in the bathtub."
> "So he can bite the bubbles."
> How did they say my face
> was pearl-gray like toe-jam—
> that I was foul
> as the gymsocks I wore a week?

This again is "the rawness that let us meet as animals" but it is also, it seems, a bodying forth of the unconscious self that inwardly has survived and thrives:

> Perhaps they had reason . . .
> even now
> my callous unconscious drives me
> to torture my closest friend.

This memory of the inner self objectified has perhaps issued to begin with from despairing self-appraisal. It does not sit well with the dream of the spirit somewhere leading the highest life, but such vast, unbridgeable disparities of experience will turn out to be a main point of the volume. Lowell's Ulysses has this bizarre, self-loathing child in him. "Ten years before Troy, . . . before Circe / things changed to the names he gave them." Upon his return to Ithaca, age and survival have made him into what Circe could not, "a foolish but evil animal," a shark, circling to destroy for no purpose other than to express the only form of machismo that survives in his senility; and he is imprisoned in the brute role of "vocational killer".

> his gills are pleated and aligned—
> unnatural ventilation vents
> closed by a single lever
> like cells in a jail—

If this Ulysses is Lowell in some form, some part, other desuppressed memories of *Day by Day* show us how and why this could be. Dr. Merrill Moore, "the family psychiatrist" (as normal a role in the context as "family doctor"), is reported to have informed the young Lowell that he was an "unwanted child." Carl Jung in the same year supposedly told Lowell's mother that "If your son is as you have described him, / he is an incurable schizophrenic." His mother herself tells him later that when she carried him in her womb, hating pregnancy as a curse, she had roamed the "refusey Staten Island beaches . . . / yearning seaward, far from any home, . . . saying, / 'I wish I were dead, I wish I were dead.'" Eventually, Lowell the child learns how to cope, by finding things to love and then destroy, lest he become unwanted by what he wants—and thus does "our fear of being unwanted" become the "unpardonable sin."

> Then I found the thing I loved most
> was the anorexia Christ
> swinging on Nellie's gaudy rosary.
> It disappeared, I said nothing,
> but mother saw me poking strips of paper
> down a floor-grate to the central heating.
> "Oh Bobby, do you want to set us on fire?"
> "Yes. . . that's where Jesus is." I smiled.
>   ("Unwanted")

"Anyone is unwanted in a medical sense," he had said to Merrill Moore, struggling to abate the pain—"lust our only father," and this he comes to believe is as true of ourselves in the universe as at home. Lowell's God has been an unwanting God whom he strives to destroy, and he succeeds, leaving a self who is only a particle in space. In another poem he says to his mother: "It has taken me the time since you died / to discover you are as human as I am . . . / if I am." The doubt is genuine, not mere flippancy. Ontological insecurity in this form is the next thing to psychic self-extinction, and the imprinted thought that he does not deserve to exist cannot be rationalized away. Time correspondingly becomes a punishment instead of remaining a simple fact—becomes deified, Nietzsche would say.

The poems of *Day by Day* are closer to us than Lowell's other work, more immediate and more intimate. The claims that the poems make are more subjective and tentative, like their station in reality, and the claimer is more modest. They are often, in effect, dramatic monologues. "Autumn is my favorite season— / Why does it change clothes and withdraw?" Such a question as this seems fatuous unless we recognize it as a dramatic utterance, occurring in the poem at the moment of the thought, the effect of a temporary aphasia and a loss of contact with necessity. Lowell types letters to his students that "they burn for fear of my germs." He does not say "I imagine" that they do this, but he *is* imagining; it is not fact. Three lines later in the same poem ("Death of a Critic") he writes, "my tragedy / delights the dawdling dawnbirds," projecting again in the moment: he is engrossed in self-pity, the dawnbirds sing cheerfully, and the connection is made in the mind. In his momentary self-absorption, he fills up and motivates the world; and in such moments there is no world apart, in itself. This shows on a small scale what happens on a much larger scale throughout *Day by Day*: the poet's whole perception of time and human life seems to him to be an extension from the center of his own defeated ego. The intimacy of the poems, which on the one hand declares his unwillingness to pretend to be standing back for the detached view, makes a point on the other hand of his need to achieve freedom from his own outlook. What tends to happen instead is that the self clawed away by the turtles becomes more and more of the human world. "Our elders," seen in photographs, he says in one poem, seem to be "thinking, like us, their autumn / the autumn of the world." They may in fact have been thinking nothing like this. But the fact that "we" think it implies that "we" fill up not only others' selves but time, too: our elders become us, and our autumn the final autumn of time. "In our unfinished revolutionary now," he says elsewhere, "every thing seems to end and nothing to begin," running together *the* age with his own experience of aging. Lowell is not disingenuous about the relativity of his own perspective and he builds elaborately inclusive, self-entrapping structures from the subject. It is one point in having himself so embarrassingly visible in the poems, in both narrative and the idiom.

An ironic but predictable consequence of this modest solipsism is that he is unable not to see his own life subsumed into the pattern of all lives and thus again diminished and made nugatory. "There is the humility of the generic about this volume," Helen Vendler says. "Lowell tells us that each generation, and each person in each generation, leads the same life, the life of that time. No one in the present is wiser or more foolish than those in the past or in the future. No fresh perfection treads on our heels; nor do we represent any decay of nature."[4] There are no long-run consolations and no special dispensations for the meek, the ambitious or the worthy, for achievers or failures. The larger patterns that consume individual human lifetimes do not relent. Lowell makes such simple truths idiomatically his own, discovers them in his own life; yet each such observance presses from its own logic toward abstraction and cheerless generalization. "Their faces, no longer faces, adorn / the golden age of photographs" ("Realities"). Here the interceding "no longer faces" typically, and delicately, averages out all of the other illusions that flourish in the language of the lines—"adorn"; "golden age." A few lines farther down he adds the inevitable association. He has become an "elder" himself: "I cannot believe myself them, / my children more skeptical than I." The peculiar double bind of time in this view is that, by repeating itself, it robs us of our uniqueness while moving us toward our deaths to accomplish the same effect in another way. Remembering the moment forty years before when he and Frank Parker, together at school, dreamed their careers into life, he remembers thinking also at the time, smugly, that the aged are "another species," kept like pets or on view like animals at a zoo: "The very old / made grandfather look vulgarly young, / when he drove me to feed them at their home." But then the momentum of such a thought is irreversible:

> We will have their thoughtful look,
> as if uncertain
> who had led our lives . . .
>> ("To Frank Parker")

and again the other impression also arises—a kind of surcharge—that one progressively loses contact with the essence of one's identity. In *Day by Day*, time's processes are characterized as so abstracting and impersonal that Lowell seems often—in his idiom, in the dispassionate tone—to be speaking for, or *as*, that force rather than against it.

Doublings of different kinds persist throughout *Day by Day* with the impersonal redundancy of dreams. Most are reflections of aging and impending death. Each has its own hallucinatory eidetic edges. All collectively undermine the security of the ego. In "Our Afterlife II" he naturally sees his own aging reflected in the face of his old friend Peter Taylor, but for a moment the impression is stranger: he thinks his face *is* Peter's:

> I saw my own face
> in sharper focus and smaller
> watching me from a puddle
> or something I held—your face
> on the cover of your *Collected Stories*
> seamed with dread and smiling—

The dreamlike quality in this episode is enhanced by the gradually adjusted perceptual distortions; and that Taylor's face should be seamed, as if stitched, with both dread and smiling therefore gives his likeness to Lowell a nightmarishly lurid emphasis. When the two become more intimately one in the poet's thoughts, it is infirmity that links them. "My thinking is talking to you— / last night I fainted at dinner / and came nearer to your sickness." In "Endings,"Lowell remembers a last visit to Harriet Winslow in Washington and falls prey again to foreboding empathy:

> You joked of your blackouts,
> your abstractions,
> . . . . .
> You woke wondering why
> you woke in another room,
> you woke close to drowning.
> . . . . .
> A month later you were paralyzed
> and never unknotted . . .
>
> A small spark tears at my head,
> a flirting of light brown specks in the sky,

explosive pinpricks,
an unaccountable lapse of time.

In "Unwanted," he reads an "article on a friend" (John Berryman) "as if
recognizing my obituary." In "To Mother," he says, "I see myself change
in my changed friends." The husband and wife in Van Eyck's *Arnolfini
Marriage* are like himself and Caroline, "crowded together in Maidstone, / patriarch and young wife / . . . to pose in Sunday-best"—one
point of that association being that "Giovanna" will outlive her
"Giovanni" "by 20 years." In "Death of a Critic," he reflects upon a
chastening irony: older writers, "Dull, disagreeable and dying" had been
"setups for my ridicule"; now "time, the healer [has] made me theirs."
Even the old wine baron of "Ear of Corn," who cannot be cured of "his
hallucination / he can bribe or stare / any woman he wants into orgasm,"
mocked in the poem for senile lechery, becomes at the end an admonitory
true reflection of the mocking poet as he ironically perseveres in perceiving
illusory reflections of sexual youth:

Is this substance hoped for,
after a grasshopper life of profit—
to stand shaking on fine green legs,
to meet the second overflowing of Eros,
himself younger in each young face;
and see in that mirror
a water without the life of water. . .?

This last image is wryly so much like Lowell's own progressively thwarted
erotic career that he and the wine baron seem virtually to have changed
places. "Like belief," he has said twenty lines earlier, "he makes nothing
happen." In "In the Ward," Lowell reconstructs the last days of Israel
Citkovitz, to whom he is linked both by virtue of their being artists—and
failed ones, each in his own mind—and by each having been the husband
of Caroline Blackwood (though this point is not established or relevant in
the poem). Without his teeth, Citkovitz appears to have aged ten years in
an hour. He is frightened by the strangeness of the public ward, by its
foreignness to the life of the mind and art, to what he knows, and he finds
refuge in the pure form of a glaring lightbulb. Citkovitz is dying in intent
silence, and he has failed only by having envisioned work that is richer
than he can achieve, by having rejected "the art of the possible / that art

abhors," cutting his losses until he has no losses to cut. The implied connection between the poet and the old composer is made more secure in the preceding poem, called "The Art of the Possible." In that poem's opening lines, Lowell is admonished by a friend for his "profession of making what can't be done / the one thing you can do." In "For Sheridan," this theme is broadened and extended to the past and the future by Lowell's seeing himself at two stages of his life identified with his son:

> Three ages in a flash:
> the same child in the same picture,
> he, I, you,
> chockablock, one stamp
> like mother's wedding silver—
> gnome, fish, brute cherubic force.

The one has failed to bring his life into accord with his *a priori* vision of it, and the other will fail not for lack of will or desire but because it is a convention of human life. The poem sounds surprisingly like Eliot of *Four Quartets*—in its opening lines, "We only live between / before we are and what we were," and in its conclusion:

> Past fifty, we learn with surprise and a sense
> of suicidal absolution
> that what we intended and failed
> could never have happened—
> and must be done better.

Day by Day indeed has a great deal of *Four Quartets*'s kind of fatalism in it (as does *History*),though Lowell's version is not redeemed, and markedly not orchestrated to serve a larger rhetorical and theological end. The unembellished statement in "Endings" on Harriet Winslow's illness ("Effects are without cause; / your doctors found nothing") presents itself in such a context as a judgment not just of the limits of human knowledge but of ontological fact. An aphoristic rhetorical question in"Endings" neatly encapsulates the lesson of all the doubling poems: "Why plan; when we stop?" The images of other lives at their ends serve to draw the personal future down into the present in the mind, thus foreshortening the spaces between *now* and *ultimately* in which the imaginary self is otherwise free to range. The illusion of freedom is conditional upon a compatible illusion of time, and the will to act is contingent upon both. If, as Sartre says, "subjectivism means . . . that an individual chooses and makes himself" and that man "is the being who hurls himself toward a future and who is conscious of imagining himself as being in the future," with Lowell this process has malfunctioned and appears to have worked in reverse.[5] The effect for him of "subjectivism," of unalienated self-consciousness—which is not oblivious to the signals flashed from its human environment—is to demystify the ideologies of freedom and will on purely empirical grounds. Thinking of Harriet Winslow dying, and by extension of others as well, Lowell says, "My eyes flicker, the immortal / is scraped unconsenting from the mortal." The psychology of freedom is as fragile as that, the symbolic "immortal" self as perishable as any. The undertone of, "Why plan; when we stop?" is regressive and expresses exhaustion under the strain of becoming; the instinctive projections into other people's lives seem to stem from an impulse away from individuation, toward self-elision.

Lowell's poems have always been fatalistically uncurious about why things happen in human experience in the way that they do. Their syntax is not the syntax of analysis and synthesis. For the defeated and receding ego of Day by Day, there is not only no will but also no means for making even a factitious order from the heaps of empirical data from past and present. ("Grassfires" is an interesting variation on this theme.) Anomie without is in one respect a projection of the anomie within, and in another aspect a cause of it; the two are thus perversely symbiotic. This dispiriting condition takes its most obvious dramatic form in the strangely subdued poems in Day by Day that recount Lowell's last serious mental breakdown, and the period of his hospitalization in Northampton, England. Whatever else madness may symbolize, here it is less a metaphor than simply an extension of the loss of understanding and control—and finally failure, in its most humiliating form. In one of these poems, the hospital is called "Home." A doctor calls Lowell a "model guest" and adds with unthinking irony, "we would welcome / Robert back to Northampton any time, / the place suits him . . . he is so strong." To himself, he is a mere "thorazined fixture" for whom, as he anticipates in a preceding poem, "heaven and hell," through the magic of medication, have become the same. The doctor says, "remarkable breakdown, remarkable recovery," but the patient has reason to be less sanguine: "the breakage can go on repeating / once too often."

> Since nature,
> our unshakable mother, will grow impatient with us,
> we might envy museum pieces
> that can be pasted together or disfigured
> and feel no panic of indignity.

Nature's growing impatient with us seems not to imply impending death but instead the growing fear of discontinuity with the world, of reification, that comes from having been put back together one too many times. Lowell perceives himself, and is apparently perceived by Caroline, as one who has deserted his wife and his children (in this case without choosing to) by temporarily ceasing to be, by having failed, unlike normal people, to consolidate an identity by transcending the world.

> *If he has gone mad with her,*
> *the poor man can't have been very happy,*
> *seeing too much and feeling it*
> *with one skin-layer missing.*

The "visitors" who come to take him away, police or paramedics, say to him, "'Where you are going, Professor, / you won't need your Dante'"— perhaps deliberately insinuating the difference between the imagined and the real world, mythic and authentic hells.

The last irony of the narrative in *Day by Day*, and the final insult of fate to the dreamed life, is the transformation of Caroline from a lithe deliverer to a crippled companion in suffering, as if she had indeed been invented by Robert Lowell. The dolphin-woman-mermaid of *The Dolphin*, who spouts " 'the smarting water of joy in your face' " and " 'cuts your nets and chains,' " (p. 54), a "whole spirit wrought from toys and nondescript" (p. 56), a "baby killer whale / . . . warm hearted with an undercoat of ice" (p. 36), is no longer magically discontinuous with fate but expressive of it. She suffers stoically from an incurable wound, the effects of a broken back sustained thirty years before in a car wreck, driving with her cousin for the first time with her "learner's" card. Her life is regulated by pain, by her "spine's spasmodic, undercover life": "Putting off a luncheon, / you say into the telephone, / 'Next month, if I'm still walking.'" In bed she says,

"Not now—
my spine is hurting me,
I can only lie face down,
a gross weight innocent—
if you will let me sleep—
of seduction, speech, or pain.
I'm too drugged to do anything,
or help you watch the sky.
I am indifferent to the stars—

By simultaneously rejecting her husband-lover and the stars, she identifies them: "what woman has the measure of a man, / who only has to care about himself / and follow the stars' / extravagant, useless journey across the sky. . . / Because they cannot love, they need no love." If by "stars" is meant also "constellations," then an analogy to poems is apparent, too: human orderings of chaos moving otherwise pointlessly from one horizon of our experience to the other. Caroline in this poem is given the words for Lowell's indictment of himself—fixing upon the stars to "divert" them both, really, though she says "me," from "the absence of the sun." This erratic and fervent relationship began with bodies as the measure of freedom and now ends with bodies as necessity: another characteristically ironic progression. Lowell says in "Last Walk?" that they had thought "to last with joy as long as our bodies." Now even "rain lashes and sprinkles / to complete its task— / as if assisting / the encroachments of our bodies / we occupy but cannot cure." And "the present" is "the infection / of things gone" ("We Took Our Paradise"). The attraction of the stars' distant and pointless beauty is one of the signs in *Day by Day* of the end of the poet's wavering infatuation with human life on earth. Caroline's less otherwordly version is the imagining of a godlike lover, "too young to be frightened of women", who "can only appear in all my dreams."

Body determinism in *Day by Day* is both a fact and a metaphor, one of those cases, however, where tenor and vehicle are hardly distinguishable. In its figural role, it keeps before us the perverse scheme of things by which we are wed in joy to life and betrayed in the end (or along the line) by the same power that brought us to such a state to begin with. The mania of Lowell's illness is thus a metaphor, too: "*Why is it so hard for them to accept / the very state of happiness is wrong?*" ("Home"). Medically, in the case of manic-depressive illness, the "state of happiness" *is* wrong, as it is in other physical conditions as well—for example, in hypertension. Happiness is therefore now *primarily* a warning signal. "We are dangerously happy," he says, addressing Peter Taylor in "Our Afterlife I," alerted by the happiness of reunion with Taylor to the thought of the recent deaths of other writers (Ezra Pound, Edmund Wilson, and W. H. Auden), then to his own progressive deafness, and to "the ladder of ripening likeness" by which he and Taylor begin to resemble each other in age. They are, he thinks, only provisionally "alive in flight," as if tossed. Happiness is equally problematic with Caroline; the humor of a moment is perhaps also mania: "I grow too merry / when I stand in my nakedness to dress" ("Ten Minutes"). When their joy together is unalloyed, he must will his existential paranoia into defensive service:

> Is our little season of being together
> so unprecarious, I must imagine
> the shadow around the corner. . .
> downstairs. . . behind the door?

And, he adds, deprecating his own life-abridging anxiety, "I will leave earth / with my shoes tied / as if the walk / could cut bare feet" ("This Golden Summer"). Later, he acknowledges that it is childish to think that imagining the worst is a way of warding it off:

> Darling,
> terror in happiness may not cure the hungry future,
> the time when any illness is chronic,
> and the years of discretion are spent on complaint—
>
> until the wristwatch is taken from the wrist.
> ("The Withdrawal")

The humility of *Day by Day* represents paradoxically both a defeat for the self and a release, and this ambiguity partly explains the volume's peculiar richness of tone and its generically human resonance. The poems are morbid and demoralized and yet tender, wistful, and affirming. The pace of experience in the volume has slowed virtually to a standstill. Most commonly, in fact, the poet himself appears in watchful, unmoving states—often in bed, otherwise sitting, thinking or talking, absently trout-fishing—though these states may be troubled or impinged upon by anxiety breaking through or by resented human entanglements. As in "Shadow," Lowell may be called at such moments "to the world" by the narcotic beauty of the night. The objects he is drawn to and contemplates are nearly static, picturelike: the drifting stars, houses, paintings, grazing cows ("one sex, one herd, / replicas in hierarchy"), sunlight on an open field, an aged oak tree, an unmoving, munching, "ageless white horse." Apart from the discontinuous syntax of *Day by Day*, with its unbridged associational spaces, and apart from the volume's unhappy human story, these things remain in place. "Ants," he says, "are not under anathema to make it new," bringing the point home, with reference to the labor of the artist and to human restlessness generally—and no doubt to his own appropriated but mismanaged life in particular. "They are the lost case of the mind," he adds, in a thoughtful summation, meaning *case* probably in both the juridical and grammatical senses. In *Notebook*, nature was change; here it is stability: "Placed chestnut trees flower mid-cowfield, / even in harvest time, they swear, 'we always had leaves and ever shall' " ("For Sheridan"). In *The Dolphin*, Lowell would say, "My eyes have seen what my hands did," affirming responsibility for choice and act. In *Day by Day*, he is accused by dream figures of being incapable of love "and luxuriously nourished without hands." The handless state in *Day by Day* begins as helplessness and ends as the state of passive receptivity to the world.

In "Shifting Colors," Lowell invokes as an acceptable alternative to writing "only in response to the gods" a mode of writing that he calls "universal consolatory / description without significance." The phrase conjures up the notion of a style that really does submit (as that of *Lord Weary's Castle* had not) to what Jarrell had represented as the "senseless originality and contingency" of things, one of textured objectivity and clarity. And although the style of *Day by Day* does not achieve, or even attain to, that concrete simplicity of utterance, it reflects what might be called another epistemological retrenchment, the last embodiment in form of Lowell's antiteleological vision. It expresses a willing identification with a life that is not purposive and it is therefore a notational style, not one of syntactical rigor that imparts a structure of meaning. The monumental authority of *History*, and historical prospects generally, have receded. The poems cohere with one another remarkably because of their unity of theme and their prevailing, elegiac sadness, but they seem often to be built themselves of bits and pieces of things and ideas, sometimes cryptically associated. People, friends, are only seamed faces, reaching arms, brave smiles. The idiom seems like prose because its diction is responsibly natural and colloquial, but Lowell's impatience with conventional exposition—and by extension his unwillingness to establish a poet-audience relationship and thus a rhetorical presence for himself—makes of proselike elements an elliptical, suggestive medium that is virtually the opposite of the prosaic. He seems intent to forego all but the most indispensable syntactic resources of the language, as if free-climbing, without rope and pitons. What is lost in clarity is gained in austerity, delicacy, and dignity of tone. This style—minimalist, calligraphic—is itself the subtlest and most affecting expression of his unrationalized and receptively experiential world view, and yet its reticence makes it seem at times as if the substance of the world were receding before the poet's eyes. "This year for the first time, / even the cows seem transitory": he makes a kind of joke of the issue, recalling from *Notebook* his massive symbols of complacent groundedness. He frequently represents himself as becoming progressively unretentive. And where once he had filled up his world, now he begins to worry that he is missing from it:

> Sometimes
> I catch my mind
> circling for you with glazed eye—
> my lost love hunting
> your lost face.
>
> Summer to summer,
> the poplars sere
> in the glare—
> it's a town for the young,
> they break themselves against the surf.
> No dog knows my smell.
>
>   ("Homecoming")

This may seem paradoxical, that the world in these poems is both indefinite and patiently observed; but it is less enigmatic if we suppose that when one's ego no longer fills the nonhuman world, the world recovers its naturally inchoate form, and that one must then reobserve what is there in order to adjust a new position in relation to it. The style of *Day by Day* is the gesture of this observance.

   The world-in-itself in *Day by Day* is cherished largely to the degree that it is not human. Human life in *Day by Day* is characterized by isolated moments of achievement and joy that are all too easily subsumed into a larger, prevailing pattern of guilt, physical illness, defeat, and dread. There are no margins left in which we can believe other normative human lives to be flourishing. On the other hand, there are margins, if not human ones, and they remain open precisely because they are not encroached upon by ordinary human experience. A protected space remains in these poems, elusive as music with "its ever retreating borderlines of being," and, like music, unaligned with any empirical element, "science," "systems," "fecundity," and opposed to the final nihilistic surrender of "silence." "Somewhere," Lowell says of Israel Citkovitz, "your spirit / led the highest life; / all places matched / with that place / come to nothing"—and the "places" that come to nothing are real places where human beings are required to dwell and act and therefore become fragments, alienated from their dreamed selves. When the other marginal, ideal "place" is not music, it is wordless emblems in nature, escaping human containment, or—appropriately for the vaguely Heideggerian drift of this interest in *Day by Day*—light.[6]

> It's amazing
> the day is still here
> like lighting on an open field,
> terra firma and transient
> swimming in variation,
> fresh as when man first broke
> like the crocus all over the earth.

In this first stanza of "The Day," the light of an earlier happier day is perceived to have remained fixed in time, stationary and Edenic (like Yeats's wild swans, "still" in two senses); but though irony is implicit, the love having failed that gave the original light its enchantment, the conventional irony is not all that emerges. The poem itself is about the death of love, but it is paradoxically lyrical in feeling, the regret complicated by the realness, the presence of the beauty of the light. The light remains, separated from the bitterness of human failure, uncontaminated and possessing the autonomous quality of something revealed rather than subjectively imagined. The discontinuity between what is human in the world and what is not is affirmed as well as observed, and this pattern emerges as the prevailing one in the last section—part three—

of *Day by Day*. It is affirmational, but only with the restrained unhumanistic skepticism that Auden intended when he wrote, "Life remains a blessing / although you cannot bless."

"The Day" is the first poem in part three to introduce this pattern. "Domesday Book," which follows, extends it. The poem's title refers to the irony that England's country houses—"stately homes" as they are called now, being mainly artifacts—are falling "under the ax of the penal taxes / they first existed to enact," and, more broadly, to the universal, unsentimental process by which the human achievement they represent is undone.

> Lathom House, Middleton Manor,
> New Hall, Silverton,
> Brickling with its crinkled windows
> and rose-pink gables
> are converted to surgeries, polytechnics,
> cells of the understaffed asylum
> crumbling on the heads of the mad.

The scene is both particular and universal, and on its surface the poem is conventionally elegiac: the chimney stacks of the houses are "cold," the statuary "greening," the formal gardens "parceled to irreversible wilderness / by one untended year." And although the images are primarily architectural ones, the meditation remains firmly political and historical in its interest. So as the poem begins with Harold falling, "with an arrow in his eye at Hastings," the thought of things moving "from something to nothing" becomes a common denominator by which, toward the end of the poem, beheaded Charles I and his adversary Cromwell (the first adversary and taxer of the royalist houses) are brought to mind and linked. And as Charles and the Protector shared a "strange / fibered Puritan violence," of which they were both perpetrators and victims, so the houses connect still with the "calculated devastation"of William the Conquerer, "never improvidently / merciful to the helpless," though we tend to forget this when we regard them aesthetically, only as picturesque, separated from the political function that brought them into being in the first place ("the old follies, as usual, never return"). This foregrounded theme of a retributive determinism inherent in historical process is reiterated by a laconic joke alluding to Cromwell's being disinterred, hanged, and beheaded months after his natural death: "If they have you by the neck a rope will be found." The theme is then secured by an equally terse summary of historical fact: "The reign of the kingfisher was short."

Read with the attention focused exclusively on these historical elements, the point of "Domesday Book" seems plain enough, though by no means simple. But "Domesday Book" has a characteristically inter-calated structure. Main areas of attention are interrupted by secondary areas, which compete for interest by appealing to our consciousness at a different level. Before the last line about the brevity of Cromwell's reign, this seemingly extraneous comment disrupts the poem's anticipated resolution:

> Only when we start to go,
> do we notice the outrageous phallic flare
> of the splash flowers that fascinated children;

and before that, these two lines: "the houses still burn / in the golden lowtide stream of Turner."[7] The statement about starting to go is the first clear indication we have in the poem that the poet is with someone at one of the estates and that instead of being a relatively abstract meditation upon history, the poem is inspired by a particular occasion and setting (though we never know what that setting is). The suggestion, then, is that what the poet notices only at the end, "when we start to go," is representative of an aspect of this event—a tour, a visit, a potential buyer's inspection—that has passed unnoticed up to this point, and this takes *us* back to the body of the poem for a second examination. What we then notice is that the "house" that stands for all houses seems disproportionate and out of place in its own setting and that its "elephantiasis" is now "smothered in the beauty of its English garden / changed already to a feathery, fertile waste." The emphasis seems to be on the beauty of the change back toward the original, prehuman state, "waste" modified by "fertile" functioning in its earlier innocent form as *uninhabited* or *unused*. The formal man-made lawns are "drenched" in "gold-red sorrel," the unconstrained, "hectic" rose "climbs a neglected gravel drive"; "wild flowers take root in the kitchen garden." Of course these details have been noticed in one sense—otherwise they wouldn't be there in the poem; but so long as they are serving the theme of the vanity of human wishes, they are being seen only as they would be by someone who is older and declining himself, projecting his own sense of futility onto the world. It is seeing them as the undemoralized child would see them that makes the difference—or seeing the houses as Turner had, suffused in light. So an important distinction is thus achieved, albeit obliquely: if we see what we get, we also get what we see; and what a child would see here, or a Turner, would be a vivid and robust beauty in the world, which is innocent altogether of human purpose or pain. "But we must notice," Lowell will say later, "we are designed for the moment." The rich light of "The Day" was first revealed "when we lived momently / together forever / in love with our nature"—not, that is, despising or regretting it—and its scenes were, significantly, a "child's daubs in a book / I read before I could read." The quality of his alienation from the world, otherwise, has been suggested in "Notice," where he addresses to someone at Northampton the bemused question, " 'Is this what you would call a blossom?' " With *Day by Day* alone as evidence, it would not be hard for us to understand how noticing, living in the moment, and innocence of perspective should have come to symbolize for Lowell a desired status in the world.

Both the images of light and of the "feathery, fertile waste" of the natural world are consistently identified with the influence of Caroline upon the poet's way of seeing. This point is made explicit in "Logan Airport, Boston." Suffering from Caroline's recent departure, the poet "in the brown air of our rental" decamps "from window to window / to catch the sun," wondering if it is "cynical to deliquesce, / as Adam did in age," and thus linking the loss of Caroline with a fall from grace and the attendant temptation of despair. But by the end of the poem his spirits have lifted, not as an effect of reasoning or thought but because of a mysterious, spontaneous incandescence of the world:

> I cannot touch you—
> your absence is presence,
> the undrinkable blaze
> of the sun on both shores of the airport.
>
> Bright sun of my bright day,
> I thank God for being alive—

It is Caroline's absence that makes this "presence," just as in "The Day" the light has mysteriously held, long past the waning of love. That the blaze is also "undrinkable" implies that its region of being is apart from, even though revealed by, human meaning. Both of these poems show how complicated and ambiguous the phenomenology of *Day by Day* can be,

for before part three ever begins we know that this marriage has failed—
"Last Walk?," "Suicide," and "Departure" at the end of part one have told
us this—and *in* part three, as we have seen, the marriage itself is
progressively damaged by existential paranoia and by the dividing anxieties
of sickness of body and mind. As Lowell says in "Caroline in Sickness,"
"on the threshold of pain, / light doesn't exist," though he bids the hidden
moon at the end of this poem to "stop from dark apprehension" and to
"shine as is your custom, / scattering this roughage to find sky." But again,
the very point being made of this seems to be that even in suffering there is
accessible a vision of beauty and possibility in the world that human life
infallibly falls short of.[8] This expanding context turns random images at
least toward the status of metaphors, as with the drought summer that is
paradoxically "bountiful" for its seeming "golden" in the sun, its fields
yellow with a preternatural "fertility," which, like the "undrinkable blaze"
in "Logan Airport, Boston," is "too rich to breathe." Or, three stanzas
further into the same poem:

> I see even in golden summer
> the wilted blowbell spiders
> ruffling up impossible angers,
> as they shake threads to the light.
> ("This Golden Summer")

On the other hand, by virtue of the same subtle thematic influence, such
figures can also take on the sharper significance of paradigm:

> The struck oak that lost
> a limb that weighed a ton
> still shakes green leaves
> and takes the daylight,
> as if alive.
> ("We Took Our Paradise")

Accumulating, these images affirm subliminally a kind of phenomenal
grace, which seems (perhaps because it is so indistinct) like Heidegger's
"Being," which in turn is forever both hidden and manifest, no-thing and
all.

The spirit of this grace, whatever its autonomous properties might
be, prevails cryptically in the poem "Marriage," which commemorates the

innocent *idea* of marriage as a sacrament of human life by the means of associating Van Eyck's *Arnolfini Marriage* with Lowell's own. The comparison comes to mind for the poem on the occasion of posing for a family photograph at Maidstone—"Patriarch and young wife"—and because the finished product shows "a rousing brawn of shoulder / to tell us you were pregnant," like Giovanni Arnolfini's bride, whose condition (in Lowell's view) is visibly more advanced. Lowell reads Van Eyck's painting so as to show that its nuances express an unambiguous trust in life, that things will remain as comfortable as they are. "Giovanni" in "an age of Faith" is "not abashed to stand weaponless"; both bride and bridegroom "in an age of costumes. . . seem to flash their fineness," as if faith and fineness were somehow akin. The two are delicate and beyond doubting. Giovanni holds up a hand—"thin and white as his face" to bless Giovanna, who smiles, swells, blossoms. His raised hand is "like a candle"; her hand in his other is "like china." They are in a bourgeois Eden, a "crisscross" of "petty facts," so exquisite that the rawness of Giovanni's slippers and the *sang-de-boeuf* color of hers, matching the "restless marital canopy," are slightly ominous. But a candle still burns in the candelabrum; peaches blush on the windowsill. Light and color rather than mass and shadow prevail. It is as if, Lowell says finally,

> the airs of heaven
> that blew on them when they married
> were now a common visitation,
> not a miracle of lighting
> for the photographer's sacramental instant.

Putting the difference this way—between marriage as it starts out in faith and eventually, somehow, ends—brings the Arnolfini portrait and the Lowell one ingeniously together, mention of the photographer at the end of the sentence being the only indication that the time reference has subtly changed. But that change is decisive in the poem, for it introduces change as an attribute of real, human life outside of paintings and photographs and thus the meaningful fact of the poem's last lines, that Giovanna will outlive her bridegroom by twenty years. The implications of this outcome are not drawn out, as they might be by Lowell in a darker mood. The facts are stated in order to stress the miraculousness of the "miracle of lighting," its "as if" quality; and this miracle—though it partakes of the love and trust of the bride and groom and of the care painted into objects and light by the painter—is made finally to seem detachable from the merely human, from the *course* of human life.

Thought of in these terms, "Marriage" is a kind of sun, around which the other poems in the last section of *Day by Day* orbit, partaking of its light variously. And, indeed, the next poem ("The Withdrawal") begins:

> Only today and just for this minute,
> when the sunslant finds its true angle,
> you can see yellow and pinkish leaves spangle
> our gentle, fluffy tree—
> suddenly the green summer is momentary. . . .

These are images of approaching fall, but the tone is scrupulously unautumnal. The light, the color, the delicately changing (and precisely observed) leaves are themselves only, involved in no human extrapolations regarding aging and approaching death. The light, again, is set apart from the human, which means it must be immune, too, from the metastasis of human concepts. And so when Lowell writes, toward the volume's end,

> I see
> horse and meadow, duck and pond,
> universal consolatory
> description without significance,
> transcribed verbatim by my eye—

it is a kind of act of faith, an effort to meet the world on its terms, for a change, and to stand before it both unabashed and weaponless. Even such a minimal openness would have been unthinkable in the threatening environments of *Life Studies* and *For the Union Dead*. *Day by Day* is not a spirit-lifting breakthrough in Lowell's canon, but it does show remarkably a striving on Lowell's part, at the end, to make himself at home in the world.

In the volume's last poem, unappeased desire and the will to faith in the world mix with each other in an explicit restatement.

> I hear the noise of my own voice
> *The painter's vision is not a lens,*
> *it trembles to caress the light.*

The artist's merely observing the world is not an adequate metaphor, this says, for the reach of his being toward it: what is yearned for is an intimate and absolute union of subject and object, which are otherwise forever apart. Art itself in these terms is a reaching toward the world for whatever it is that the light stands for, which, being helplessly human we are excluded from and cannot touch. This theme of the last section of *Day by Day* is reinforced, as I have said, by the volume's organization as well as by the augmenting images and statements of the individual poems. The failure of Lowell's last marriage has been conceded at the end of part one, and since that marriage and its inception have symbolized since *Notebook* the hope for choice and the will to enrich one's actual life by appropriating it, it would seem that exhausted hope, and chastened pride, would dominate the tone of what Lowell seems to have anticipated would be his last book.[9] But by altering and transcending the actual chronology of this sad and troubled story, he manages to relegate to a lower priority the significance of individual human fortunes, including his own, and to separate the dream from the dreamer, the not-human from the fallible human, to send the living dream, still alive, free into the world. We seem always in Lowell's work to be in the presence of the Lowell who wrote "Till Christ again turn wanderer and child" or who was accessible momentarily to psychic healing by the thought of forsythia distilled from the image of policeman's oilskin slickers. In *Day by Day*, that presence is more vivid than anywhere else in his work. He is compelled to admit defeat in this phase of his personal life; he does not now conclude that his own defeat expresses, finally, the world-in-itself. In "Epilogue," the last poem, the subject begins as his needing "to make / something imagined, not recalled," and that tension is resolved by his deferring, instead, to the world: "Yet why not say what happened? / Pray for the grace of accuracy"—and much is implied in the second of these two lines: that "grace" and "accuracy" (an accurate rendering of the world) may turn out to be the same after all. To pray for that grace implies self-effacement, humility in its presence, negative capability. So the poem ends with the evocation of still a third symbolic master of the love of light: the "grace of accuracy" is Vermeer's, who gave it "to the sun's illumination / stealing like the tide across a map / to his girl solid with yearning."[10] The abstracted elements of this composition—light, the world as a map, and a person yearning in intransitive being—seem alone to compose in the poem the reticent, pared down, affirmation upon which *Day by Day* comes to rest. "Solid" is the true qualifier for the girl: she is of the world, no pre-Raphaelite yearner. And Lowell adds, to distinguish finally between what is human and mortal in this image from what is not, that we are "poor passing facts." Saying photographically "what happened" does not ensure "the grace of accuracy"; that is why we pray for it. In fact, comparing his own art to Vermeer's (implicitly), it seems to him a "threadbare art" of the "eye" merely, like a crude snapshot—"lurid, rapid, garish"—heightened but "paralyzed by fact." But, he says, our being poor passing facts enjoins us to "give / each figure in the photograph / his living name"—his name as he is most alive, rather than paralyzed as fact—as being alive is finally ironically, yearning "to caress the light." The poet or the painter may capture the mystery and wonder of being in the world or he may not, but he does not make it. The poet's synaesthesia symbolizes the paradox: it is an imagined mode of being in the world—a mode that both depends upon the senses and transcends them.

This last stage of Lowell's life and work brings to mind two analogous cases, one odder than the other. The first, once again, is Yeats, who managed almost never to think of his own aging or the disappointments and failures of his personal life without also affirming an autonomous beauty and power in the world, which, unaffected by individual lives, endures apart. This is why, for example, "The Wild Swans at Coole" is elegiac in sense and not in feeling, why the counted swans cannot for the poem be the original swans, since it is not they that matter but instead the glimpsed and revered mystery of being that they embody and that survives them. Therefore, Yeats makes a point of distinguishing between the autonomous quality of being and his vision of it in reverie by imagining that when he "awakes" the swans will fly away and nest again and "delight men's eyes" somewhere else, rather than disappear. Yeats's symbolist guides did not release him to nature utterly, to be "paralyzed by fact."

The other analogy is to Mann's Aschenbach, who is granted a vision of what he thinks to be perfect form, of spirit made visible, in the ironic embodiment of Tadzio. Being a boy, Tadzio is for Aschenbach a symbol of the ultimate inaccessibility of the beauty toward which he yearns. That this perfect form reveals itself in a setting of corruption, reeking of mortality—and indeed revealed *through* Aschenbach's moral and intellectual confusion—only intensifies the power of its hold upon Aschenbach's being and makes him know that which he can never attain. "He [Tadzio] paced there, divided by an expanse of water from the shore, from his mates by his moody pride; a remote and isolated figure, with floating locks, out there in sea and wind, against the misty inane...It seemed to [Aschenbach] the pale and lovely Summoner out there smiled at him and beckoned; as though, with the hand he lifted from his hip, he pointed outward as he hovered on before into an immensity of richest expectation."[11] In the course of Mann's narrative, events force Aschenbach to abandon his metaphysical mode of understanding in order to come to terms with life dialectically; for Tadzio, finally, is neither a visible aspect in nature of a spiritual world beyond nor a way into the "abyss" but an immanence, indivisible being, both near and remote, radiant and sickly, concealed in paradox. Gazing both upon and beyond Tadzio, Aschenbach dies at peace in absurdity, longing to "caress the light." Lowell would have understood this aspect of Aschenbach's story, because he had passed through such stages himself, and because in the end his whole mode of being and understanding was—far from being cleanly binary—dialectical in a dense and irresolvable way. For dialectical understanding of that modern kind, there is no stable true world, and therefore no truth—nor beauty nor love—hypostasized; and for dialectical being, as Lowell knew and reported, even acquiescence to the world may finally be only a form of unrequited desire. The crux of this issue he had rendered parabolically some twenty years before in a prose version of what later became "The Neo-Classical Urn":[12]

> My life... raced into pure actuality each morning. The white front of the house was still mobile with dew, the green shutters were almost black with the early morning shadows, the ant tracks on the great S of inset and spaced out red tiles on the lawn path had not yet turned to dust, the elms were dewily alive, even the... telephone poles seemed kindred to the trees, growing and casual. I would run and run. Past the pansy beds, under the little rose arbor, through the field path leading under dry, pollarded poplars, and into the pine grove. First I passed the quarter of a mile stretch of tall spaced Germanically clean and cleared pine trees. Not a twig was allowed to lie ungathered, and on my left I could see clearly the play-cabin with its log window binds [sic] and dived [sic] log door and on my right was the unsightly, ten foot wire fence that separated Mr. Leland's land from my grandfather's. Then I was passing the [statue] of Hebe, her cup dewy, one breast showing and the base of her plastic chiton a little green at the edges. And on either side of the built up path there was still water, four to six feet wide and four to six feet deep. And here time after time I could catch the yellow-spotted black turtles, as they flopped off a fallen sapling or moved encumbered through the concealing but stubbornly retarding [moss]. Then I would run home, drop each new turtle into the garden well—not a real well,

but a sort of plaster barrell [sic] about as big around as a mill-wheel and ornamented with Greeks in procession. It was an urn: after the number of turtles reached the thirties, they began to die. Despite my putting bit [s] of old meat green crab aples [sic] and buckets of fresh water in the urn, the turtles died and stank. Then did the joy of catching more turtles grow tedious, meaningless, and at last the sickly survivers—ten or so—were released. And the hunt, the single track of my appetite led nowhere, and I could not understand.

Notes

Introduction

1. Friedrich Nietzsche, *The Will to Power*, trans. Walter Kaufman and R. J. Hollingdale; ed. Walter Kaufman (New York: Random House, 1967), pp. 12–13; see also Book One generally.

2. Frank Kermode, *The Sense of an Ending* (New York: Oxford University Press, 1967), p. 133.

3. Hayden Carruth, "An Appreciation of Robert Lowell," *Harper's* 255 (December 1977): 110.

4. Alan Williamson, *Pity the Monsters* (New Haven: Yale University Press, 1974), p. 103.

5. Or so paraphrased by Kermode, in *The Sense of an Ending*, p. 145.

6. Robert Lowell, "Christmas Eve under Hooker's Statue," *Lord Weary's Castle*, p. 17. See Bibliographical Note for the editions of Lowell's works that are referred to here.

7. "Sailing Home from Rapallo," *Life Studies*, p. 77.

8. "Che Guevara," *Notebook*, p. 53.

9. David Kalstone, *Five Temperaments* (New York: Oxford University Press, 1977), p. 200.

10. Randall Jarrell, "From the Kingdom of Necessity," *Poetry and the Age* (New York: Random House, 1959), p. 193.

11. Steven Gould Axelrod, *Robert Lowell: Life and Art* (Princeton: Princeton University Press, 1978). pp. 6–7.

12. A. Alvarez, "A Talk with Robert Lowell," *Encounter* 24 (February 1965): 39–43.

1. Subduing Disorder

1. In the revised edition, *Notebook*, "surrealism" becomes, awkwardly, "unrealism."

2. Randall Jarrell, *Poetry and the Age* (New York: Random House, 1959) p. 196.

3. Alan Williamson, *Pity the Monsters* (New Haven: Yale University Press, 1974), pp. 158–159.

4. Stephen Yenser, *Circle to Circle: The Poetry of Robert Lowell* (Berkeley: University of California Press, 1975), p. 16. Tate's essay, "The Symbolic Imagination," is reprinted in *Essays of Four Decades* (New York: William Morrow, 1970), pp. 424–446.

5. Jarrell, *Poetry and the Age*, p. 196.

6. I am indebted to Helen Vendler for this information.

7. In Matthew 7:9–11 (the "Sermon on the Mount").

2. Effigies of Kings and Queens

1. Robert Lowell, "Four Quartets," *Kenyon Review* 51 (Summer 1943): 432–433.

2. Stephen Yenser, *Circle to Circle: The Poetry of Robert Lowell* (Berkeley: University of California Press, 1975), p. 90.

3. Dissociation and Authenticity

1. Charles Altieri, "From Symbolist Thought to Immanence: The Ground of Postmodern American Poetics," *Boundary* 2 vol. 1 (Spring 1973): 615–616.

2. Steven Gould Axelrod, *Robert Lowell: Life and Art* (Princeton: Princeton University Press, 1978), pp. 114–115.

3. M. L. Rosenthal, *The New Poets: American and British Poetry Since World War II* (New York: Oxford University Press, 1967), p. 28.

4. Axelrod, *Robert Lowell: Life and Art*, p. 129.

5. Jonathan Raban, ed., *Robert Lowell's Poems: A Selection* (London: Faber and Faber, 1974), pp. 165–166.

6. Sören Kierkegaard, *The Concept of Irony*, trans. Lee M. Capel (Bloomington: Indiana University Press, 1968), p. 312.

7. Stephen Yenser, *Circle to Circle: The Poetry of Robert Lowell* (Berkeley: University of California Press, 1975), pp. 156–157.

8. Norman O. Brown, *Life Against Death* (New York: Random House, 1959), esp. chs. 8, 9, and 12.

9. R. P. Blackmur, "The Loose and Baggy Monsters of Henry James," *Accent* 11 (Summer 1951): 129.

10. Yenser, *Circle to Circle*, pp. 144–145.

11. Virginia Woolf, *To the Lighthouse* (New York: Harcourt, Brace, and World, 1955), p. 117.

12. Axelrod, *Robert Lowell: Life and Art*, p. 132.

13. Martin Heidegger, *Being and Time*, trans. John Macquarrie and Edward Robinson (New York: Harper and Row, 1962), pp. 232–233.

14. Ibid., p. 233.

4. The Death of Union

1. Stephen Yenser, *Circle to Circle: The Poetry of Robert Lowell* (Berkeley: University of California Press, 1975), p. 210.

2. Ibid., p. 203.

3. Steven Gould Axelrod, *Robert Lowell: Life and Art* (Princeton: Princeton University Press, 1978), p. 143.

4. Stephen Spender, *World Within World* (London: Hamish Hamilton, 1951), pp. 312–313.

5. A detailed summary of this can be found in Axelrod, *Robert Lowell: Life and Art*, pp. 146–151.

6. Yenser, *Circle to Circle*, p. 223.

7. Axelrod, *Robert Lowell: Life and Art*, p. 168.

5. The Monotonous Sublime

1. W. H. Auden, "September 1, 1939," *Selected Poems*, ed. Edward Mendelson (New York: Random House, 1979), p. 89.

2. Robert Lowell, "Waking Early Sunday Morning," *New York Review of Books* 5 (August 5, 1965): 3.

3. Philip Cooper, *The Autobiographical Myth of Robert Lowell* (Chapel Hill: University of North Carolina Press, 1970), pp. 129–130.

4. *Webster's New International Dictionary*, 2nd ed., s.v. "sublime."

5. Stephen Yenser, *Circle to Circle: The Poetry of Robert Lowell* (Berkeley: University of California Press, 1975), pp. 267–268.

6. Steven Gould Axelrod, *Robert Lowell: Life and Art*, (Princeton: Princeton University Press, 1978), p. 193.

6. The Ground of Being

1. Philip Cooper, *The Autobiographical Myth of Robert Lowell*, (Chapel Hill: University of North Carolina Press, 1970), p. 47.

2. Theodore Roethke, "Weed Puller," *The Collected Poems of Theodore Roethke*, (Garden City, N. Y.: Doubleday, 1975), p. 37.

3. Virginia Woolf, *To the Lighthouse*, (New York: Harcourt, Brace, and World, 1955), p. 67.

4. This elliptical mode of indicating dialogue is used frequently in poems involving conversations with writers and other figures, and it appears to be borrowed, appropriately enough, from Dante. The stylistic echo from the *Inferno* and *Purgatorio* is faint but unmistakable.

5. See Julia Ward Howe, *Margaret Fuller* (1833; rpt. New York: Haskell House, 1968), p. 268: "She had a vague expectation of some crisis, she knows not what; and this year, 1850, had long appeared to her a period of pause in the ascent of life, a point at which she should stand, as 'on a plateau, and take more clear and commanding views than ever before.' She prays fervently that she may not lose her boy at sea, 'either by unsolaced illness, or amid the howling waves; or if so, that Ossoli, Angelo, and I may go together, and that the anguish may be brief.'"

6. Randall Jarrell, *The Lost World* (New York: Macmillan, 1964), p. 27:

. . . "the dailiness of life"
. . . is well water

Pumped from an old well at the bottom of the world.
The pump you pump the water from is rusty
And hard to move and absurd, a squirrel-wheel
A sick squirrel turns slowly, through the sunny
Inexorable hours.

7. Robert Lowell, "Randall Jarrell," in *Randall Jarrell: 1914–65*, ed. Robert Lowell, Peter Taylor, and Robert Penn Warren (New York: Farrar, Straus and Giroux, 1967). p. 102.

8. Thomas Parkinson, *"For the Union Dead,"* in *Robert Lowell: A Collection of Critical Essays*, ed. Thomas Parkinson (Englewood Cliffs, N.J.: Prentice-Hall, 1968), p. 150.

9. William Meredith, "The Lasting Voice," in *Randall Jarrell: 1914–65*, p. 119.

10. Dante, *The Divine Comedy*, trans. Laurence Binyon, in *The Portable Dante*, ed. Paolo Milano (New York: Viking, 1947), p. 126. All subsequent references to Dante are to this edition.

11. Sören Kierkegaard, *The Concept of Irony*, trans. Lee M. Capel (Bloomington: Indiana University Press, 1968), p. 312.

12. See Steven Gould Axelrod, "Robert Lowell and the New York Intellectuals," *English Language Notes* 11 (March 1974): 206–209.

13. Donald Davie, *Ezra Pound: Poet as Sculptor* (New York: Oxford University Press, 1964), pp. 86–87. In his review of *History*, *The Dolphin*, and *For Lizzie and Harriet* in *Parnassus* (Fall / Winter 1973), Davie is very harsh on Lowell's "sludge and waste" and "scribble and doodle."

14. Michael Wood, "Ezra Pound," *New York Review of Books* 20 (February 8, 1973): 7.

15. Fredric Jameson, *Marxism and Form* (Princeton: Princeton University Press, 1971), pp. 14–15.

16. Alan Williamson, *Pity the Monsters* (New Haven: Yale University Press, 1974), pp. 142–143.

17. W. B. Yeats, Introduction to J. M. Hone and M. M. Rossi, *Bishop Berkeley: His Life, Writings and Philosophy* (London, 1931), p. xxiii. Quoted in Alex Zwerdling, *Yeats and the Heroic Ideal* (New York: New York University Press, 1965), p. 19.

18. Alain Robbe-Grillet, *For a New Novel: Essays on Fiction*, trans. Richard Howard (New York: Grove Press, 1965), p. 32.

19. Ibid., p. 29.

20. Helen Vendler, "Lowell's Last Poems," *Parnassus* 6 (Spring / Summer 1978): 84.

21. Leonard Meyer, *Music, The Arts and Ideas* (Chicago: University of Chicago Press, 1967), p. 159.

22. Ibid., p. 171.

23. "A Conversation with Robert Lowell," *The Review* 26 (Summer 1971): pp. 14, 17–18.

24. Donald Hall, "Robert Lowell and the Literature Industry," *Georgia Review* 32 (Spring 1978): 7–12.

25. T. S. Eliot, "The Metaphysical Poets," in *Selected Essays* (New York: Harcourt, Brace, & World, 1960), p. 247.

26. F. O. Mathiessen, *The Achievement of T. S. Eliot*, 3rd ed. (New York: Oxford University Press, 1959), pp. 12–13.

27. Occasionally the expressive possibilities of idiom are manipulated more overtly, as in this concluding reflection on Waterloo, and on history since: "*La Gloire* changing to *sauve qui peut* and *merde*"; or in this laconic report on the "restoring" of Grayson Kirk's chambers after the Columbia riots:

> The old king enters his study with the police;
> . . . . .
> frames smashed, their honorary honors lost,
> all the unopened letters have been answered.
> He halts at woman-things that can't be his,
> he says, "To think that human beings did this!"
> The sergeant picks up a defiled *White Goddess*, or is it
> *Secret Memoirs of the Courts of Europe*?
> "Would a human beings do this things to these book?"
> *(Notebook, pp. 185–86)*

The *Notebook* poems are often characterized by the deceptive iridescent character illustrated here. Simply as a political statement in a charged political context, the representation of the sergeant's dialogue might seem mean-spirited and polemical; but read as the resolution of an autonomous poem, this same line deftly extends the chaos of the setting to a point of hopeless black-comic confusion.

28. Ishmael has been momentarily transfixed by the evil-seeming whale-blubber fire in the *Pequod's* try-works, and has got himself turned about with his back to the tiller, prow, and compass. Reflecting in fear on the words of Solomon ("the man that wandereth out of the way of understanding shall. . . remain in the congregation of the dead"), he says "give not thyself up, then, to the fire, lest it invert thee, deaden thee; as for the time it did me. There is a wisdom that is woe; but there is a woe that is madness." *Moby Dick* (New York: Rinehart, 1948), pp. 418–421.

29. Frederick L. Gwynn and Joseph Blotner, eds., *Faulkner in the University* (Charlottesville: University of Virginia Press, 1959), p. 199.

30. For some of these details, see Donald Newlove, "Dinner at the Lowells'," *Esquire* 72 (September 1969): 128ff.

31. The sequence called "Five Dreams" should be at least mentioned in this context, though it defies exegesis. The poet there figures bizarrely as Orestes in a modernized reexperiencing of the Agamemnon-Clytemnestra story.

32. See "Introduction," in *William Carlos Williams: A Collection of Critical Essays*, ed. J. Hillis Miller (Englewood Cliffs, N.J.: Prentice-Hall, 1966), p. 7; also J. Hillis Miller, *Poets of Reality: Six Twentieth-Century Writers* (Cambridge, Mass.: Harvard University Press, 1965), pp. 285–359, the chapter on Williams.

33. *Collected Earlier Poems of William Carlos Williams* (New York: Mac-Gibbon and Kee, 1951), pp. 11–12.

34. "It is necessary to create sober, patient men who do not lose hope before the worst horrors and who are not excited by rubbish. Pessimism about the intellect, optimism about the will." Gramsci translated and quoted in Alastair Davidson, *Antonio Gramsci: The Man, His Ideas* (Melbourne: Australia Left Review Publication, 1968), p. 53.

35. R. P. Blackmur, *Form and Value in Modern Poetry* (Garden City, N.Y.: Doubleday, 1957), p. 322.

36. These lines, modified, are carried forward from "The Mills of the Kavanaughs," p. 93.

37. Evidence here and elsewhere suggests that Lowell tended to work from imperfect memory when dealing with historical figures and events.

38. Bidart reports this in conversation.

39. Williamson, *Pity the Monsters*, p. 214n.

7. "My Eyes Have Seen What My Hand Did"

1. Stephen Yenser, *Circle to Circle: The Poetry of Robert Lowell* (Berkeley: University of California Press, 1975), p. 318.

2. Or apparently Domenico's portrait. See *La Divina Commedia Illustrata* (Milan: Selezione dal Reader's Digest, 1967), p. 7. The "tower" is clearly the mountain of Purgatory.

8. The Authority of the Ordinary

1. Jean-Paul Sartre, *Existentialism and Human Emotion*, trans. Bernard Frechtman and Hazel Barnes (Secaucus, N.J.: Citadel Press, 1971), p. 16.

2. Warner Berthoff, *A Literature Without Qualities: American Writing since 1945* (Berkeley: University of California Press, 1979), p. 173.

3. Helen Vendler, "Lowell's Last Poems," *Parnassus* 6 (Spring / Summer 1978): 88.

4. Ibid., p. 90.

5. Sartre, *Existentialism and Human Emotion*, p. 16.

6. In *Being and Time*, Heidegger uses various permutations in German of the noun *Licht* to identify the state of "clearedness" or "disclosedness" or "re-

vealedness" of Being. See *Being and Time*, trans. John Macquarrie and Edward Robinson (New York: Harper and Row, 1962), esp. pp. 401–402.

7. Lowell probably refers here to Turner's commissioned "house portraits" from the early period, around 1809–1812. Typically, the houses are harmoniously subordinated to the larger prospect of the grounds, water, and sky, and are lit by morning or evening light. Those of Petworth House (1810) and Somer-Hill (1811) are characteristic.

8. It is fitting that in Lowell's papers his perhaps last "imitation" is a lovely rendering of Horace's "Intermissa, Venus, diu," fragments of which he has worked into his own poem "Departure." The ode's last haunting stanza seems to be the story of a good many more lives than just Lowell's and Horace's: "In the night's sleep, I hold you captive, / I follow you flying over the grass / of the Campus Martius— hardhearted / you escape me in the Tiber I cannot hold."

9. "Less than ever I expect to be alive / six months from now— / 1976, / a date I dare not affix to my grave" ("Home").

10. This appears to be a composite of several of Vermeer's paintings, not a particular, identifiable one.

11. Thomas Mann, *Death in Venice and Seven Other Stories*, trans. H. T. Lowe-Porter (New York: Random House, 1964), pp. 74–75.

12. This passage is a part of an unpublished prose memoir in Lowell's papers in the collection of Houghton Library, Harvard University.

BIBLIOGRAPHICAL NOTE

No intelligent study of Lowell's career can be undertaken without access to the two pioneer studies in the field: Hugh B. Staples, *Robert Lowell: The First Twenty Years* (New York: Farrar, Straus and Cudahy, 1962); and Jerome Mazzaro, *The Poetic Themes of Robert Lowell* (Ann Arbor: University of Michigan Press, 1965). Those two critics who patiently unearthed sources and parallels and carefully delineated Lowell's creative methods, have made everyone else's work inmeasureably easier. My own debt, to Staples especially, is assimilated, but it will be apparent to anyone with even a rudimentary knowledge of the field. Both Alan Williamson, *Pity the Monsters* (New Haven: Yale University Press, 1974), and Stephen Yenser, *Circle to Circle: The Poetry of Robert Lowell* (Berkeley: University of California Press, 1975), a wonderfully thorough and intelligent book, have refined my perceptions and cleared up many obscure passages. Steven Gould Axelrod, *Robert Lowell: Life and Art* (Princeton: Princeton University Press, 1978) provided valuable biographical information as well as ideas. Besides those critics cited in the notes, others who have influenced my judgments in variously significant ways are: William Barrett, *Time of Need* (New York: Harper and Row, 1972); Ernest Becker, *The Denial of Death* (New York: Free Press, 1973); Northrop Frye, *Anatomy of Criticism* (Princeton: Princeton University Press, 1957); R. K. Meiners, *Everything to Be Endured* (Columbia, Mo.: University of Missouri Press, 1970); Marjorie G. Perloff, *The Poetic Art of Robert Lowell* (Ithaca, N. Y.: Cornell University Press, 1973); Irvin Ehrenpreis, "The Age of Lowell," in *Robert*

Lowell: A Collection of Critical Essays, ed. Thomas Parkinson (Englewood Cliffs, N. J.: Prentice-Hall, 1968), pp. 74–98; and Gabriel Pearson, "Robert Lowell," *Review* 20 (March 1969): 3–36.

I have used the following editions of Lowell's poems: *Lord Weary's Castle and The Mills of the Kavanaughs* (New York: Meridian Books, 1961); *Life Studies and For the Union Dead* (New York: Farrar, Straus and Giroux, 1967); *Prometheus Bound* (New York: Farrar, Straus and Giroux, 1969); *Near the Ocean* (New York: Farrar, Straus and Giroux, 1971); *Notebook* (New York: Farrar, Straus and Giroux, 1971); *History* (New York: Farrar, Straus and Giroux, 1973); *The Dolphin* (New York: Farrar, Straus and Giroux, 1973); and *Day by Day* (New York: Farrar, Straus and Giroux, 1976).

CREDITS

INDEX